LSE MONOGRAPHS IN
INTERNATIONAL STUDIES

The politics of oil in Indonesia

LSE MONOGRAPHS IN INTERNATIONAL STUDIES

PUBLISHED FOR THE CENTRE FOR
INTERNATIONAL STUDIES, LONDON SCHOOL OF
ECONOMICS AND POLITICAL SCIENCE

The Centre for International Studies at the London School of Economics and Political Science was established in 1967 with the aid of a grant from the Ford Foundation. Its aim is to promote research and advanced training on a multi-disciplinary basis in the general field of international studies.

To this end the Centre sponsors research projects and seminars and endeavours to secure the publication of manuscripts arising out of them.

Whilst the Editorial Board accepts responsibility for recommending the inclusion of a volume in the series, the author is alone responsible for views and opinions expressed.

The politics of oil
in Indonesia:
Foreign company–host
government relations

KHONG CHO OON

Laski Senior Scholar, St John's College, Cambridge

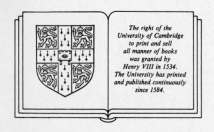

The right of the
University of Cambridge
to print and sell
all manner of books
was granted by
Henry VIII in 1534.
The University has printed
and published continuously
since 1584.

CAMBRIDGE UNIVERSITY PRESS

Cambridge
London   New York   New Rochelle
Melbourne   Sydney

Published by the Press Syndicate of the University of Cambridge
The Pitt Building, Trumpington Street, Cambridge CB2 1RP
32 East 57th Street, New York, NY 10022, USA
10 Stamford Road, Oakleigh, Melbourne 3166, Australia

First published 1986

Printed in Great Britain at the University Press, Cambridge

British Library cataloguing in publication data

Khong, Cho Oon
The politics of oil in Indonesia: foreign
company–host government relations. – (LSE
monographs in international studies)
1. Petroleum industry and trade – Political
aspects – Indonesia
I. Title II. Series
338.2′7282′09598   HD9576.I52

Library of Congress cataloguing in publication data

Khong, Cho Oon.
The politics of oil in Indonesia.
(LSE monographs in international studies)
Bibliography: p.
Includes index.
1. Petroleum industry and trade – Government
policy – Indonesia. 2. International business enterprises
– Government policy – Indonesia. I. Title.
II. Series.
HD9576.I52K48 1986   338.2′7282′09598   85-22416

ISBN 0 521 30901 8

WD

For my parents

CONTENTS

vii

FIGURES

ACKNOWLEDGMENTS

I am grateful to Michael Leifer for his generous help and advice over the writing of this book. I would also like to thank the Ford Foundation for a Graduate Fellowship and the London School of Economics for an ICERD (International Centre for Economics and Related Disciplines) research grant. In addition, the Ford Foundation provided a grant which enabled me to be attached to the Centre for Strategic and International Studies in Jakarta, and to conduct research in Indonesia, Malaysia and Singapore. The people in Indonesia who helped me are too numerous to list, though I would like to thank in particular Johannes Soedjati and Juwono Sudarsono. Finally, I would like to thank Professor Susan Strange for going over the manuscript.

C. O. KHONG

St John's College, Cambridge
April 1985

1. THE IMPACT OF THE FOREIGN COMPANY ON GOVERNMENT POLICIES IN LESS-DEVELOPED COUNTRIES

THE PROBLEM OF PERCEPTION

Investment by foreign firms in less-developed countries tends to give rise to political tensions which are the product of corresponding perceptions held by companies and host governments of a manifest imbalance in their respective bargaining strengths, whether economic or political. It is argued here that the problems arising from this sense of 'imbalance' are largely of a political nature and can only be resolved through the development of an underlying political consensus providing a basis on which common interests can coalesce, that is, constructive reciprocal relations between the purveyors of capital and technology on the one hand and the proprietors of natural resources and labour on the other. Economic concerns and market forces are in a sense peripheral to the issue.[1] What matters most is the development of a convergence of interests, and the evolution of a shared perspective over principles and practices. Such a perspective requires the transformation of the narrow sectarian sense of confidence in the 'rightness' felt by each party into a genuine sense of partnership within broader more inclusive dimensions.

In stating that the problem is one of perceptions, it should be realised that this expresses itself in very basic dilemmas over choice of appropriate policy and attitude. Multinational firms are generally regarded by host governments as increasingly important actors in contemporary international affairs. Yet, faced with the difficult task of formulating policies to deal with their activities, there is an even greater inability to agree on what impact it is that such firms are supposed to have on the host countries within which they operate. The proponents of multinational enterprise claim that it provides vital social services, raises national income, educates

1

management and labour, promotes production and abundance; in short, that it is a key instrument of national development for the less-developed country. But its critics argue that, among other things, it prevents the transfer of technology, contributes to even greater inequality of income distribution within such countries, and creates serious balance-of-payments problems.

This incompatibility of perceived roles has meant that it is difficult to draw clear and firm conclusions as to what government policies and objectives ought to be, much less, given the complex nature of the problem, what their ultimate effects are. In practice, it has resulted in government activity being characterised by an uncertain dialectic whereby the interaction between the two perspectives of economic nationalism on the one hand, and some sort of dependency relationship on the other, results in a constant bargaining process. How these perspectives appear to the government concerned will determine at any one time how far it attempts to go in trying to renegotiate contracts and conditions of operation of foreign companies.

As for the outlook of the multinational firm itself, a similar insecurity exists on its part over its operations within the less-developed world, as it seeks to balance its appraisal of risk against anticipated benefit. While extremely conscious of its economic strength, especially when set against the underdeveloped nature of its host country's economy, it is also aware of the fact that economic power is not of the same quality or kind as political power, and therefore cannot be equated with it. In the last resort, it is the host government which has ultimate authority, whether in monitoring and controlling new investment, determining levels of dividends and remittances allowed, imposing production and price controls, or passing legislation which could control any aspect of a foreign company's operations, from its accounting practices to the proportion of local people it employs.

Yet, paradoxically, the position of not being a free agent able to do as it chooses can give the multinational firm considerable bargaining strength. For the more its activities are interlocked into the host country's economy, the more indispensable it becomes, both to that economy's efficient operation as well as to the general impression which it presents over what others see as its attitude towards foreign investment. The multinational firm may not ultimately have political power, but it can still exercise considerable influence which, if not explicitly political, has significant political implications. For it can create a need for its presence and a sense of dependence within the less-developed country.

The impact of foreign firms on less-developed countries induces a corresponding necessity for host governments to regulate their activities. This interaction results in a conflict of perspectives which is generated, at least in part, by corporate definitions of the appropriate conditions for efficient operation as opposed to nation states' understanding of the conditions essential for their own development. To understand how both sides see their respective interests and how they intend that these interests may be realised, it is necessary to focus on the bilateral relationship between foreign multinationals and local host governments as it is shaped by the different power positions of the two sides. The crux of the issue is the shifting power relationships between them.

But before setting the power relationship just outlined in the context of the political environment of less-developed countries within which it operates, a number of caveats ought first to be entered. First, this relationship cannot be considered in isolation. It must be set within the general international system of which it forms a part, consisting of a triangular relationship between the transnational business companies, the home countries from which they originate, and the host countries where they locate their operations. The composition and relative power of these groups varies in each case, affecting the bargaining process between foreign company and host government. And these shifts in relative strength act on each other through a process of adjustment, as a change at any one point of the triangle affects in turn both other points. This system is understood to be 'transnational' in that it incorporates non-government actors which have organised relations across national boundaries that are not explicitly directed by central government decision-makers. It also includes governmental activities, and does not preclude the sort of inter-government relations assumed by conventional foreign policy and state-centric international relations. Indeed both governmental and non-governmental activities are intertwined and may closely affect each other.[2]

It should be noted that the framework of this system, as it is employed here, by no means encompasses the activities of multinational firms in general, most of whom concentrate the bulk of their assets and the major portion of their activities within what is regarded as the developed world, in countries which themselves act as home states for multinationals. Just as no clear distinction can be made in every case between home and host countries, nor can a line be drawn delineating exactly which policies and activities of their respective governments arise from interactions within the triangle, that is, are motivated primarily by the concerns of dealing with the multinational firm.

Second, it should be made clear that none of the groups involved forms a homogeneous entity. Multinational companies are a diverse lot, being different in structure and operations as between home countries and between industries in which they are involved. Host countries too break down into a variety of different interest groups, which have widely differing relations with foreign companies. The same situation applies for home countries as well. It should therefore be noted, in contrasting the multinational enterprise with the nation-state (whether home or host), that there are important alignments which cut across this distinction. Thus, within the state, different groups may align themselves differently in relation to the foreign firm, and it can be misleading to speak of the interests of the host country when it is not made clear to whom in particular they apply.

The foreign company for its part may seek to exploit these differences in order to strengthen its own position, setting off one interest group against another; or alternatively it can attempt to influence those groups it judges to be most important for its activities. However it is also vulnerable to similar actions on the part of governments, as although the company possesses a more tightly knit internal structure, yet it is itself in competition with other firms within the same field, a rivalry open to exploitation. Differences in methods of operation between companies and in the source countries from which they originate further widen the possibilities for host governmental action.

Third, it may be noted that the foreign-firm–host-country relationship advanced above sets the multinational corporation against the government of the country within which it operates in a juxtaposition of a microeconomic entity against a macro-economic body. This apposition may be justified in that, in most less-developed countries, the multinational, through its sheer size within the local economy and its links with its home country, often constitutes a 'macro' and not a 'micro' problem for the host government in terms of its impact on the domestic society and economy. Yet it should be noted that this in no way implies that the latter will remain anything less than a powerful and difficult economic unit for the multinational to deal with. When many states have become politically independent for the first time, and are under the comfortable impression that for them, at last, the age of self-determination has begun, the presence of the foreign firm often strengthens nationalist feelings and the sense of independence of host-country governments, as they attempt to assert their economic and political autonomy against it.

Conversely, the strength of the reactions which the multinational generates from the government it deals with can also be seen as an indication of its own importance to the host economy. In fact, in playing a role of near-macroeconomic dimensions, the foreign firm goes further in acquiring a political importance through the implications which it poses for the shaping of government policies covering a very wide spectrum of activity, and in the way fundamental political attitudes have sometimes even been determined by it. This brings us to our next consideration.

IMPLICATIONS FOR GOVERNMENT POLICY

The operations of the foreign firm within the host economy of the less-developed country present difficult problems for its government, of both a general nature as well as a more specific character. These problems in turn have both internal as well as international ramifications.

As such governments have developed a clearer picture of what they intend to achieve in ordering their domestic societies and economies, they have been able to identify more specifically their priorities and have also become more aware of how foreign investment may be used to help attain these social and economic objectives. They are therefore able to be more explicit in setting out what they require from the foreign firm. Yet, underlying this growing self-confidence, there is still a fear, usually subconscious and not often openly expressed, of foreign domination. And this unease is coupled with a certain distrust, even dislike, of foreign investment and its intentions, and some disenchantment as well with its effects. So if host governments in less-developed countries have come to recognise the capabilities of foreign multinational companies, in doing so, they have had to overcome their habit of viewing such companies as a manifestation of foreign intrusion reminiscent of colonialism.

The reasons shaping attitudes and policies towards the foreign firm have thus arisen not just from purely economic consider-ations, but also from non-economic and specifically political con-siderations. And these political considerations are often decisive in shaping governmental initiatives and responses in this field. Simi-larly, the effects resulting from such investment are fraught with political implications, and attendant domestic political pressures in turn contribute to shaping government policies.

In examining the relationship between host governments and foreign multinational companies, the political implications that this relationship entails for the formulation of policy by govern-ments is therefore of particular interest, whether these policies are aimed in particular at dealing with foreign investment or are directed towards the economy as a whole. As governments assess the costs and benefits of alternative foreign investment strategies, the influence of such political considerations is a factor not usually explicitly recognised nor sometimes even implicitly acknowledged. Yet these considerations are reflected not just in basic industrial strategies and general outlook towards foreign multinational companies, but also in more specific policies applied within par-ticular industries and to particular investment projects.

At a basic level, the very decision to pursue a policy of national development in which foreign investment plays an important part is in itself a political choice, even if made ostensibly on mainly economic grounds. Internationally, the host country's ability to attract the foreign multinational depends, at least in part, on its having a particular foreign policy. This policy would include such priorities as the development of good relations with the govern-ments of the home states of foreign companies within the western world and the projection of an impression of amenability to their foreign policies and ideas. In general, it requires an awareness, when formulating foreign policy, that such features are often used as a litmus test indicating the conditions the prospective foreign investor is likely to encounter within the host country.

The host country having set out on this path, its foreign policy may further be influenced by the fact that investment from outside has been accepted. This need not necessarily mean that strong multinationals expressly attempt to lean on or to pressure host governments over the setting of policy, though this is a possibility which may occur and cannot be excluded. It rather implies that a long-term policy of attracting and retaining foreign investment is crucially dependent on the international image and economic status of the country as perceived from the outside.

Host-government concern can arise over the activity of source-country governments in representing the interests and supporting the operations of their firms abroad. This involvement, though often suspected by governments jealous of maintaining their own independence of action, is not usually definitely proved. For home-country leverage, whether political or economic in nature, is seldom applied in an explicit manner. But it makes relations with foreign governments an extremely sensitive issue for the host; even more acutely so when much of foreign investment in any particular country comes from only one source country, as is sometimes the case. Of course the policies of the company's home government will to some extent, even unintentionally, affect the behaviour of subsidiaries located abroad. While for the host government, policies such as those aimed at creating employment, securing tax revenues, or safeguarding national security would be complicated by the involvement of specifically foreign companies, given the multiple jurisdictions within which they operate.

The implications extend internally as well. Within the domestic economy, the foreign firm has the ability to impede government planning and to evade governmental attempts at controlling economic activities, through measures such as transfer pricing and capital-flow policies. More generally, its strength is often concomitant with an important or dominant position within some particular geographic region or sector of activity of the host economy. It may on the other hand have some favourable implications in raising the host government's bargaining power against that of local entrepreneurs, who could well be occupying a favourable position within the local economy as suppliers of capital or through their business enterprises. This group itself would resent the increased competition that a multinational company brings, quite apart from its being foreign, and the threat that it may pose to a comfortable monopoly position.

Given this background, and turning to the broad conjunction of political climate and the multinational firm, there is the possibility which ought to be considered that a link could be established between the acceptance of foreign investment and a commitment to political stability maintained perhaps through the adoption of measures by the host government that may be generally regarded as authoritarian or even repressive. If foreign investment is what is strongly desired and if a low cost and quiescent labour force is regarded by foreign firms as an important component of a favourable investment climate, then a trend towards authoritarian policies could be set in motion to bring this about. The urgent need to attract the foreign investor would thus influence the government's willingness to tolerate or to allow the existence of powerful labour unions or of domestic political opposition, among other things, and will shape to a certain extent its attitude towards such matters. And foreign investment may well accentuate any divisions that could exist within the host society by further affecting the distribution of income or of social élitism.

This is not in any way meant to suggest that foreign investment necessarily results in host governments pursuing authoritarian policies. Clearly these policies could arise and indeed have arisen by themselves, without the stimulus any foreign multinational might provide and in societies where such investment is not even allowed. Nor is it intended to pass judgment in any absolute value sense on such governments, which may very well be effective in their task of governing, despite or perhaps even because of an inherent movement in their policies in the direction of authoritarianism.

It could well be that, in some cases, the problem lies more with the host government than with the multinational companies. It may be too ready to grant monopoly positions and other privileges to the multinationals. And it may have a bureaucracy insufficiently sophisticated and experienced to match the persuasiveness of those representatives of the foreign firms with whom it negotiates, together with politicians also too easily susceptible to their influence.

The foreign multinational probably desires more order and stability than is inherent in the host country's political process and socio-economic circumstances. Foreign investors are naturally attracted to a stable and friendly economic and political environment. And in less-developed countries, this tendency of companies has often been translated into a preference for what may be viewed as 'rightist' governments.

It is necessary and only natural for the foreign company to seek to advance its own interests, and hence the political problems associated with it are in a sense inevitable. It would not be possible or fair to expect the company not to attempt to use its power to influence the political environment in which it finds itself or not to try to affect domestic policy, while just passively accepting the conditions which exist.

Being foreign, it may lack certain basic political rights, but the multinational will still participate formally or informally to the fullest extent possible in the political process. It is for the host government to decide which of its political initiatives warrant attention. If any improper influence of government policies ensues, this will probably reflect the fact that the government concerned is weak and corrupt, or lacks clear and specific objectives. Thus while the foreign firm may exacerbate existing conditions, it cannot be said to be solely responsible for them.

The final position that must logically be considered is the absence of foreign investment in any country, a situation which may also have political implications. In such cases, the government may wish to be free to increase its monopoly power within and control over the local economy, and to expand its influence through increased regulation of political affairs. It is in a better position to promote radical social change and reform, unencumbered by the necessity of allowing for and coping with external economic influences. But such a situation, associated with a closed society and economy, is also likely to lead to the imposition of authoritarian and restrictive government policies.

The discussion so far has focused on issues affecting those broad policies that determine the character of the basic development strategies pursued by different governments. It has therefore been concerned with that complex of general attitudes held by host countries towards the foreign investor that go to shape the prevailing investment climate in both economic and non-economic, primarily political, senses. But government policy-making has been affected in a different and more direct manner. Given the inflow of foreign investment, it becomes extremely important for host governments to closely regulate their activities. Governments have had to devise specific policies affecting particular aspects of their relationship with the foreign investor. These policies are aimed at directing the entry of foreign investment as well as scrutinising the operations of the multinational enterprise within the host economy.

Such policies, though formulated with a common object in mind, cover a wide range of activity, which makes it difficult to clearly discuss them as a whole. For convenience, they can basically be divided into five broad groups.

The first group, comprising policies on ownership and control, lies at the very crux of the host-government–foreign-investor relationship itself. On it this relationship may be said to pivot, for the question of control is central to the operations of the foreign multinational. This is so because these policies operate at the fundamental level of perception, motivated by the desire of both sides to have effective control over and to reap maximum benefit from the joint undertaking. Such attitudes are inspired by the suspicions of each as to the intentions of the other. For host governments, they almost always provide the pretext for intervention. Such policies as are adopted attempt to exercise effective control over firms by limiting foreign ownership, enforcing levels of local participation for both capital and management, as well as laying down such requirements as those which restrict business participation within particular areas of the host economy to certain forms, such as joint ventures or managerial and technical contracts. In this last case, the varying stringency with which host governments apply legislation on local participation coincides with their own economic motives, desires, and fears as to where they most perceive a supposed threat to their control of the economy emanating from foreign multinationals.

The second group comprises those other government policies (apart from the ownership policies of the first group) which any multinational investor initially encounters on entering the host country. These policies might be thought of as the government's part in setting the context of its relationship with the foreign firm. They comprise the general laws and regulations which attempt to give the host government closer observation and control over the actual inflow of foreign investment. They determine the conditions under which all multinational firms are allowed into the country in the first place, channelling them into certain desired areas where possible, and out of other fields where they are deemed unacceptable, and tying their presence in with overall government economic policy. Measures aimed directly at the foreign investor may include equity restrictions, various locational and operational restraints, exchange and price controls, and certain economic incentives such as, for instance, the selective provision of credit or tariff protection. Most host governments have even gone further in setting up specific governmental bodies to supervise and to assess more closely this foreign economic influx.

The third set of policies, consisting of the operational restraints imposed on the foreign multinational, is closely related to the second in effect. For it is through the conditions placed on its operations that the host government is able to ensure some form of control over its activities. These policies function on a more practical level, having to do with the everyday management by the host government of the foreign firm's operations, and with each restriction relating to a particular aspect of its activities. As they are aimed at specific aspects of the company's operational functioning, these policies are also distinct from the requirements on ownership and forms of participation set by the first group of policies. General restraints apply of course to all firms, both foreign and local, but foreign companies in addition are subject to a further series of restraints. These encompass controls on such matters as the employment of expatriate personnel, the running of training programmes and checks on financial flows, and restrictions within particular areas such as those on the size of operations and their location and integration into the host economy. Such government measures extend to specific restraints on terms and conditions applying in individual cases.

Fourth comes the issue of investment incentives and guarantees, both in the form of tax exemption and other similar measures, as well as the provision of administrative assistance. While the desirability of these policies has been the subject of considerable debate, such incentives can and have been used to structure foreign investment in line with general economic and social objectives. They are not then simply used as direct attraction devices. Straightforward guarantees attempting to reassure foreign investors are provided over a wide range of issues. These may for instance include the possibility of nationalisation and expropriation, the repatriation of profits or capital, and the protection of specialised technical knowledge. Incentives also take many different forms, whether of exemptions or deductions from certain taxes or duties, the provision of credits or non-financial benefits such as tariff protection, and priority over various matters. There is an international dimension as well to these policies with agreements worked out between host governments and home governments covering general issues such as the promotion of trade and investment, as well as more specific issues such as the prevention of double taxation or the protection of foreign investment. These policies tend to be superficial rather than substantive in their impact on company–government relations. Still, the host government often believes that they enable it to more easily obtain the cooperation of foreign firms, making the latter more amenable to its control.

Fifth and finally, there is the question of those policies worked out between governments, usually on a regional basis, dealing with the problem of international cooperation by host governments over the issues raised by multinational investment. As host governments tend to be in a competitive position to each other, the evolution of joint policies looks like being a long-drawn-out process for most, though there are signs that it may be becoming more widespread. Early attempts at such inter-governmental cooperation were often motivated by the desire to set up a common front against multinational firms, to reduce mutually disadvantageous competition for their investment, and to evolve systematically agreed policies over such matters as financial cooperation, terms of entry and eventual divestment. But expectations have tended to exceed achievement. Cooperation has also begun to evolve in an effort to provide common services and to increase the potential for investment. Cooperative measures may include complementary arrangements, involving the setting up of systems of production for related products where these can be divided across countries, or inclusive package agreements involving inter-governmental negotiations to establish new investment projects. But disparities in social systems and a competitive desire to attract foreign investment still hinder governmental efforts to formulate common policies, to synchronise existing policies, and to cooperate against the multinational firm.

THE ENVIRONMENT OF THE LESS-DEVELOPED COUNTRY

The peculiar characteristics of the social, political and economic environment of most less-developed countries impose certain distinctive features on the nature of the operations of foreign multi-national companies within them, and a number of these special characteristics have to be borne in mind when interpreting company actions.

To begin with, it should be emphasised that the activities of foreign multinationals are confined to clearly defined areas of the host economies, most of which have a distinct dualistic structure. This dichotomy usually arises from the economic history of these countries, and it comprises a modern economic sector separate from an indigenous agrarian sector. The former is shaped both by the production of primary export products of minerals and commercial crops as well as the development of manufacturing industries often in distinct export enclaves, while the latter sector remains relatively untouched by external forces. With growing disparities in technologies employed, productivity achieved and income earned, differences between the two sectors could become more pronounced.

The growth efforts of host governments, while intent on modernising the economy on a national scale, have often in practice meant using the modern sector as the principal base for diversification and development. It has been hoped that development forces would be able from this base to permeate the entire society, thus changing the pattern of dualistic growth with consequent integration of both sectors. The role of foreign multinational companies within this transitional strategy is confined by the very nature of their activities to the more modern market sector, where their capital and technology can be effectively employed.

There is thus a large part of the economy, varying in size for different host countries, not touched by the foreign company. Its activities may indeed form a vital part of that sector of the economy where political power, capital and economic wealth are concentrated. But large sections of the host country's population will not be affected by these activities. Their direct effects on social processes must therefore be seen from an overall perspective as limited to some extent, no matter how important these effects may at first appear to be. But indirectly, the presence or absence of foreign investment in any given situation may well have profound and wide-ranging political implications for the structure of the host society. Several concerns for governments ensue from this consideration. One is to ensure as far as possible that the operations of multinationals are sufficiently integrated both vertically and horizontally into local economic activities for there to be stimulant effects reaching out into the rest of the economy, beyond its immediate area. Another is to make certain that the acceptance of multinational investment in a development strategy does not imply too excessive a reinforcement of the existing bias in favour of the modern sector, with the political consequences that may result from this. Some strengthening of this bias is, however, inevitable.

Related to this concern, and also possessing clear political implications, are the large social differences to be found in many less-developed host countries, differences which may be further widened by the activities of the foreign multinational company. These differences impose an additional obstacle to the integration not only of what may be termed the governing social groups with the general population, but also of these groups themselves with each other.

The multinational company is often thought of as being associated with the idea of an open economy based on a rapid and changing flow of ideas. It is, however, more usually the case in such countries that it represents the intrusion of a new model or set of values extrinsic to what is, for the majority of the population, a closed social system. But for that part of the society exposed to the influence of the external world and to the ideas which it brings, an outward orientation of attitudes often results. This stimulus, further strengthened by foreign investment and what it brings, may provide an important catalyst for encouraging development through the adoption of new methods and approaches, and is therefore no drawback in itself. Yet this inclination to look outside the system, if carried too far, could encourage a tendency to disregard the social and cultural realities of the local society and lead to a breakdown in communication between different levels of society.

There is another and more direct way in which the host society is divided by the activities of foreign multinationals. Insofar as politics in these countries operates to a large extent on a personalised rather than institutionalised basis, foreign firms often find they are obliged to align themselves with certain social groups, and hence, by implication, against others.[3] Further, while expanding the influence of those sections of the bureaucracy charged with controlling or working with them, they may also cause resentment and provoke complaints from domestic entrepreneurs, suffering from increased competition. Through operating on a personal level, therefore, foreign investment may strain social cohesion in a number of ways, as various groups or individuals are affected by its presence. This problem may be thought of not so much as arising from the multinational presence, but rather as reflecting the particular functioning of the internal political and social process.

All this is part of a more general picture wherein host governments in less-developed countries fear that foreign investment poses a threat to indigenous practices and cultural values, as defined by them. Tending to be concerned with building up national identities and to have the concept of central planning very much as the core of their development philosophy, they view the foreign multinational, with a certain amount of unease, as huge, alien and obtrusive. This is not just a matter of actual physical size. It is sometimes the case, for instance, that although a particular investment project is small, by carrying the name of a major multinational it could attract attention and acquire a significance not really deserved.

The problem is really in part one of foreign 'visibility', in the sense that, operating in a far different social environment than that of its source country, the foreign company's activities tend to stand out and its presence becomes more noticeable. This prominence is compounded by the degree of concentration of foreign investment in the host economy's growth sectors and the general impression it often gives of being larger and more profitable than local rivals. The visual impact of foreign companies is further emphasised and spreads out into the general society through their public relations efforts, in which advertising and the dissemination of ideas play a crucial role. To the extent that they are able to influence the habits and values of those with whom they deal, they begin to acquire a power of at least potential importance for shaping their host society.

The multinational's capacity to adapt and adjust is therefore vital. Attitudes towards foreign investment have often appeared remarkably stable in certain less-developed countries despite extreme political change. Yet even this invariability does not absolve multinational firms from a need to be aware of political and cultural factors which could lead to difficulty in their relationship with host governments and societies. They may be required to cope with activities and approaches quite different from those to be found in their traditional environment and to manage political as well as economic risks. Procedures employed within more-developed countries may hence not be suitable when negotiating elsewhere.

The problem of foreign companies blending in with their host environment is also partly a matter of dissipating suspicion through making more open their decision-making processes. Further, they need to convince host-country politicians and businessmen that their local organisations have some independence of action, even if circumscribed, rather than having them be seen as mere affiliates. Specific problems will still remain. The issue of corruption, for instance, which can usually be regarded as a matter of routine when connected with the speeding up of bureaucratic procedures, becomes much more complicated when payments are expected in order to gain new contracts.

The relationship between foreign firms and less-developed host countries is hence a volatile if not unstable one. It can be maintained only if there is a conscious effort to narrow differences in outlook, interests and needs between the two sides. This does not mean foreign firms should have to operate in a non-commercial manner. But if they do not act with some awareness of the impact of their actions outside their immediate area of concern, their role will be limited by political and economic nationalism.

Finally, an additional consideration needs to be raised when drawing generalisations from the particular experiences of individual less-developed countries. In applying theoretical concepts and in determining the results and judging the merits of various policies within such countries, difficulties will be encountered where social forces in a very different institutional framework may not be readily amenable to conventional forms of analysis. An unfamiliar social setting, with often very different institutions, values and accepted practices, may distort the perceived importance of various observations, making it more difficult to discern their validity and significance. Then there is the tendency of host governments to make details of agreements reached inaccessible, being extremely reluctant to publish any information which may disadvantage themselves. And even general statistics, if not absent, are often inadequate and cannot be relied upon to fully reflect social changes that have occurred.

THE SPECIAL CASE OF THE MINERAL INDUSTRIES

The evolution of the company–government relationship emerges more clearly within the mineral industries than elsewhere. This clarity results from the process of mineral extraction being distinguished by a number of individual characteristics which sharpen the negotiating concerns of both host government and mineral company.

To begin with, natural resources, whether fuels or minerals, possess a unique character through their essentially non-renewable nature and the special 'only once' aspect of their exploitation. This acts in two ways, to make especially clear-cut the policy positions of both negotiating sides in the resource-development process.

First, through the finite nature of the resource, at least as it applies to a given country within a short- to medium-term period, it poses in particularly stark terms the issue of the distribution of gains which lies at the heart of the negotiating process. This specific concern over profit sharing acquires a distinctive importance from the element of economic rent in the exploitation of natural resources. Put simply, this rent element comprises that part of the marginal gain derived from working a given mineral deposit over its next cheapest alternative.

Host governments naturally wish to secure as much as possible of the value of the economic rent, and this desire has led most of them to lay down the concept of a national claim to ownership of their minerals. But while holding sovereign control over the resource, host governments commonly lack, to a greater or lesser extent, the other factors required to make mineral exploitation a viable commercial proposition. These other factors comprise access to the required expertise and technology, capital to finance the venture, and a market for the output. Hence such countries are driven to seek a collaborative working arrangement with a foreign mineral company to supply the necessary capital, expertise and managerial competence. But the introduction of a foreign entity into the extractive process sharpens attitudes within the host country over the division of proceeds. For as governments have assumed increasing responsibility for regulating their domestic economy, a heightened economic role for the state, within a climate of rising economic nationalism, has to be asserted against the resident foreign enterprise.

Adding to host government suspicions and part of the economic rent component of overall profits, are what are viewed as large monopoly gains deriving from the imperfect nature of the mineral industries. Whether or not such fears are justified, it still remains that situations of oligopoly in production and oligopsony in market distribution are often to be found. Further gains relating to changing circumstances and conditions within the host country or in foreign markets are also possible. Such gains could take some time to adjust for if the host government lacks essential information or if negotiating practices are too inflexible to allow for immediate responses, as is generally the case.

Indeed, traditional bargaining theory is here deficient if it assumes a smoothly downward-sloping marginal productivity-of-investment curve, relating different levels of investment by the foreign company to expected rates of return for the government. For, given the 'lumpiness' of mineral extractive activities, the foreign company will not automatically adjust its investment according to the level of government taxation. In practice the company will make a given level of investment for a finite determinable range of profits, set by the company's minimum acceptable return at one end and what the government regards as its own minimum acceptable return at the other. Where the rate of return finally settles will of course depend on the bargaining skills of the two sides. But the level of profits which the government is prepared to allow the company will depend on its being aware of the financial flows resulting from the extractive operation, and on how readily it can act upon receiving the relevant information.

The second consideration involves the host government taking a time perspective and determining the rate of exploitation, as this element of time has close relevance for its basic development strategy. The options open to the government are clearly defined and limited by the fixed-quantity character of the given resource. In making its choice over timing resource development, it has essentially to decide, within the context of general economic growth, what the estimated extent of its gains and incurred costs are and will be, as production of a given quantity of any mineral resource at one time will preclude its exploitation at another. It may be thought that the more advanced the economy, the better able it is to absorb profits and to benefit in general. But host governments have to bear in mind a whole variety of considerations, including such matters as the possible future demand for the mineral in question and the trend in the terms of trade, what their own future negotiating strengths are likely to be, the ability of their economies to absorb the real returns from mineral sales, the extent to which local participation is and will be possible, and whether further resource processing is or might become feasible.

Apart from the individual details involved in the deliberations of both sides, the mineral industries also deserve particular consideration for the position they hold within the whole global economic system. Within this system mineral and fuel resources have a vital place, underpinning all economic activity in that they provide both the raw material as well as the energy to make this activity possible. The process displays certain distinctive characteristics. While about half of mineral production is accounted for by the developed countries who themselves comprise its principal consumers, there has been a vast increase in the scale of both mineral investment and resources which are traded internationally. And with many of the low-cost resource deposits being found in less-developed countries, where they tend to constitute an important if not indeed the main component of their economies, an increasing portion of resources traded internationally moves from them to the more advanced countries.

This change in mining activities has coincided with the political independence of many less-developed host states. While host-government intervention in the mining sectors of less-developed countries is not a recent phenomenon, its form and content have changed dramatically as government control over natural resources has come to be seen as a strong characteristic of nationalism. Foreign companies in the mineral industries hence became a target of nationalist movements. Thus the problems of resource extraction become especially complex and intractable, as they acquire a wider political significance.

The problem for host governments is more complicated than merely reducing or even eliminating foreign involvement in their resource sectors. For government policy may have to be directed towards maximising revenue which may well require cooperation with foreign companies on a stringent supervisory basis; while policy has also to be formulated with a view to securing the consent of certain sections (not necessarily the majority) of local society, which may well not hold a unanimous view on the presence of foreign investment. The government has after all to consider its own stability, and a difficult balancing act may be required. Host-government policy could indeed vacillate between giving relative freedom to foreign mineral companies and attempting to strengthen national control over their activities.

Conventional theory on foreign-company–host-government relations generally holds that, at least so far as mining activities are concerned, there has been a decisive shift in favour of the latter in the content and operation of the agreements which are reached.[4] As new contractual forms between host governments and foreign companies become established in the mineral industries, so the negotiating process and the shift in the balance of relationships have gone further to the advantage of governments as compared to such contracts in other fields. These new agreements purport to involve the host government more directly in asserting its owner-ship of the resource, controlling the extractive operation, and benefiting from the financial proceeds. How true this presumed shift in power is in practice warrants investigation, because host governments have come to base their actions in dealing with foreign mineral companies, and to legitimate their own nationalist credentials, on its validity. Especially in the mineral industries, less-developed-country governments have demonstrated an increasing sense of political self-awareness and economic initiative as they have attempted to assert their greater bargaining strength. And as resource-producer groupings and other economic associ-ations begin to emerge among less-developed countries, the earlier methods and strategies that have been employed by some mineral-producing governments are beginning to be studied by others in their dealings with foreign firms. And previous successes, especially in the extreme case of petroleum, are clearly regarded as at least reference points if not necessarily targets by these other host governments.

Though the power of the relatively resource-rich countries may be thought of as unique, yet the example which they have set has general implications in demonstrating a cogent functional process in action, which is both economic and political in its content and import, and which has had a compulsive influence on other host-country governments moving along the same path. In looking at the mineral industries, the negotiating process may be seen to have developed to its fullest extent so far. By examining how this has occurred and by evaluating its actual as opposed to its presumed achievements, a pointer could be provided for other host governments as to what they might realistically expect to achieve in other fields. It may be possible to go further in determining to what extent these results can illuminate those other more general political issues that are then drawn into the process of contract negotiation.

Such an evaluation is especially important with host governments being increasingly alive to the activities of each other. For as governments become aware of each other's moves to increase their respective bargaining strengths, and as various alternatives become more widely known, so these same methods are adapted with high expectations for use elsewhere. Also, with an inclination by almost all host governments towards planning overall development, close and growing similarities in policies to regulate foreign investment will in any event ensue. An assessment of what these structural trends can obtain for host governments may well introduce a sobering note of caution into host-government expectations based on a shift in bargaining power, if this presumed shift turns out to be less effective in practice than is at first thought.

It cannot be strictly objected that the process in the mineral industries is too atypical for inferences to be drawn elsewhere. While different fields of activity exhibit a wide diversity of economic circumstance, state of development, and market characteristics, generalisations are possible insofar as there is a recognised similitude between many of the specific demands made by host governments in different areas. There might almost, even, be said to be a common ideological dimension to these policies which cuts across wide divergencies in political outlook. With the broad politicisation of the whole negotiating process, the choice of objectives and strategies open to less-developed host countries can in this regard be contained within a common framework, uniting the mineral producers in particular and other host governments in general. Concerted policies and alignments of position are not ruled out despite individualistic nationalism, though common objectives are limited to different degrees in various fields by dissimilar market conditions and disparities in political will and economic strength.

So by illuminating the functioning of the foreign-company–host-government relationship within different contexts, the foundations are laid for a more broadly based approach to the problems of mineral development. A clearer picture will also be provided of the overall working environment of this relationship, within societies with very different basic problems, attitudes, endowments and styles of action. It is therefore particularly important to question prevailing assumptions on the foreign-company–host-government relationship, as the introduction of new factors and dimensions could well lead to different conclusions.

2. THE INDONESIAN PETROLEUM INDUSTRY: FORM AND CONTENT OF AGREEMENTS

INDONESIAN ATTITUDES TO FOREIGN INVESTMENT

In looking at successive Indonesian governments, the range of opinion to be found on the issue of foreign investment is not extreme. Considering the wide spectrum of Indonesian politics, a surprising degree of consensus obtained on the need for external economic support of some kind. Practically all Indonesian leaders, whatever their political background, held an almost implicit assumption that considerable foreign aid and investment was necessary, indeed indispensable, for national development. While most politicians were strongly inclined to change the structure of the economy, which had been shaped by the previous Dutch colonial administration, they had to reconcile national feeling with an underlying if contradictory regard for the importance of foreign investment in maintaining essential export earnings.

This dichotomy of attitudes had two effects. First, while efforts to remove foreign economic influence and to radically reorder the economy became a constantly reiterated theme of Indonesian political leaders, there was a tacit acceptance of foreign enterprise. Actual policies dealing with foreign firms were to prove much milder than public statements made in respect of them. Thus political conditions encouraged a divergence between the general tenor of public rhetoric and the actual concerns of the government of the day.

Secondly, while there was considerable public debate concerning the conditions under which foreign firms should be allowed into the country, their actual terms of operation were set by the limits of the economic structure. This fact of life tended to encourage a certain inertia in the implementation of government policy on these matters, which delayed effective policy formulation on foreign investment for almost two decades. The lack of resources, both financial and in expertise, of successive Indonesian governments meant that while their own weak position was due to the existing nature of foreign ownership and investment, it also prevented them from undertaking any major restructuring of the economy. Attitudes on the subject remained notably constant despite perceived major turning points in December 1957, with the seizure of Dutch investments, and the rise of Soeharto's military-dominated New Order from March 1966. Radical and far-reaching though these changes were in many ways, the previously existing economic configuration was in many respects to sustain continuity through these changes.

Where differences have arisen has essentially been over the conditions that can or should be imposed on the operations of foreign capital at any given point in time, that is, on issues which are relative in nature. On such absolute questions as the need to look outside the country for some form of support for national development, or the necessity to maintain control over this aid, there has always appeared to be wide agreement.

The uncertainty on the first of these issues meant that, up to 1966, no agreement on a unified economic policy could be found, and Indonesian political leaders turned away from the specific concerns of economic growth toward much broader questions of politics and ideology. Indeed, even the agreement achieved under the Soeharto régime did not mean that a consensus was reached either on the way political leaders viewed economic matters, or on the policies which they wished to pursue with regard to foreign investment. So long as fundamental agreement could not be reached on the kind of social and economic system that the country should have, particular economic issues were left unsettled. Reaching this basic consensus is a concern of the political process. And so, economic differences acquired a political focus and economic issues tended to be considered within an ideological context.

In this way, at least until the advent of the Soeharto régime and to some extent after that, economic policy did not change as much as the shifting political power structure appeared to suggest. Prevailing thoughts on the economy always kept within reasonably consistent limits, with economic development as a principal objective and with Indonesianisation of the economy invariably paid some deference. The economic system had remained a mixed one, even under the radically nationalist policies of Sukarno; while under Soeharto there has always been a latent suspicion of foreign investment carried over from the preceding Sukarno era, though it remained unexpressed in the events accompanying the transfer of power in the latter half of the 1960s.

From about 1970, however, foreign investment came under sharper criticism, the substance of which pointed to a revival of the former Indonesian viewpoint that resources were 'drained away' by being exported abroad. Criticism was generally directed at the more appropriate use of foreign capital, especially through the introduction of intermediate technology. There was little public criticism to call the whole government strategy into question or to seek the removal of all foreign capital.

Restrictive measures on foreign investment were gradually introduced over the years by the Soeharto government. These included the laying down of greater controls on the forms of investment allowed and their areas of operation, on equity transfers, on foreign workers, and on promoting the transfer of technology. Foreign firms complained that the investment climate had become extremely uncertain.

Faced with the recurrent dilemma of either appeasing foreign investment or appearing to restrict it severely, the authoritarian nature of the Soeharto régime thus enabled it to suppress overt opposition and to introduce a number of palliative measures, but without changing what it believes is still the most potent practical source of development. In this sense, 1966 marked much less of a fundamental change in attitudes than is generally supposed. And just as in the past, while restrictive measures against foreign and non-indigenous interests may have overtly strengthened the ruling régime, its legitimacy is predicated in great part on its assertion that the military is the force best able to provide stability and promote development. Hence the régime's own stability still remains subject to the maintenance of general economic growth, which in turn is a process dependent on economic factors not entirely under the government's control.

THE PETROLEUM INDUSTRY AS A CASE STUDY

The Indonesian petroleum industry may be chosen as an appropriate subject in an examination of the wide range of issues raised by Indonesian aims and attitudes towards host-government–foreign-investor relations. The varying attitudes manifested have here given rise to different types of formal relationship. This multifarious connection serves to point up the factors underlying conflict and accommodation between the two parties, and may be seen in a broader sense to determine the nature of the contribution of foreign resource investment to the country's overall development process.

The approach adopted reflects this fact. In examining the issues posed by company–government relations within the Indonesian petroleum industry, we look first at the form and content of the various types of agreement that have been reached. We shall view them within the context of those aims and attitudes which have determined Indonesian government policies on foreign exploitation of its mineral reserves. This examination not only takes account of the legal form of governmental policies, but also other resulting arrangements, both formal and informal, agreed upon by both sides.

The Indonesian petroleum industry provides a good example of the impact of political and economic considerations on the foreign-company–host-government relationship. That relationship has developed over a relatively long period of time, and so can show how changes in bargaining abilities and positions are translated into different contractual arrangements. Furthermore, the choices of policy posed for host governments emerge with particular distinctiveness for those middle-level oil producers such as Indonesia, with limited petroleum reserves to set against ambitious development plans for a large population and territory. The Indonesian example is especially complex, however. South-east Asia's largest oil producer was for many years the only country in the region with a well-established state oil corporation which was instrumental in formulating policies which enabled the petroleum sector to attain its present dominant position. The methods adopted to regulate relations with foreign oil companies reflect on the Indonesian political process itself. In addition, the central role of oil in the Indonesian economy raises issues which derive from the tremendous influence and importance both of the state oil company and of the foreign contractors working with it. In particular, for the government the pattern of relations within the oil industry is crucial to its primary concern of harnessing development of the oil industry to meet broad national goals.

Looking at the pattern of relationships in the Indonesian oil industry, it is clear that the central issue of contention, with a dominant influence over the various courses of action pursued, is that of control over exploitation of petroleum reserves. Bargaining over control finds practical expression in the negotiating process in three main areas of concern to both sides.

First there is the fundamental question of the division of net revenues or profits between government and foreign company. This is not as straightforward as may first appear, for such division can depend on the imposition of a variety of often complex taxes, with the host government seeking to serve a number of different and possibly even conflicting objectives through taxation. Uncertainty and even confusion in the implementation of taxation policy and frequent and seemingly arbitrary changes in tax laws may introduce further complications, turning negotiations on the division of profits into a major source of conflict.

Closely related to this issue, as it also derives largely from the financial provisions of the contract, is the determination of the absolute level of total revenues and those matters which affect it, such as export prices and the level of output. Both sides may hold different opinions on the maximisation of returns, especially when transfer pricing (the pricing of intra-firm transactions) plays a large part in the operations of the multinational company. Or both may view the future trend of resource prices differently, while attaching different weight to the desirability of maximising present revenue at the expense of future production.

Third, the domestic impact of the foreign company's operations, in both economic and political terms, is also an issue. The problem here is one of integrating resource activities into the local economy so as to maximise its contribution to economic development. This broader aspect of the extractive operation also encompasses the influence which the multinational company may have on labour relations and the domestic political situation. Both sides have to take into account the diversity of domestic political forces and the manoeuvrings of various interest groups, whose influence might persuade the government of the day to take a stiffer negotiating attitude than is feasible. Such an attitude might on the other hand render company positions more flexible if the government is seen to be as moderate as domestic opinion will allow.

The settling of differences in these areas of concern is achieved through modes of control, both formal and informal, over various aspects of petroleum exploitation agreed by both sides. In fact, the agreements which are reached, while bearing different titles such as concession arrangement or work contract, address themselves basically to the same concerns which any oil-extractive operation must face. Where they differ is in the mechanisms which they embody to safeguard the interests and secure the objectives of both parties to the contract. The revision of these mechanisms provides the means to resolve differences of opinion on outstanding issues. Procedures for dispute settlement and for the renegotiation of contract terms enable solutions to conflicts arising from the above three issue areas to be reached.

It should be pointed out that the issues of conflict inherent in the company–government relationship may not be of a type amenable to rational analysis if looked at strictly in cost-benefit terms. Indeed the legal forms arrived at may have as much political as economic or operational significance. Popular accounts of foreign investment in resource extractive activities may well have emphasised seemingly irrational elements in the course of oversimplifying these issues. But these elements may only seem irrational if looked at purely in terms of the economic issues involved. We must consider, on the one hand, the whole socio-political milieu within which the host government is operating and, on the other, the foreign company's point of view in taking into account its overall global operations of which any one producing affiliate forms only a part.[1] In the Indonesian case, issues of dispute with foreign oil companies have in the extremity effected changes in the nature of the company–government relationship within the domestic political economy, with further repercussions touching the internal economic and political structure.

THE GENERAL LEGISLATIVE FRAMEWORK

In their various attempts at establishing a legal framework for the operation of foreign mineral extractive companies, Indonesians claim to take as their starting point article 33 of the country's 1945 constitution which states that 'branches of production which are important to the state and which affect the life of most people, shall be controlled by the state'. It goes on to affirm that 'land and water and the natural riches therein shall be controlled by the state and shall be exploited for the greatest welfare of the people'.[2] While this may indicate an ultimate goal of national control over all natural resources, circumstances have required the adoption of a somewhat more modest programme allowing foreign companies access to these same resources. The effective degree of state control resulting from such an arrangement may not be as great as might have been envisaged within the terms set out above. But, accepting this qualification, the Indonesians have had to determine the most suitable relationship with the foreign companies that is achievable in practice.

The first decision any host government has to take is to determine the extent to which it can rely on general legislation in its dealings with foreign companies, as opposed to determining individual conditions through separate negotiations and contractual arrangements. For having laid down the basic objectives it wishes to secure, a legal structure has to be devised which can provide a framework incorporating appropriate directing mechanisms to guide company involvement in petroleum development. The comprehensiveness of this structure would depend on the extent to which the host government wishes to rely on such a general framework. It therefore follows that general legislation and individually negotiated contracts are not mutually exclusive alternatives.

In the Indonesian case, all extractive activity in the petroleum industry comes within the legal framework set by Presidential decree, which became Law No. 44, passed as a government regulation in October 1960.[3] Theoretically the extraction of oil and natural gas is therefore covered by general legislation. Yet it is striking that this Law has almost nothing to say on the relationship between government and foreign company. While laying down that all extraction of petroleum 'shall be undertaken solely by the state . . . (and) shall be implemented solely by state enterprises' (article 3), who may in turn reach work agreements with various contractors to implement this work where the state enterprise was unable to carry it out (article 6), the Act is otherwise content to concern itself solely with the relations between government and the state enterprises through which it acts. Moreover nowhere in the law is there any definition or specification of what constitutes a 'work agreement', or even any general description of its form or nature. An accompanying commentary merely noted that the content of individual contracts was left entirely to the discretion of the government, as circumstances would be expected to vary in each particular case.

The actual contracts between foreign oil companies and the state oil company Pertamina (as well as its predecessor, Permina) have in fact been contracts with the state enterprise and nothing more. This is despite having a law which addresses itself exclusively to regulation of the petroleum sector within the economy, the result of an explicit decision made in the 1950s that this industry should be governed by a separate law from that of the mining sector in general.

Furthermore, the production-sharing contracts, as introduced in the 1960s, were not subject to parliamentary ratification even though article 6 of Law No. 44 calls for the validation of working agreements between contractors and state enterprises in the petroleum industry through 'legalisation by law'. Instead their legitimisation had its origin in various policy statements made by President Sukarno, construed to imply support for the production-sharing form and which conferred legal endorsement in practice. They were neither formally embodied in laws nor did they displace any laws previously enacted on this matter. The early production-sharing contracts which Permina and later Pertamina signed with various oil companies thus rested in a significant sense on a dubious legal basis.

The anomalous status of these contracts was further clouded when a new foreign investment law was enacted in 1967. This law was intended to encourage foreign investment by clarifying its validity, but succeeded only in achieving further obfuscation. Article 8 of the law states that foreign investment in the mining sector would be 'on the basis of a working contract or some other form of cooperation'.[4] An accompanying commentary does little to elaborate this statement. It runs as follows: 'To facilitate economic development, the Government determines forms of cooperation between foreign and national capital which are most profitable for each field of activity. Such cooperation may be in the form of a work contract, joint venture or another type.'

While it may be argued that this by no means excludes production sharing, it should be noted that the term itself is not even mentioned. The law cannot therefore be seen as strengthening the legal basis of such contracts. And the only possible conclusion which can be drawn is that investment in the oil sector is not bound by any clearly defined national legal framework, even if one is supposed to exist. In the last resort, foreign companies have the status only of contractors, employed on the basis of specifically negotiated agreements.

General Ibnu Sutowo, one-time President-Director[5] of Pertamina, was adamant in insisting that relations with foreign companies should take the form of contracts with the state oil company and should remain outside the legislative prerogative of Parliament. His nominal superior, the Minister of Mines, Bratanata, took a diametrically opposite view. He was a strong advocate of subjecting all relations with foreign companies to parliamentary approval. The issue was only resolved in January 1967 when President Soeharto removed Migas, the Oil and Gas Directorate, from the Ministry of Mines and placed it directly under cabinet control. In this way, indeed almost by chance through the settlement of an internal difference of opinion as to the form of foreign-company–government relationship desired, the petroleum sector acquired a special position within the Indonesian economy. And the state oil company, Pertamina, also acquired a special status within the political hierarchy. All oil contracts were approved by the President, bypassing the Ministry of Mines, and Sutowo acquired considerable freedom of action for himself and the state enterprise which he headed. Migas was returned to the Ministry of Mines in October 1967, with the appointment of a new more pliant Minister. But the oil contract approval procedure remained unchanged, the new Minister not having authority over his formal subordinate. Pertamina's irregular position was made formal when a law governing its operations was passed in September 1971. This law, known as the Pertamina Law, allowed for 'production sharing contracts', whose terms were not defined, to become effective when approved by the President.[6]

It is usually argued that under a system of general legislation, governments can ease the process of company–government negotiations by incorporating detailed provisions within an overall mining code. By investing such terms with legal sanction, the scope for bargaining during contract negotiations is reduced. To standardise their form and features through this means may result in more effective supervision and enforcement of contracts. Furthermore such legal ratification simultaneously protects terms from becoming the object of company attempts at contract revision, while still allowing governments to enact legislation within the general legislative framework. This legislation may introduce new financial provisions which take into account what governments regard as changed circumstances surrounding their relations with foreign companies. The argument applies with even more force within the petroleum industry. And the tendency towards the general and away from the particular has been even more pronounced, as host governments (to which the Indonesian government is no exception) have greater experience upon which to draw and as many contract provisions have acquired a uniform character.

The conventional argument may therefore be said to favour a general legislative system for governments. In states such as Indonesia, where terms are fixed by individually negotiated contractual provisions, governments can only enforce changes by renegotiating specific contractual terms. Such renegotiation is a more cumbersome process and one in which companies can and have put up stronger opposition. For this reason, companies have generally preferred a system based on individually negotiated contracts. While perhaps conceding the case for a revision of terms along mutually agreed lines where operational conditions have altered significantly, they regard the unilateral power which general legislation provides governments, to change contract terms or extract an increased share of profits at their expense, as generally unacceptable. This preference is more strongly marked when companies operate in less-developed countries, where there is much greater uncertainty as to how the political process and hence general legislation will develop in the long term. Companies are therefore keen to seek even greater guarantees of stability over their period of operation, and prefer incorporating these guarantees within individual contracts.[7]

In the Indonesian case, Pertamina has advanced two main arguments for relying on individual contracts which run directly counter to the above opinion. First, the relationship between Pertamina and the foreign company is depicted as a dynamic one which requires constant monitoring and modification over time. If this relationship were to be bound within a general legal framework, contracts would have to be submitted for parliamentary ratification. This procedure would mean losing the flexibility necessary for governing such a relationship by subjecting it to a cumbersome legislative process, with the government as a whole being required to act in the event of a dispute between Pertamina and a foreign company. The reasoning appears somewhat singular when set against the standard argument. But it may be seen to fit cultural traditions in a country whose political system is characterised by the enactment of decrees, which are strongly directive in nature and which derive from general laws which provide broad and indeed somewhat vague and ambiguous guidelines. The individual contract may therefore be regarded as analogous to a particular administrative regulation elucidating a general policy directive.

Secondly, it is claimed that foreign oil companies might assert that prior parliamentary ratification of contracts had made them irrevocable and unalterable, even though the legal basis of this somewhat specious argument is admittedly rather doubtful. Companies might resist changes whether imposed through the enactment of new legislation or through abrogation and revision of contract terms. However, where a contract clause possesses the authority of law, it is more readily accepted by companies. Indeed some companies have admitted that their opposition to Indonesian attempts in 1976 to revise the financial terms of their contracts was all the greater because these attempts did not have the backing of parliamentary legislation.

Ibnu Sutowo had an additional implicit reason for favouring specifically negotiated agreements outside the purview of the legislative process. This arose from his rivalry with the Minister of Mines, Bratanata. He consequently desired to retain full control over Pertamina, with the freedom of action to implement his concept of production sharing against a Ministry more concerned with such orthodox objectives as maximising financial returns from the extractive operations of foreign companies.

The companies too had an additional reason within the Indonesian context to favour basing their relationship with the government on ad hoc agreements with the state oil company. By interposing Pertamina between themselves and the governmental apparatus, they hoped to reduce to some extent bureaucratic delay and corruption which they had already experienced in dealings with government.

THE TRADITIONAL CONCESSION SYSTEM

Having determined the basis on which its relations with foreign companies are to be regulated, a choice has then to be made by the host government of a particular form of agreement from among a range of alternatives.

In the Indonesian petroleum industry, contractual arrangements have carried a number of different names, the differences in terminology being significant in differentiating types of agreement whose changing forms have reflected both political and economic considerations. Indeed political factors appear to have been of overriding importance in the determination of a particular form of agreement. Changes in relative bargaining strength between the two sides have however also influenced the format of contracts. And these agreements have gradually been extended in scope from covering purely financial terms to an attempt at asserting greater host-country control over the extractive process.

Three major types of agreement can be distinguished in this case. Insofar as the system was not governed by general legislation, the contract chosen would set out to specify the control over company operations which the government wished to assert. But in evaluating their respective features, it should be noted that the form of agreement adopted may have more of a notional than a substantial property, and that the formal title need not necessarily reflect the agreement's actual structure or working relationship.

Up to 1960 foreign oil companies operating in Indonesia did so under so-called 'let alone' agreements in which, pending the introduction of new legislation, the concessions, contract terms and operational arrangements agreed with the previous Dutch colonial government remained in effect. These agreements therefore extended the traditional concession system, the terms of which were shaped by the 1899 East Indies Mining Law (in its amended form of 1930) which remained operative.[8] The companies dealt directly with the Indonesian government, and the principal thrust of government petroleum policy, so far as this existed, was directed towards increased financial reward.

Under this system, the companies were granted full ownership rights, under long-term agreements ranging from 40 to 75 years, over their concession areas. Possession gave them the exclusive right to explore for, produce and market petroleum. The Indonesian government was divested of ownership rights over petroleum resources within the concession area and the companies retained management rights over all phases of their operations. To the extent that the politically disturbed conditions of the time allowed, they operated largely outside government supervision. Companies provided all their own capital requirements. And they could retain all foreign-exchange earnings from sales of oil as long as they agreed to provide from their own overseas sources the necessary foreign exchange required to restore their production facilities and oil-fields. These were severely damaged as a consequence of the Second World War and the subsequent war for independence.

A four per cent royalty was paid, which was based on the declared export price of oil produced rather than, as is more common elsewhere, the volume of output. It was therefore termed a 'gross production tax'. There was also a standard 20 per cent profit tax based on production profits, and an additional tax of 20 per cent on corporate profits for all concessions granted after 1918. These were termed 5A contract areas as they derived their legitimacy from Section 5A of the 1918 amendment to the 1899 Law which authorised the government, as sole holder of mineral rights, to dispense ownership entitlements to the companies. Both profit taxes were clearly based on declared company proceeds. An area rental was levied and various additional taxes were placed on the companies' exporting and marketing activities.

It would appear that the integrated character of the internal structures of petroleum companies, under which oil was exported to processing and marketing subsidiaries abroad, gave them considerable room for manoeuvre. They could reduce both royalty and profit tax payments by fixing sales prices in order to reduce local profits. The Indonesian government lacked the resources to administer even this basic system, and the term 'let alone' seemed applicable in more than one sense. The main source of government revenue was clearly through its tax on profits, and even royalty payments required the checking of price levels. In order to assess taxes and royalties accurately, the government would have had to verify both the sales price of the petroleum produced and (for tax purposes) the companies' calculations of expenses to be deducted from gross income. And with transfer-pricing practices whereby firms could fix artificial prices in inter-affiliate sales in order to shift profits between various tax jurisdictions, the administrative machinery for this investigation just did not exist. Even today it is doubtful if the Indonesian authorities have the tax administrative capacity necessary to supervise such complex financial flows.

The sole reason for relying largely on profit taxes rather than royalty payments would have been the greater willingness of the companies to accept an arrangement under which payments would only be made if profits materialise. They would hence be more willing to concede better terms to the government, at least on paper. In this light, the small royalty payment might be seen to serve the purpose of assuring the government of at least a minimum payment when company profitability was low or non-existent. It only required the administrative authorities to keep a check on the actual physical volume of oil production attained, a much easier task than tracing financial flows. But in this case, as the royalty too was dependent on submitted prices, company payments could still be reduced through price fixing.

Beset as it was with conflict between various political groups unable to agree on how the oil companies should be treated and the petroleum industry organised, the Indonesian government was not in a position to assess the companies' degree of tax compliance. It is not surprising that the government was content to receive what revenues it could, while devoting its attention to other matters. There was probably something to be said for adopting an even simpler form of concession, basing royalties, for instance, solely on tonnage of crude oil produced. But no doubt the political exigencies of the time would not have allowed it.

The formal position of the concessionaires was therefore extremely strong, and their situation was reinforced by two additional factors. First, the petroleum industry was dominated by only three large oil producers. The concession system had been used by the Dutch to restrict competition, and the Indonesian government inherited its structure from the colonial administration. This concentration of ownership helped the companies to coordinate their efforts against government attempts to assert greater control over the petroleum sector.

Secondly, while its relative importance may have varied over time, Indonesia has a long history as an established oil producer. This fact is significant for the assessment of relative risk undertaken by companies when making an investment decision. For the risk when an investment is made without prior knowledge of an area's potential, and the risk after commercial quantities of petroleum are discovered are both different, and in turn affect the projected minimum returns which companies are prepared to accept. This basic conflict over the supply price of capital did not exist, as production areas were well established and prospective operational areas existed which were already surveyed. (It should however be noted that this situation applied only in the 1950s, before exploration interest moved either offshore or to less accessible onshore areas.) Even so, the position of the companies was in effect far less secure than their formal position might suggest. Formally they were protected under the 1949 Round Table Agreements. These Agreements set the terms for the transfer of sovereignty to an independent Indonesian government, recognising and restoring all previous concessions and licences, thus assuring the companies of the continued retention of their assets. Yet the government remained too weak to enforce these conditions in practice, and was itself clearly divided over the legitimacy of their position. Conflict arose between various political groups over such fundamental issues as retention of production facilities and oilfields, rivalry between themselves over their control, and occasional arbitrary interventions in the management of company activities. Such uncertainty resulted in an extremely insecure environment within which companies operated.

WORK CONTRACTS AS A MODERN CONCESSION ARRANGEMENT

The development of other forms of contract occurred as a reaction to the concession system and in response to claims of national ownership over natural resources. Their protagonists have sought to achieve more than just an improved profit share for the government. The terms have been devised to secure two additional objectives: increased government ownership of petroleum resources and production facilities, and a greater role in the management of the extractive operation. The forms of these agreements reflect this trend towards increased state participation. They therefore differ significantly in structure both from traditional arrangements and also, depending on whether they have placed greater emphasis on ownership or on management, from each other.

In the Indonesian petroleum industry, a new type of agreement replacing traditional concessions came into effect after the passing in 1960 of Law No. 44 covering oil and gas development. Agreements based on this Law and termed 'work contracts' were reached by the three state oil enterprises operating at that time, acting on behalf of the Indonesian government, with the existing three foreign oil companies in 1963, and with one new entrant to the local petroleum industry in 1962.

The use of the term 'work contract' is misleading. It implies that the foreign firm is in some sense a contractor to the host government or state enterprise, the government purchasing its services, with the company itself claiming no ownership interest in any part of the extractive process. In actual fact, the line dividing these work contracts from previous concession arrangements has proved to be less than distinct. The substance of these agreements may be deduced from the terms set out in the 1962 contract between Pan American Petroleum Corporation and Pertamin, then one of the Indonesian state oil companies.[9]

While the asserted principal feature of the work contract is that sovereignty over natural resources is vested in the state until the point of sale, this is only true insofar as the company does not hold formal title over its concession area. In other respects, there was little difference in practice from the traditional concession.

The contract was of shorter duration than for previous concessions, covering thirty years. And it encompassed a smaller geographic area, some 35,000 square kilometres in central Sumatra and adjacent territorial waters. It incorporated an area-reduction clause, providing for mandatory relinquishment of one quarter of the contract area after a period of five years and another quarter after ten years. And it laid down various minimum expenditure requirements totalling US$28.5 million which the company would have to incur.

These provisions might at first be seen as radical alterations of the traditional concession structure. Yet they were less than effective in ensuring government control of company activities through securing a commitment from the company to a minimum work programme in real measurable terms. The relinquishment clause stopped short at half the contract area. And the contract stipulated that full management control was retained by the foreign company, which therefore effectively controlled all extractive and processing activities. The company kept full responsibility and assumed all risks. It could plan its exploration in the manner it wished, as a commitment to minimum expenditures is less effective in ensuring compliance with government intentions than palpable requirements setting out specific survey and drilling obligations. Failure to specify these conditions was, though, probably no more than a reflection of the weak bargaining position of the government and the low level of information available to it. Furthermore the ownership of all production facilities was retained by the company.

The provisions on government taxation were even more interesting. To conform with the illusion that Pan American was no more than a contractor to Pertamin, all the financial arrangements were expressed in terms of petroleum as shares of production to be received by the company and Pertamin. But the company was appointed as Pertamin's exclusive sales agent, and authorised to take over the government's 'share'. It then paid the value of this share to Pertamin, the title to the oil passing to the company at the point of export shipment.

Operational costs, calculated in monetary terms, were deducted from gross production value. And a 60:40 division of profits in favour of the government, valued at realised prices, was agreed. This therefore amounted in effect to a profit tax. When taken in conjunction with a bonus of US$5 million payable to Pertamin at the time of signature, and a further production bonus of the same amount payable at the end of the first year in which production averaged 15,000 barrels per day, the government's financial position was significantly improved over previous concession arrangements. To guard against transfer-pricing abuses, the oil was to be appraised on the basis of realised prices in sales to third parties, even if sold to an affiliate of the company. It remained doubtful however if the government possessed the necessary expertise to determine an appropriate third-party price. And the decision to valuate sales prices in the last resort on the minimum f.o.b. prices of other petroleum companies selling Indonesian oil represented an unsatisfactory solution to the problem, given the inter-affiliate nature of those sales. Significantly, though, Pertamin did reserve the right to take 20 per cent of gross production in kind if it so chose, as an additional safeguard. Furthermore Pertamin retained the full 20 per cent of production, even if this exceeded its 60 per cent share of net profits. This was an important and hard-won concession, as companies tend to attach substantial import-ance to retaining control over the actual disposition of their oil production.

As this agreement served as an example of the form of contract which the Indonesian government was trying to establish, the other oil companies were reassured that their proposed new 'contractor' status was in fact not dissimilar to their previous 'concessionaire' one. This realisation hastened their own signing of work contracts with the various state oil enterprises.

This form of work contract remained primarily a profit-sharing arrangement, with payment in financial terms. Pertamin and the other state companies maintained a passive role as tax collectors and supervisors of company activities. Indeed the government was so dissatisfied with their performance in this role that it later appointed further control and supervision teams to check on the foreign companies, though with little effect. As an attempt to secure control over petroleum operations by foreign companies, reflecting the doctrine of national sovereignty over natural resources, these work contracts were ineffective. An important objective was that ownership of petroleum resources was retained by the government. Yet this achievement became somewhat symbolic when full management rights and control over operations were transferred to the company, with no provision for effective supervision. Indeed the actual passing of title over the petroleum amounted to little more than a legal distinction, without practical effect.

As a declared departure from concession agreements, more significance was imputed to these work contracts than is warranted from an examination of their terminology. They may have been based on the premise that the oil company was merely a hired agent carrying out services specified by the government. But the government achieved no improvement either in terms of a more direct influence over management or, discounting the illusory transfer of ownership over petroleum reserves, of increased ownership of assets. Certainly it did realise a larger financial share from company operations. The agreements, though, worked in practice in much the same manner as concession arrangements had done and were therefore better classed as modern concession arrangements.

THE PRODUCTION-SHARING CONTRACT AND ITS DERIVATIVES

A further form of contract, which has since come to dominate the operations of foreign petroleum companies in Indonesia, is that of the production-sharing agreement. This contractual form arose out of dissatisfaction over the terms and operational conditions of the contracts of work. As the title implies, it was an attempt to devise an arrangement whereby the output of the extractive operation was shared by the foreign company and the state enterprise in predetermined proportions, the former serving in some way as a contractor to the latter. However, although the structure and terms of the new contract appeared to represent a radical departure from previous agreements, the actual distinction between this and the preceding work contracts was, at least initially, less than clear. Indeed it would now seem that the term has come to be loosely applied to almost any form of contract in which there appears to be at least an option for both participants to share production rather than fix payments entirely in monetary terms. The causes of this blurring of definition may be traced back to the original reasons behind the setting up of such contracts, and the terms in them which were agreed upon.

The principle of production sharing was first enunciated in a presidential statement on 3 August 1962, and further elaborated in official statements over the following two years. It reflected the nationalistic policies favoured by the Sukarno régime, which was not prepared to accept any foreign equity investment in the Indonesian economy. Foreign participation was to be allowed only through the provision of foreign credits, which would be repaid from an agreed share of production. The concept of production sharing therefore emerged as an association purely between a foreign creditor and an Indonesian investor for the establishment of a specific project. It was not a joint venture as the enterprise was to be owned, managed and operated entirely by Indonesian nationals, and there was to be no financial payment to the foreign creditor.

As a contractual device for regulating the relationship between foreign company and host government, the classic application of production sharing worked best in areas where there was no pre-production risk of loss (because there was no exploration risk), typically in activities such as timber felling or agricultural estate production. For in such cases, the foreign investor was assured of some future return on his investment. But even in these early ventures, the application of production sharing was seen to diverge significantly from the principles which had been enunciated.

These early production-sharing contracts required the Indonesian party to provide for a bank guarantee to meet the balance of account, should the total value of production fall short of the amount required for the amortisation of the foreign company's loan. This situation could presumably result either from low prices or from a shortfall in production. Furthermore, although ownership and management were unambiguously vested in the Indonesian party, yet extensive foreign 'assistance' was provided for, even to the extent of allowing the foreign partner to wield a dominant role in the overall management of the project. Marketing, except for traditional export products, was undertaken entirely by the foreign company, with the Indonesian company selling its share of production to its foreign partner. This arrangement continued even after the original foreign credit had been repaid. Yet, even so, the price received by the Indonesian side was generally at a level below accepted world prices, as the foreigner was deemed to provide a service in undertaking to market the product. Thus, even from the beginning, production-sharing agreements incorporated elements of profit sharing, and were not clearly distinct in practice from those previous equity investment contracts they were intended to supersede. In this respect too, they were quite different from those coproduction agreements negotiated for manufacturing projects in East European countries by western firms. Such projects required the company to provide patent rights, machinery and technical assistance, for which in turn it received an agreed quantity of the resulting production.

It was Ibnu Sutowo who took this concept of production sharing and applied it to the different context of the petroleum sector in an effort to improve on the contract of work as a means of regulating petroleum company operations.[10] Sutowo's stated intention was to devise an arrangement for balancing the conflicting demands of the oil companies and nationalist sentiments: 'I tried to find a system reasonable for us and yet still worthwhile for companies to gamble their money.'[11] He described it as a 'new conceptual approach to working with a foreign company'.[12] But while Sutowo acknowledged the influence of discussions he had in 1961 with government officials in Saudi Arabia, Venezuela, Iraq and Iran on how national interests were best secured in the petroleum industry, his description minimised the importance of early production-sharing precedents in the primary production sector of the Indonesian economy.

The first oil production-sharing contract was signed in 1966 with the Independent Indonesian American Petroleum Company (IIAPCO), a consortium of various American interests. The format of the IIAPCO agreement was to provide the basic framework for all such subsequent contracts; though in succeeding years, the terms of later contracts did vary in some particulars and various additional provisions came to be included. As most of these changes came into force after the renegotiation of contract terms in 1976, it is possible to distinguish between a pre-1976 version of the production-sharing contract and a revised 1976 production-sharing contract. However, as the new terms were largely the result of a response to perceived inadequacies in specific details of the original form of contract, and as production sharing continued as the declared main principle of the new contractual form, they will be discussed later, when individual provisions of the production-sharing contract are examined.

The basic concepts underlying the production-sharing contract may perhaps be seen from examining the agreement reached in September 1968 between Pertamina and IIAPCO, for a contract area of approximately 122,000 square kilometres offshore from South-east Sumatra. This contract may be considered characteristic of its type in form and substance.[13]

In establishing the scope of the agreement, the contract begins by vesting responsibility for the management of operations with Pertamina. IIAPCO, though not described explicitly as a contractor, was responsible to Pertamina for executing these operations, providing all foreign exchange and technical assistance required, and assuming all operating risks. In this last respect it may be observed that in undertaking to carry the burden of risk, the company thereby acquired an economic interest in the project. It could therefore not be considered as simply a contractor to Pertamina, in the sense of furnishing its services at an agreed rate.

The key provisions of the agreement, which constitute its declared main point of departure from the work contract, are found in section VI. This section allows IIAPCO to recover all its operating costs in the form of petroleum, up to an amount equal in value to a maximum of 40 per cent per annum of crude oil produced. The balance of production was to be divided in the ratio of 65 to 35 in favour of Pertamina, rising to 67½:32½ for that quantity of daily production above 75,000 barrels a day. Although IIAPCO was liable to income-tax charges and had to comply with the requirements of Indonesian tax laws with respect to such matters as filing of returns, tax assessments and the proper keeping of accounts, the production-sharing principle was preserved as Pertamina undertook to pay all these taxes on behalf of IIAPCO out of its own share of petroleum. The title to its share of oil passed to IIAPCO only at the point of export. And all capital equipment brought into Indonesia by IIAPCO became the property of Pertamina, thus in effect nationalising many of its assets.

The effect of these provisions was however negated to a considerable degree by a requirement which obliged IIAPCO to market all crude oil produced. This requirement encompassed the 40 per cent 'cost' oil intended to offset IIAPCO's operating expenses and also Pertamina's own share, unless the latter wished otherwise. Furthermore, although the contract stipulated that 'either party shall be entitled to take and receive their respective portions in kind',[14] Pertamina could only take its portion of petroleum provided it gave adequate notice, and only if this did not interfere with any sales agreement for the petroleum reached by IIAPCO prior to this notice being given. The length of notice required was laid down as not less than 90 days prior to the half-year period in which the division of production was to take effect, and Pertamina had to specify the exact quantity of petroleum which it wished to take up. These restrictions went a long way towards safeguarding IIAPCO's control over its downstream requirements for crude oil.

It may be noted here that the 40 per cent 'cost' oil provision represented in some measure a reversion to a similar arrangement to the royalty payments of the traditional concession. For as the expenses that could be deducted before the division of production took place were limited to 40 per cent of the value of output, and company expenses were bound to be considerably higher at least for the initial years of production, those operating costs in excess of the 40 per cent limit would have to be deferred till they could be recovered in subsequent years. Consequently, the payments by IIAPCO to Pertamina resulting from the subsequent division of the 'profit' oil element of production[15] constituted in effect a royalty; for Pertamina was guaranteed some minimum payment from the extractive operation irrespective of its profitability or the market price of petroleum. Pertamina received revenue as long as production took place, an attractive proposition when considering stability of income.

The contract embodied an important safeguard against transfer-pricing practices. All petroleum sales to third parties were valued at the net realised price (f.o.b. Indonesia) received by IIAPCO, unless Pertamina was able to obtain a more favourable price, in which case this market price was to be used. And sales to affiliates were valued on the basis of prices realised on third-party sales by either side.[16] These provisions provided significant protection for the government side against the possibility of underpricing by IIAPCO. However if there were no third-party sales on which to base an appropriate valuation, the contract laid down that an adjusted price derived from the general commercial sales of Sumatran crude oil was to be used, an unsatisfactory solution, as it was vague and ill-defined. The ambiguous phraseology was compounded by allowing for commissions or brokerage costs incurred at a level which was not to exceed what was described as 'the customary and prevailing rate'.[17] The efficacy of this provision would require an ability not just to identify affiliate transactions, but also to scrutinise company accounts in close detail and evaluate myriad crude oil transactions in order to arrive at an acceptable general price. This presupposed a high level of sophistication and expertise on the part of the monitoring authority if it wished to challenge company calculations of operating costs and sales prices.

Pertamina had of course the option of taking its share in oil rather than in financial terms, which provided additional protection. And if IIAPCO was not prepared to meet a declared higher price by Pertamina, the latter was also entitled, provided it had given sufficient notice, to take and market the 'cost' oil share of production. It therefore kept open a possible course of action whereby if Pertamina was not satisfied with IIAPCO's declared oil prices, it could take payment in kind and attempt to sell this production to a higher bidder. The effect of this provision was however weakened by a requirement obliging Pertamina in these circumstances to pay IIAPCO for the 'cost' oil share of petroleum on the basis of its higher realised price, which would in effect confer a price subsidy on IIAPCO. The latter, if it so wished, was also entitled to transfer part of its 'profit' oil share for sale by Pertamina on the same basis, again receiving payment at the higher price.

It is therefore possible to see that the basic theory underlying production sharing as a system for governing company–government relations was not fully borne out by its operation in practice. Actual physical division of production need not even occur, and Pertamina still had to maintain scrupulous monitoring of all company financial transactions.

Like the preceding contracts of work, the production-sharing contract also included an area-reduction clause and minimum expenditure requirements. And the contract also provided for the payment of signature and production bonuses, though the former was termed a 'compensation' payment in exchange for information held by Pertamina on the contract area. But as the details of this information were not set out in the contract, the payment would probably be more accurately regarded as a signature payment.

Pertamina has extended its concept of production sharing to meet varying circumstances in different fields. A significant development in the Indonesian petroleum industry has been the emergence of liquefied natural gas (LNG) as a valuable export in its own right, with long-term arrangements to supply LNG to public utilities in Japan and South Korea.

The bulk of LNG production is under production-sharing agreements with foreign companies, and the terms of these contracts are similar to the initial production-sharing arrangements for petroleum. The foreign company is entitled to recover its costs, including its capital investment, in the form of a portion of the LNG produced, and the balance of production is divided between the government and the company in the ratio of 65:35, the government's share being taken to include the company's payment of its corporate tax liabilities. Unlike the initial oil production-sharing contracts, however, no ceiling was placed on the ratio of cost recovery to total production. There was therefore no limit to the extent of the company's possible 'cost' oil recovery, and the government was consequently not guaranteed a minimum payment from the commencement of production. In this respect, LNG production-sharing contracts resemble the revised post-1976 petroleum production-sharing contract form, the concession on cost recovery being necessary to induce companies to incur the very high capital investment required to start up operations in this field.[18]

Another notable application of production sharing in a different context may be seen in the technical assistance contract signed with Redco (Rehabilitation, Engineering and Development Company) in October 1968, in which the latter undertook to assist in Pertamina's existing operation of certain fields in East Kalimantan and Tarakan island.[19] Redco agreed to help rejuvenate existing fields already in production for Pertamina, to carry out repairs to production facilities and, as a secondary function, also to engage in exploration for further oil reserves in the contract area. Both sides agreed on a hypothetical projection of future production, were Pertamina to be solely responsible, and only additional production above that level, which would be achieved through Redco's intervention, would be split according to standard production-sharing terms, Pertamina retaining all production below that level (see fig. 1). It would appear that there were no major differences in determining the hypothetical projection of future production were Redco not to participate, as the line was based on known reserves and existing rates of production. This contract comes closer to giving the foreign company the contractor status laid down by Indonesian law.

In attempting to further this same aim, later production-sharing contracts have required the foreign company to agree to sell a certain portion of its production interests to a local Indonesian participant as soon as petroleum sales commence. Under a participation provision, the company was required to offer a stipulated percentage, usually five or ten per cent, of its share in the venture to an Indonesian entity nominated by Pertamina. This offer was to take effect within three months of the company's notification of its first commercial discovery. The Indonesian participant was to reimburse the contractor for its exploration and development costs at a proportion equivalent to the percentage acquired. This could be paid either in cash or taken out of production from half the participant's share of petroleum; though in the latter case the payment

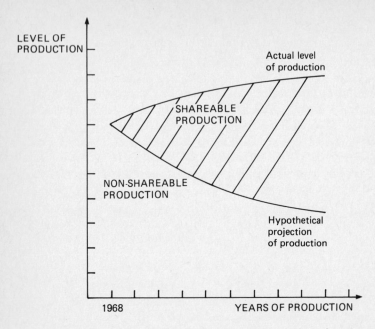

Fig. 1. Division of production under the Redco technical assistance contract. Source: private communication, Tesoro Indonesia Petroleum Company, 1980.

exacted would be one-and-a-half times the amount required in the former instance. This was to compensate for the postponement caused by its taking place over a period of time.

This participation requirement neatly allowed further financial benefits for Indonesian interests, without corresponding financial risks, as the 'participation' was of a highly selective kind. The company's managerial autonomy was not compromised either, as it remained solely responsible for the management and operation of the project. And the price it paid the participant for the latter's share of oil was fixed at a level below the realised market price, to reflect the lower price of company inter-affiliate sales, thus protecting its operating profits.

The introduction of an element of equity sharing into production-sharing arrangements through a form of limited participation was extended further with the establishment of a form of joint participation contract, on an equal-share operating basis between Pertamina and the foreign company. These contracts were brought in for the development of onshore areas previously reserved exclusively for Pertamina. The arrangement was devised by Trisulo, then Pertamina's Head of Exploration and Production. It was formulated with the intention of reducing Pertamina's own exploration costs, especially for areas which it lacked the financial resources to develop adequately, while providing the foreign companies with access to lower-risk contract areas in which they had expressed interest. These are former contract areas where Pertamina claims to have undertaken exploration work, which counted as an initial investment contribution, and the foreign contractor is committed to spend at least as much on exploration as Pertamina claims to have done. It also has to carry all expenses for the first three years, after which, providing it has matched Pertamina's declared capital contribution, costs would be equally shared with Pertamina. Oil production would be divided on an equal-share basis, and the company's half share would be further divided according to standard production-sharing terms. The foreign company would also be subject to the same incentives and tax arrangements as are in force for current production-sharing contracts, though it would have to make an additional compensation payment to Pertamina for the right to acquire its survey data on the contract area.

These agreements, in which Pertamina and its foreign partner share both the costs of developing a field and any petroleum taken from it, seem to indicate a possible shift in direction in host-government petroleum policy. As the government is now prepared to commit risk capital to petroleum exploration, albeit in limited quantities, it might move in the future to more overt forms of equity-sharing arrangements, even while retaining an element of production sharing in them.

The contract forms reached so far are contractual joint ventures rather than equity joint ventures, as the partnership is not constituted into a joint-stock operating company. However a joint structure does exist, at least theoretically, with relations between the parties regulated by the terms of the partnership contract, even if the foreign partner may seem to control the technical aspects of the actual extractive operation. As a joint-stock company is not established domestically, the partnership remains free of any restrictions which may be imposed by Indonesian company law, which would allow more flexibility for cooperation between the two sides. And the petroleum produced is not jointly owned, each partner owning its own share of production directly. This last point represents for the government a subtle but significant shift in its relations with the foreign company.

A major barrier in less-developed countries against moving in this direction is the scarcity of capital that may be used to fund petroleum extractive ventures, with their attendant high risks. The Japan National Oil Corporation has, however, offered the Indonesian government risk capital for an extremely low rate of return for oil exploration. Indeed should no oil be forthcoming, it would then be prepared to waive repayment, not just of the interest but even of the principal. This loan might provide the Indonesian government with the resources to initiate equity-sharing agreements on a more extensive scale. The joint participation format has since been extended to contracts for some offshore areas where the prospect of finding oil is especially promising. Pertamina, however, continues to prefer keeping such arrangements for existing onshore areas which it owns in Sumatra, Java and Kalimantan, rather than regarding them as providing a model for future contracts in new offshore areas. As these contracts are relatively new, however, it may be regarded as prudent to see if they prove to be a satisfactory formula for governing company–government relations, before extending their applicability.

This conspectus of Indonesian oil contracts has shown that their nomenclature does not necessarily provide a reliable guide to the manner in which the individual contract forms may be expected to function. Having conceded this point, it should be noted that the Indonesian government has been driven as much by political considerations as by financial ones, if not even more so, in determining its choice of contract form. But while it has sought to negotiate contracts which can satisfy the political requirement of being seen to assert its sovereign rights, it has also come to believe that the balance of bargaining power against the foreign companies continues to shift in its favour as these new politically-determined forms of agreement are introduced. The question remains, to what extent have changes of form induced a corresponding shift in tangible financial terms? It is therefore to the intricate problem of dividing financial rewards that we now turn.

3. FINANCIAL PROVISIONS AND CONSEQUENT AREAS OF DISPUTE

FINANCIAL PROVISIONS GOVERNING PETROLEUM
EXTRACTION

The problem of allocating financial benefits forms the focal point of the relationship between foreign company and host government. The various arrangements by which host governments seek to increase their revenue from company activities, and the practices employed by companies to defend their share of profits, are hence the subject of this chapter.

Whatever method is used to divide income, whether it be royalties, income taxation or production sharing, difficulties over allocation lie at the centre of all contract negotiations. The results of these methods, as indicated by the royalty or tax rates achieved or the division of production arrived at, were set out in the previous chapter. Yet behind these financial flows are various additional factors which have to be taken into consideration in determining the balance of financial advantage between company and government.

Indeed an assessment of relative bargaining power only from the actual outcome of the bargaining process, even though set out in the contracts agreed upon by both sides, can and almost certainly will prove to be, in effect, a misleading rather than an accurate indication of how financial profits and other benefits from the extractive operation are likely to be allocated. Actual rates alone cannot indicate the full picture of the allocation of financial benefits and risks, where the financial transactions involved attain such levels of complexity as are possible within the scope of a transnational relationship.

On the company's part, a rational calculation of the discounted cash-flow rate of return on the project might be expected.[1] Such a financial exercise would be requisite for petroleum development, where substantial capital sums would have to be expended before the operation begins to yield revenue. The object of the exercise would be to balance those annual net cash outflows with the stream of net cash inflows in order to arrive at the net return. However, subjective determinations would intrude in the assessment of the probability of each of the variables determining this expected rate of return: the exploration risk attendant upon discovering commercial-sized reserves, the economic risk in projecting levels of costs and prices over the long lead times typical of oil production, and the political risk associated with the probability of local governmental stability and the possibility of politically motivated change bearing on the company's operational conditions. It is over these issues, as they affect what might be regarded as an acceptable rate of return on company investment, that differences arise in the bargaining process with the government side. For the company will claim a premium on these risk factors in the form of a higher rate of return so as to offset the uncertainty surrounding the magnitude of future earnings.

It might therefore be expected that the government would seek to introduce as strong an objective element as possible into this subjective area. It could attempt to quantify the risks involved, and then reduce them through certain commitments embodied in the company's contract. Or it could assess the risk premiums accepted by other producer governments. The company's calculations of risk and its estimates of those factors determining the cash flow of the project would also have to be independently assessed by the government. The problem here is that the technical expertise for this evaluation, in the form of trained geologists, petroleum engineers and market analysts, is seldom readily available to the government.

The problem is further compounded for the host government if, as is usual, it would like not only to capture as large a portion as possible of the revenue flow for itself, but also to promote various social and political objectives. It might for instance wish to be seen to exercise direct control over its own natural resources, or to compel the foreign company to engage in activities which directly benefit the wider national economy. Trade-offs between such benefits and the financial costs incurred in meeting them introduce a further normative element into host government considerations, and one which may not be easily quantified in financial terms.

The end result is often a failure on the part of the host govern-ment to grasp the implications of alternative financial arrange-ments and assumptions, which may result in apparently arcane decisions when working out details of the financial régime govern-ing the operations of the foreign company. Further confusion may arise where, as in the Indonesian case, there is no indigenous tradition of codified written law, leading to a predilection for accommodating rather than resolving differences of opinion through a careful choice of terms which enthrone form over sub-stance in company contracts and legal decisions affecting their terms of operation. It need hardly be added that the converse also holds. For where the host government can determine what its financial return would be under different arrangements, it is better able to choose between them. And an improved understanding of the issues involved enables a more intelligent choice between social and financial objectives to be made.

GOVERNMENT INCOME THROUGH ROYALTIES AND TAXES

The various arrangements which constitute the financial com-ponent of a foreign-company–host-government contractual relationship need to be considered individually. Although these arrangements contribute to the overall financial settlement, they also have their own particular effects on the objectives to be secured and interests to be defended of both parties. These arrangements therefore have to be evaluated in terms of what both sides want. If surmised to be an increased financial share, some measure of this may be sacrificed by the company in return for a wider latitude of permissible activity, and by the government for thorough and efficient methods of exploitation of its petroleum reserves or other more general socio-economic objectives. A choice has to be made from such specific devices as royalties, income taxation, and those resulting from a closer involvement in the extractive venture through some form of joint contractual arrange-ment or selective delegation of exploitation rights.

An historical dimension has also to be borne in mind. Different financial provisions may derive from a conceptual framework which has altered radically over time. Thus a royalty payment derives from the basic premise that the ownership right over the actual petroleum produced is effectively ceded to the company upon payment of an agreed financial sum, the company then being entitled to receive as large a profit from the resource as it is able to achieve. A tax on profits introduces a new premise, which confers on the government the right to appropriate a share of these profits. The direct involvement of the government itself derives from a further understanding which allows the company no more than a fair return on its investment, any surplus over this amount properly belonging to the state. And this fair rate of return may be defined as that level of profitability which just suffices to induce companies to maintain the government's intended level of exploration and production.

Under the early concession agreements outlined previously, the companies may be seen to have already conceded to the government a share of their profitability, for the major portion of the latter's share effectively originated from taxes on corporate profitability and specifically on profits obtained from the extractive operation concerned. These agreements have been described as paralleling similar contracts then governing Middle East concessions.[2] However there was a fundamental difference from those other arrangements, as royalties were not the primary source of government revenue in the Indonesian case. The question therefore arises, why was the royalty or gross production tax set at such a low level and why was it calculated from the value of production rather than from its more easily determined physical volume?

The answer to this question lies with the system first operated by the colonial authorities, which endured till 1963. This system restricted capitalist enterprise through the formal control of section 4 of the 1899 Law, limiting permit and concession holders to Dutch-owned or Netherlands-incorporated companies, and through the informal practice of manifestly favouring the former over the latter in the dispensation of concessions. Restrictions extended to cover the nationality of the directors of limited liability companies and partners in joint partnership firms. What amounted in practice to an overall closed-shop policy of favouring a few at the expense of other potential entrants, worked in effect to favour specifically Dutch firms by according preferential treatment to Royal Dutch Shell and other Dutch companies, while seeking to keep out extraneous concerns. As it lacked the means to adequately supervise the terms of oil production, the colonial government could by this practice at least ensure that the oil companies worked to some extent to its advantage or, at the very least, not against general Dutch commercial interests, and that their repatriated profits, however obtained, went after all to Dutch shareholders. Deficiencies in administrative capability could in this way be rationalised, to secure a less antagonistic relationship between companies and government, and terms of operation could be designed to attain what was perceived of as common advantage for both sides.

In this light, the minor role of royalty payments within the structure of the Indonesian concession may be seen to reflect companies' reluctance to agree to significant royalty payments which would have to be made regardless of the profitability of the operation or the market price of the resource. Indeed a commitment to a large royalty from the outset of an oil-extractive venture can be particularly hazardous for a company in view of the heavy capital expenditure involved and uncertainty over the future prospect of profitable production. A commitment to pay a tax on profits involves less risk, as there can be no tax obligation if there are no profits.

On the other hand, the attraction of this royalty payment as it operated for the colonial and, later, Indonesian governments was that, irrespective of circumstances, its full value would be realised. For as the royalty was regarded as a production tax and indeed termed as such, it was supplementary to taxation income and could not be deducted from business costs nor credited against taxes on income or profits. This constraint on company action may be regarded as significant. Expensing royalty payments (by charging them as costs) or crediting royalties against taxes substantially reduces the level of revenue flows accruing to the government. Disallowing company recourse to such measures represented another important difference in the way royalties were treated from Middle East concession terms, where in the 1950s they could generally be credited against tax or, from the 1960s, set off as expenses against business costs. The companies' quid pro quo for this advantage to the Indonesian government would appear to have been to require the government to base its royalty charge on the value of production, with the attendant difficulties of administration and price determination, as it would not be possible to levy a so-called 'production tax', with its fiscal implications, on a physical unit basis. The latter form of royalty would anyway be far more susceptible to erosion in its real value as the price of petroleum increased; for as a charge per barrel of oil, it would remain constant even if the oil increased in value. This danger is avoided by the chosen method of charging royalties on value, though this consideration does not seem to have been a factor influencing the deliberations of the colonial administration which brought it in.

Turning now to the subject of taxation, a number of issues present themselves for consideration. Foremost among them is the determination of net income, through setting appropriate values both for the sales price and for production costs. Other matters of concern, including the issues of depletion and affiliate purchases, will be discussed later, as these points come up again within the context of state participation in the extractive operation.

It may reasonably be presumed that the inadequacy of general tax laws as applied to transnational business activities can be gauged by the extent to which they need to be supplemented by detailed tax provisions applied specifically to each individual agreement. The contrary may however be seen in this particular concession arrangement, where taxes applicable to the petroleum industry were incorporated within Indonesia's general body of law, rather than negotiated on a contract by contract basis. This reliance on general law obtained from colonial to Indonesian administrations up to 1963, despite the provisions on taxation relating in particular to foreign investors, these being regarded by them as lacking definition and clarity.[3] The reasons for this preference for general law derived from those which determined the original selection of method for royalty payments by the colonial administration, with a closer relationship between companies and government justifying a search for convenient and mutually advantageous arrangements. So when the system was devised by the Dutch colonial government, ease of administration took priority over close monitoring of company financial flows.

This disposition for ease of administration may clearly be seen to have governed in the aforementioned assessment of taxable income, an operation which involves first calculating the firm's gross income, and then permitting suitable deductions in order to arrive at its net income. To achieve the former, both the firm's sources of revenue and its sales prices have to be determined. Relevant income was restricted by article 165 of the revised Mining Law of 1930 solely to those sources arising from operations within the concession area, and their sales price assessed at what was termed the original market value. Though this was to be determined by the Chief of the Mining Service, his valuation was made only after consultation with the concessionaire and was based solely on information supplied by the latter, who in addition possessed a further right of appeal to the government authorities. Early Indonesian administrations might be regarded as having even less of a predilection for questioning company calculations, given their own internal preoccupations and their 'let alone' understanding with the companies. Furthermore, allowable deductions under the concession system covered not just the firm's immediate expenses directly incurred in the process of production, but also a share of its general expenses calculated in proportion to the expenses incurred by the company as a whole.

As a result of these conditions, while only locally earned revenue, delimited in the strictest possible sense, was subject to taxation under the Mining Law, the provision on general expenses, phrased in recondite terms, would appear to have opened up a loophole for transfer-pricing practices which would contrive to further reduce the profits of the locally incorporated company. The firm's position was further aided by the government's dependence upon it for data on which to base taxation charges, a situation not relieved by the latter's perfunctory powers of audit and inadequate supervisory capabilities.

Taxation practices differed further from Middle East conventions on this question of defining taxable income, most significantly in attempting to specify an actual realised value for the sales price when Middle East oil agreements from the 1950s generally relied on an artificial 'posted' price, even for sales on the open market. For Indonesian concessions, the market value of production was defined as its price at the point of departure from the concession area, this in practice being taken as equivalent to the price (f.o.b.) on the nearest available market. But with an industry structure characterised by the presence of only three major operationally integrated companies, a fair 'arm's length' price would clearly be difficult to establish, as there would be no meaningful open market transaction on which to make a reasonable appraisal.

Without any genuinely independent sales to provide a basis for establishing a free market price, and with inter-affiliate sales prices tending to favour company objectives, the problem of sales transactions within the large integrated company poses important financial considerations for the host government. While these considerations are not unique to transnational business relationships, their effects are obviously much more important in the international as compared to the domestic context. The significance of the colonial government's restrictive nationalistic policy in the granting of licences and concessions therefore lay in reducing the danger of financial loss by transforming a transnational relation into a closed internal operation; taxes on profits would be levied in the Netherlands itself if these were transferred out of the Netherlands East Indies. The serious implications of the initial 'let alone' agreements reached by the independent Indonesian government with the oil companies, under which colonial concession arrangements continued in practice, arose from not recognising that the situation had reverted to a purely international context. Profits could be shifted right out of its tax jurisdiction with a potential loss of considerable revenue, but with no compensating gain accruing to a related government elsewhere.

The actual division of profits between company and government under the concession system is not easily ascertained because of the various taxes that could be applied. It might therefore be expected to vary for the different companies involved, depending on which particular taxes affected them. In the case of negotiations to revise the early concession agreements in the 1950s, the companies claimed that they were paying in taxes and royalties more than 50 per cent of their profits, a figure which then held a somewhat mandatory status in most oil-producing countries. This assertion by the companies is, however, not easy to sustain in considering their overall position on extractive operations, for it included a 20 per cent profit tax applied only selectively to certain areas. This was the tax on 5A contract areas referred to earlier, which would for instance have left one company, Shell, largely untouched, and would for another, Stanvac (a joint subsidiary of Exxon and Mobil Oil), have affected only part of its operations. Yet even then, the Indonesian Central Bank claimed that oil company taxes had in its estimation gone up from 40 to 52½ per cent, and expressed fears that an excessive burden was therefore being placed on the petroleum companies.[4] On the face of it, this might apparently be taken as verification of the companies' position. Yet, within the political context of the time, it may more reasonably be construed as support by technocrats within the Central Bank for a government which believed in foreign investment and was committed to upholding its position within the domestic economy, against those political forces opposed to such views.

STATE PARTICIPATION IN THE EXTRACTIVE OPERATION

The increasing provision for state involvement in petroleum-development ventures made under successive Indonesian governments was a process which clearly entailed particular financial implications. The host government which proceeds along this path will soon discover that it cannot by this means escape the problems associated with conventional tax arrangements.

The contracts of work, which replaced concessions in 1963, proved to be no more than an alteration of terminology rather than a qualitative change in the practical relationship. And even the palpable change of structure effected in the late 1960s by production sharing entailed substantial qualification in practice. Neither one could be regarded by the host government as self-regulating. Nor did they obviate the need for careful auditing of financial calculations, even if ultimately expressed as payable in kind rather than in cash.

In describing work contracts, the bald statement that financial provisions were on a 60:40 basis obscures the manner in which this final result was achieved. By stipulating that the government was to be reimbursed in value for its share of production taken by the company, the division of production was effectively transmuted into a tax on profits with all its concomitant risks. Indeed the government was expected to meet all its various tax exactions on company operations out of its 60 per cent share; and should these tax demands exceed the value of this share, the company was not liable for payment of the excess. On the other hand, the government was allowed no comparable benefit in the converse situation. For of the 20 per cent production share which the government was entitled to take in kind, should this exceed 60 per cent of notional profits, the company was allowed to credit the excess against the government's 'take' in subsequent years.

Furthermore, in addition to deducting current operating costs to arrive at taxable income, a depletion allowance on preproduction exploration and development costs was also conceded as a business expense. This was to be amortised at 10 per cent, tied to the level of output.[5] While there is no generally accepted procedure for the treatment of expenses incurred before commercial production is reached, the scale of such costs in petroleum operations ensures their importance in the financial considerations of both sides. Such a depletion deduction would logically be based on a straight-forward estimation of the cost of bringing the deposit into production. But to set it as a fixed percentage associated with the production rate introduces an extraneous if not indeed arbitrary formula into its determination. This may be set in context by noting that, in general, percentage depletion results in larger deductions than direct cost depletions, with the total deduction over the life of the resource resulting from the former, not being an accurate reflection of the actual relevant cost. In any case, because of the uncertainty over the effect of depletion allowances, the general trend in oil production has been towards their reduction or elimination.

While the procedure in contracts of work for valuation of petroleum produced was imperfect, disputes over the correct price were subject to a formal determining mechanism. These differences of opinion were to be referred to a joint price committee whose decision was binding on both sides. Such a formal system provided a clear adjudicatory procedure for resolving disagreements of this nature, even if it was not fully consonant with the Indonesian preference for arriving at a consensus with an agreement in the interests of both parties as a whole. In the actual valuation procedure, however, the company could still adjust prices to suit its own particular circumstances. Discounts on the sales price could, for instance, be justified in establishing new marketing outlets.

As noted earlier, royalties based on sales prices and taxes on income require close auditing, by the government side, of both sales prices and deductible expenses, engaging administrative resources and abilities which the Indonesian government has never possessed in adequate quantities. This situation remained unchanged under the system of contracts of work. A major vindication for introducing the concept of production sharing was that it was intended to obviate this need by dividing production rather than financial profits. However, in production-sharing contracts of the kind that have been reached, the host government still has to be concerned with pricing issues. Sales to affiliates have to be monitored, because the foreign company may still remain responsible for marketing even Pertamina's share of production; while contract provisions prohibiting the oil company from transfer-pricing practices are vague and ill-defined with no effective mechanism for ensuring compliance. Operational costs must also be calculated to determine the proportion of output that the company can claim as 'cost' oil. Decrements in the income due to the state enterprise can thus occur over the calculation of operational costs or the validation of sales prices. These therefore have to receive the level of scrutiny and quality of supervision that would be given by competent tax authorities to declared income and cost deductions. This form of production sharing therefore remains as complex to administer as other types of contract, even though it claims to avoid the necessity for intricate supervisory arrangements.

The difficulty which the Indonesian system of production sharing entails in checking attempts at transfer pricing may be seen to lie in inadequate provisions within the contracts themselves for auditing the company's financial calculations. This weakness only reflects the government's limited capacities in this regard. Each contract has an accounting procedure appended to it as a separate 'exhibit', setting out those costs which the investor is allowed to deduct from gross income in its 'operating costs account'. However, there is no provision for auditing its calculation of these expenses. The contractor is merely required to 'consult if necessary' Pertamina over its purchases of materials and equipment and the procurement of services.[6]

Within the main body of the contracts, it is Pertamina, with the assistance of the contractor, which is given the responsibility for actually keeping complete books and accounts relating to their joint contract. The contracts state, though, that until the actual commencement of commercial production, this obligation is delegated to the company by Pertamina. And, in practice, even after companies have reached the production stage, Pertamina has required them to continue in charge of accounting responsibilities.[7] Early production-sharing contracts did not even give Pertamina the right to inspect its contractor's accounts, though the company was able to audit Pertamina's own books and accounts relating to its own contract. Pertamina only acquired a corresponding right in the 1970s, when contracts extended similar inspection privileges to both sides. It has, however, limited its supervision in this respect to circulating standard budget and accounting forms which the companies are obliged to fill in.

Petroleum companies supply much of the inputs required for local operations from affiliates abroad; and generally try to price these so that profits are generated where their own interests dictate, which may well be outside the host government's tax juris-diction. The supervisory problems involved in policing attempts at price manipulation have proved difficult for governments of less-developed countries. Monitoring of prices of purchased goods is clearly central to such control; and agreements which, as in this instance, make no proper provision for auditing the company's cal-culations of operating expenses only give it more leeway to fix prices at the host government's expense. In some cases, host governments have turned to independent assessors to evaluate mining company purchases, where they have lacked the expertise to calculate an acceptable sales price. This course has, however, been ruled out by Pertamina on the grounds that it further compromises national sovereignty in an area where judgments are made which directly affect national interests. Pertamina also believes that only through direct practical experience of the prob-lems involved in the whole oil-production process can it gain the necessary understanding and knowledge for more competent administration.

If the procedures for supervision have not been set out in production-sharing contracts, neither has the basis for company charges been clearly laid out. Contracts call for records which are 'kept in accordance with generally accepted and recognised accounting systems, consistent with modern petroleum industry practices and procedures',[8] which are not specified. The problem here is that accounting methods vary widely within the petroleum industry. Revenue may be allocated across time in a seemingly arbitrary fashion, and the generation of profits can depend merely on internal bookkeeping. Furthermore, it is not only a matter of agreeing on what accounting standards should be applied. In less-developed countries, few such standards exist, especially with regard to international transactions. And procedures worked out in developed countries which might conservatively underestimate profits may well be against the interests of a host-government tax-ing authority.

It is not just over purchases from affiliates that transfer pricing can be practised. Profits may also be shifted through fixing charges for services provided by the parent company or other affiliates, set-ting technical or other consulting fees for the provision of specialised information, and charging for a proportion of general administrative costs in the company's home country.

On charges for technical services, production-sharing contracts call for 'a fair rate for charges . . . provided such charges shall not exceed those currently prevailing or performed by outside techni-cal service companies'.[9] In this way, the charge is compared to the cost which would be incurred if the service was provided by a party not affiliated to the local company. This would be straightforward enough where comparable third-party transactions existed, though it would require constant verification by the host government of comparative charges across a wide range of activities. Where no such comparisons exist, however, contracts provide no clear course of action to determine what 'currently prevailing' charges are.

A different principle is used in assessing general administrative costs, more restrictive than that allowed under the previous con-cession system. Here production-sharing contracts only allow charges to be based on the actual costs incurred (a method which incidentally might be beneficially extended to cover charges on technical services where there are no equivalent external compari-sons). They do not, however, lay down the manner in which these costs are to be calculated and apportioned among the company's different subsidiaries. This drawback is met by requiring the 'esti-mated cost' to be 'determined by a detailed study' on which the company would consult with Pertamina.[10] Such an approach, placing the onus on the company to determine its charges with sufficient care and detail that the results reached are clear to the other side, can only reflect the hope that, under these circum-stances, the company would make a choice which is reasonably satisfactory to Pertamina.

As for technical fees charged by the parent company, it is again very difficult for the government side to know what a reasonable charge is. The production-sharing contract calls for a 'fair rate' to be charged, but there can be no external constraint on the amount the parent company charges apart from what may be imposed by the government. In the last resort, such payments to the parent company simply represent a reduction in the host government's effective tax rate, and will have to be accepted as such in effect if they are not disallowed altogether for tax purposes.

The extent to which foreign oil companies have engaged in transfer-pricing practices by fixing costs is difficult to assess objectively. The Indonesian government has been warned, though, that production costs and factor payments were far in excess of comparable payments elsewhere, and this matter therefore needed thorough investigation in order to ensure observance by the companies of their contract terms.[11]

Transfer pricing may be practised not only on the input side of extractive operations but also on the output side, where sales commissions may be charged and marketing discounts permitted on exports. The problem here for the host government is to ensure that the applicable price deduction is paid to the affiliate actually effecting the relevant transaction, and that the amount paid is consistent with accepted practice. For the large transnational oil company may well be able to pay a sales commission to an affiliate different from the one really dealing with the ultimate purchaser. Again the host government can choose either to allow such price deductions on inter-affiliate sales at a rate equivalent to similar third-party transactions, or to disallow such charges on inter-affiliate sales in every instance. The standard production-sharing contract sets down that 'commissions or brokerages incurred in connection with sales to third parties, if any, shall not exceed the customary and prevailing rate'.[12] Commissions on inter-affiliate sales are debarred, this being probably the most sensible course of action, and price deductions at an appropriate level allowed only on sales to independent third parties. Pertamina, however, still has to be able to judge what rates of commission would be proper and acceptable within the context of oil-industry practice.

As a guard against transfer pricing, it must be stressed that whatever the provisions may be within contracts, there can be no substitute for knowledge of the industry and continual auditing of all financial transactions. Pertamina's predecessor, Permina, therefore took an important step when it began a small independent marketing programme for its crude oil in May 1965 by establishing a joint-stock trading company with a group of 21 Japanese companies, comprising independent oil refineries, public utilities and industrial users. This, the Far East Oil Trading Company, was initially intended to channel Permina's own oil production to its Japanese partners. But it had the long-term aim of developing a market for its entitlements of production from contracts of work and, later, production-sharing contracts. A second company, the Japan–Indonesia Petroleum Company, was formed by Pertamina in March 1973 as the result of an inter-government loan, to market an agreed supply of oil guaranteed to Japan. It therefore served the same purpose, thus widening the scope of buyers. Though its effect was not evident till the 1970s, the programme did eventually provide some basis for checking on company pricing policy by providing Pertamina with its own information on costs and market prices. Furthermore, the activities of both companies were not confined to marketing crude oil. They were also involved in raising finance and buying equipment for extractive operations, thus giving Pertamina a working knowledge of pricing across a wide range of oil-company activities. The Indonesian marketing efforts were, however, hampered initially by the peculiarities of the Japanese market, which required Pertamina to incorporate purchasers within the trading companies and to deal with them directly, thus reducing its own sales flexibility. Pertamina therefore found it very difficult at first to market its production; and when sales conditions improved in the mid 1970s, it was unable to increase exports, as Indonesian oil production had levelled off.

Under the 'realised price' concept of production sharing, the establishment of independent marketing outlets is essential for two reasons. It provides not just a means of checking company financial calculations, but also helps establish, if possible, a higher sales price which the company would have to match in disposing of the 'cost' oil element of production. This requirement, however, is not entirely advantageous to Pertamina as it is obliged to reimburse the company at the higher price. It should also be noted that this provision may constitute a disincentive for the company in its marketing efforts if it leaves Pertamina to set the price. And it tends to undermine the price structure of Indonesian petroleum exports as a whole, given Pertamina's own limited opportunities for marketing crude oil.

Although prices continue to remain relevant under the production-sharing contract, it has to be conceded that production sharing does reduce the importance of working prices. The volume of production is an important factor as revenues from the 'profit' element of production are derived from fixed percentages of petroleum produced, rather than those profits which may result from artificially depressed prices set by a large vertically integrated company. Fixed production payments also reduce the accounting problems encountered by taxing authorities seeking to verify the taxable proceeds of companies, as these, like royalty payments based on physical levels of production, are more easily measurable and less subject to company manipulation.

As for the 'cost' component of production, the use of f.o.b. prices in valuing petroleum has helped simplify price verification. This was at first an issue of contention between Pertamina and the oil companies, who would have preferred the c.i.f. landed price as the initial basis for valuation, deducting an appropriate charge for transportation costs. It proved difficult, however, to agree on such charges, which are relatively high for Indonesian petroleum, as smaller tankers generally have to be used because of inadequate onshore storage capacity and port facilities.

Finally, it should be mentioned that transfer pricing can affect taxable income not only in the calculation of revenue or costs but also through debt-financing transactions with affiliates. If the parent company provides part of its investment not in the form of equity but as debt, the local company may be able to deduct the interest charged from its taxable income. It would therefore seem appropriate not to allow any deductions for interest payments when these are made to affiliated parties.[13] Such a policy would generally not be difficult to administer, and the distinction between types of loans provides reasonably fair treatment of company borrowing policies by still allowing interest charges on non-affiliated loans. The production-sharing contract allows for costs 'not including interest on any monies borrowed for oil field exploration or development'.[14] It therefore goes further in disallowing, for income determination purposes, deductions for interest payments not only to affiliates but all such payments as a whole.

While this approach is feasible, it is perhaps only appropriate where the government finds difficulty in distinguishing between affiliates and independent parties. This problem would presumably arise for the Indonesian government first in the case of

Japanese investors, where the links between firms and especially with banks are so complex that the relationships are virtually impossible to unravel, and, secondly, over the large number of small 'independent' firms[15] which characterise the Indonesian petroleum industry today. In the latter case, contract areas have been parcelled out by contract holders in a farm-out procedure which confers an interest in possible production from the contract area in return for an obligation to participate in actual work operations. Companies have also engaged in a farm-in procedure by selling an equity interest to other companies, thus providing only an interest in the contract area for those companies without the capacity to engage physically in oil operations.[16] This fragmentation process has arisen because many independent companies possess neither sufficient capital nor adequate expertise to fulfil the whole of their individual contractual obligation. And it has created an extreme diversity in the number and type of companies within the industry and a network of relationships which is difficult to elucidate.

A blanket policy of proscribing all interest payments may be the only viable solution to deal with this situation. It should be noted, though, that contracts deal with this problem in a separate addendum to the main contract, added for the purpose of determining the company's allowable costs. The Indonesian government therefore recognises that it need not actually attempt to alter the manner in which the investment has been funded in the company's records. It need only specifically disallow such transactions for its own purposes, leaving the company to retain if it can any tax advantages which its debt may afford in its home country. In any case, despite the comprehensive coverage of the prohibition against charging interest payments, some companies have managed to circumvent it by taking their loans from affiliates or companies from which goods or services are also purchased, and then charging the interest on the loan within the price of the goods.

The problems associated with affiliate transactions are met again in the later joint participation contract, and indeed can be more significant under it. This is a contractual joint-venture arrangement and there is no sharing of equity. Consequently, the government does not draw any part of its receipts from dividends, and issues of transfer pricing remain relevant. The company may still attempt through such methods to draw off profits that would have to be shared with the government. However, under these contracts development and operating costs are equally divided, and the government may therefore find not only income from the joint venture reduced if the company can raise costs by fixing prices, but in addition be obliged to meet half of the increased costs. Thus although the actual production split achieved under these agreements is more favourable to the government than for the standard production-sharing contract, their greater complexity, incorporating as they do elements of both production sharing and joint participation, requires even closer supervision by government authorities.[17]

OTHER FINANCIAL PROBLEMS

Examination of the standard production-sharing contract reveals other financial disabilities. Thus, when crude oil prices rose after the 1973 Middle East war, an inherent inflexibility was revealed when foreign oil companies found themselves receiving what amounted to windfall profits as prices outstripped production. Of course if the principle of production sharing was to be strictly adhered to, the companies were as much entitled to reap the benefits of higher oil prices as the government was, in proportion to their share of production. The government, however, advanced the somewhat presumptive argument that it could not have envisaged such massive profits for the companies when the contracts were first negotiated.[18]

Pertamina therefore negotiated an amendment which in effect imposed a ceiling on revenues. This amendment was first applied to Caltex (a joint subsidiary of Socal and Texaco and the largest oil-producing company, operating under a contract of work), and subsequently extended to the other companies operating under production-sharing contracts. A base price was set, initially at US$5.00 per barrel, and the 65:35 'profit' oil split was retained only for this first $5.00 received. Any revenues realised above that ceiling were subject to an upwards sliding scale, being split 85:15 in Pertamina's favour for production under 150,000 barrels a day, 90:10 for production ranging between that and 200,000 barrels a day, and 95:5 for even higher production levels. To allow for price inflation, the base price itself was not constant, but rose in proportion to the change in both the weighted average value of crude oil and of the United Nations price index for manufactured exports.[19]

This amendment had been foreshadowed in contracts signed as early as 1967, when a graded increase in the government 'take' was introduced upon attaining certain production levels. The revision may therefore be seen also to work in a different direction, serving to eliminate another inflexibility in the contracts by establishing a series of production thresholds, increasing the tax return as the production of individual companies increased. It also represented yet a further dilution of the production-sharing principle.

Determination of the absolute level of total revenues, as noted earlier, is also an issue of concern in financial bargaining. This would be most affected by the rate at which work is to proceed. Since management theoretically remains with Pertamina, this ought to be a management decision. In practice, it is related to the resources of the particular petroleum company, as well as to the nature of the deposit.

As the Indonesian case is characterised by relatively small but numerous fields, the issue of relative extraction rates is therefore transformed into one of relative exploration rates. As fields are usually exhausted within seven to fifteen years, companies find that they have to keep exploring for new deposits so as to counter-act the decline in production from existing fields. In Indonesia, production curves are bell-shaped, and the decline rate is regarded as significantly high. Furthermore the percentage increase in production must be higher so as to meet the same percentage decline, because the latter starts from a higher base rate. It is therefore difficult to keep production levels constant, and the rate at which companies are prepared to develop new oil-fields depends in the last resort on their economic profitability, and hence relative size. It should, however, be noted that the existence of numerous small deposits is itself no especial disincentive to companies, so long as their existence is not in doubt and they are not difficult to work. For oil companies tend to exhibit risk-averse behaviour, setting a greater weight on certainty as against the size of potential returns.

Approval of exploration programmes is a management issue within the context of the oil-company–Pertamina relationship. And the possibility of conflict became evident after the Pertamina financial crisis of 1976 when the Indonesian government sought to step up the rate of production while companies were winding down their exploration programmes.

The problem of tax payments also became an issue of contention despite the intention of production sharing to avoid this by dividing production. Contracts generally stated that

> [the company] shall be subject to the Indonesian Income Tax Laws and shall comply with the requirements of the law ... Pertamina shall pay on behalf of [the company], [the company's] Indonesian Income Tax out of Sixty-Five per cent (65%) or Sixty-Seven and one-half per cent (67½%) as the case may be of the value of Crude Oil produced and saved and not used in Petroleum Operations after deducting Operating Costs ... [20]

In standard contracts, while the contractor was therefore liable to meet its tax requirements, Pertamina undertook to meet these tax liabilities out of the proceeds of its own share of production, furnishing the company in return with receipts issued by the appropriate tax authorities. Significantly, the contract indicates but does not explicitly guarantee that the company's tax liability is absolved by the actual division of production. In outlining the tax procedure in this manner, the terms might be construed to imply that the foreign company retains liability in the event of Pertamina not meeting its tax obligations for any reason.

In a very few contracts, this key provision is worded differently. These agreements state that

> the portion of crude oil which [the state company] is entitled to take and receive hereunder shall be inclusive of all income taxes payable to the Republic of Indonesia, such as Company tax, income taxes or taxes based on income or profits including all dividend, withholding, and other taxes imposed by the Government of Indonesia on the distribution of income or profits by [the foreign company]. [The state company] agrees to pay and discharge such taxes for the account of [the foreign company] ... [21]

It might therefore seem that the above argument would not apply in those cases where contract provisions definitely confirm that the company's tax liability is discharged when production is divided and the state company explicitly agrees to meet these taxes without qualification. The tax status of the foreign company is, however, not so easily resolved. For if the foreign company is obliged by existing legislation to meet various taxes enacted in law, it would be difficult not to comply on the ground that another party had contractually agreed to meet these payments on its behalf. Basically, the issue is whether or not a contractual provision in an agreement between two parties is ultra vires under general law, and can obtain despite being challenged by a contravening legal requirement. In this case, the ultimate authority must rest with the law. Therefore even if the contract states that the company's income-tax liability is fully discharged when Pertamina receives its share of the 'profit' oil, it would appear that the Ministry of Finance can levy any taxes on the company which Pertamina has not remitted on its behalf to the Ministry.[22]

The position of the companies with regard to tax payments was strengthened by later changes in general legislation and in the form of contracts, though neither change settled the issue decisively. First, legislation was passed, as part of the 'Pertamina Law' of 1971, with the intention of ensuring that Pertamina fulfilled its tax-paying obligations on behalf of the companies. This stipulated that Pertamina had to deposit with the State Treasury: 'sixty per cent of the net operating income from the operations of Production Sharing Contracts prior to division between the Enterprise [Pertamina] and the Contractor', and that this would 'discharge the Enterprise and the Contractors and [would] constitute the payment' of those taxes required by law.[23] For good measure, this was reinforced by a Presidential Decree conferring executive approval on the procedure, and stating that the financial transfers under it were 'tantamount to payment' of all stipulated taxes.[24] The procedure agreed upon was for Pertamina, after having received payment from the company, to deposit the relevant sum with the Ministry of Finance, which issued an acknowledgment in return. Pertamina then sent this acknowledgment to the Directorate of Taxes, which in turn gave a receipt to the company. The legislation did not provide, though, for a situation in which Pertamina failed to deposit the required sums with the Ministry of Finance.

Secondly, the revised production-sharing contracts which resulted from their renegotiation in 1976 provided for a pre-tax 'profit' division of 65.91:34.09 in favour of Pertamina. The foreign company share is fully taxable under Indonesian tax laws at the normal corporate income-tax rate of 45 per cent, and a further 20 per cent dividend tax is applied to the income remaining after corporate taxation. This constitutes an effective tax rate of 56 per cent, the remainder of production being shared between Pertamina and the company according to the above pre-tax profit ratio. When applied to the company's share, the tax charge results in a final 'profit' split at the agreed new rate of 85:15.[25] As the ratios are expressed in value terms, the foreign company is therefore entitled to 15 per cent of the market value of the 'profit' oil. The new contractual form would presumably enable foreign companies to argue that their tax requirements were met when production was divided. It would seem that the Finance Ministry could, however, still insist that contract provisions did not exempt a company from complying with existing legislation.

On the face of it, the government proper appeared to take the position that Pertamina and not the companies bore final responsibility for their tax payments. The Ministry of Mines stated that Pertamina 'shall pay all taxes and duties arising from [production-sharing contracts], except for income taxes and other taxes of subcontractors'.[26] There had previously been unconfirmed reports in which Pertamina did on occasion fail to meet its tax payments and the Ministry of Finance then sought redress from the companies concerned, on the basis that unpaid taxes were their responsibility. The status of the production-sharing contract, as an agreement between foreign company and Pertamina outside the legislative process, was taken to support the Ministry's view, the Ministry arguing that a contract with a state enterprise possessing no power of legal amendment cannot exempt a company from complying with general legislation.

After Pertamina got into financial difficulties in 1975, the Indonesian central bank obtained withdrawal rights from Pertamina accounts in order to secure government revenues from oil production. But in the last resort the situation can only be resolved by the exigencies of political reality. The Indonesian government cannot afford to allow the status of production-sharing contracts, which are approved by the President, to be compromised, or the understandings reached between Pertamina and foreign petroleum companies to be discredited, as this would result in unacceptable damage to the country's investment climate. It is therefore ultimately unable to force its case. With the companies in such a nebulous position, however, Pertamina has apparently been able to make frequent requests for extra-contractual payments, either to fund specific projects of its own or even to be channelled to the government for the latter's own purposes.

MATTERS OF DEPRECIATION

The issue of depreciation has come to form a prominent feature of Indonesian petroleum agreements. The simple concept of depreciation as an accounting principle which reflects the loss in value of capital assets hides the fact that allowing it as a deductible cost reduces company profits and hence the government's tax income. The understanding behind depreciation, and justifying it, is that the firm's capital deteriorates in value, and that this loss should in fairness be written off against profits. In this sense, annual depreciation should strictly be based on the yearly loss in value of the company's operational assets. This, however, would involve considerable problems of estimation as the resale value of assets seldom follows a linear declining course and different types of assets depreciate at different rates. It is therefore usual for reasons of administrative expediency to estimate the value of assets and write them off over their assumed life through the course of the company's operations, either in equal annual instalments taking straight-line depreciation, or following some simple non-linear formula such as the declining-balance method, that reflects their more rapid loss in value in the initial stages of their life.

Both practices may be encountered in Indonesian petroleum agreements. Under the concession system the latter practice was adopted, with firms depreciating their capital assets according to their declining value in the balance sheets. These were written off each year at the level of seven per cent of their book value, the book value itself being determined by taking the average of the book values at the beginning and end of the assessment year. It can be seen that this method allows for much greater depreciation in earlier years and less in later years as the average book value of the capital stock declines, and companies therefore enjoy a lighter tax burden initially, though this is compensated for in subsequent years.[27]

Contracts of work on the other hand choose the former course of linear depreciation, allowing companies to depreciate capital assets out of current production 'at commercial rates which in the aggregate will average ten per cent (10%) of original costs per annum'.[28] The write-off therefore occurs in equal amounts each year, though not over the assumed life of the asset, but instead over a specified period of ten years. As a safeguard to ensure that companies recover the full value of their capital investment, contracts of work allow them, during the last ten years of the term of their contract, to depreciate newly introduced capital assets at rates which allow full recovery of their investment during the remaining period of operation. Though work contracts may appear to provide a more generous depreciation margin than concession agreements, it should not be forgotten that straight-line depreciation does not take account of the greater decrement in value of capital assets during their first years of use; and hence does not allow companies to postpone some of their tax payments by reducing initial profits.

The production-sharing system also provided at first for straight-line depreciation, but under a highly complex procedure which took into consideration both Pertamina's nominal management of the extractive operation and the need to provide some sort of financial inducement to encourage oil companies' acceptance of the new contract form and investment in the offshore contract areas that were being opened up. To begin with, contracts stated that all equipment defined as 'movable physical assets', purchased by the company and brought into the country for use in oil operations, automatically became the property of Pertamina, to whom rental payments would have to be made for their use. These payments were to commence only upon attaining commercial production, and were to be made at a rate commensurate with the estimated life of the relevant asset, though not to exceed ten per cent of their original value per annum, until total payments equalled the purchase price. Though companies were therefore in effect required to pay again for the major part of their required capital equipment, these rental payments were recoverable out of operating costs and could hence be written off against operational profits.[29]

Contracts included a further depreciation clause which provided for 'the initial cost of all normally depreciable physical assets' to be written off in equal amounts over a five-year period. Just as for recovery of rental payments, these too would only begin when the operation reached the stage of commercial production. It should be noted that the clause is phrased to allow a straight-line depreciation over five years, not only for that portion of capital assets regarded as 'fixed' in nature and hence not taken over by

Pertamina, but also for 'movable' assets, on which the company would already be making rental payments to Pertamina and including these payments in operating costs.

It would seem that petroleum companies can therefore both depreciate their capital assets and at the same time recover rental payments on the bulk of this same equipment, including the two sums in their operating costs. In practice, this is what the companies do. They are therefore not as adversely affected by the rental payments clause as might at first appear. Thus accounting manipulations can inflate operating costs, and as these costs are recovered from current production, the net result gives the foreign companies a larger share of overall production from the extractive operation. It has been noted, though, that so far as Pertamina's management function is concerned, it is able to avoid all preproduction risk by requiring the companies to accrue capital payments on their books, allowing depreciation to begin only if and when commercial production commences.[30]

As depreciation was recovered from operating costs, and as contractors were in turn entitled to take these costs as petroleum out of a maximum of 40 per cent of the oil produced annually from the extractive operation, problems of depreciation were in a sense circumvented in the standard production-sharing contract. Most companies concede that, even for its time, this was a relatively generous provision, allowing most of them to recover the bulk of their costs in less than five years. It was a major factor in influencing their decisions to engage in oil exploration in Indonesia in the 1960s, with its then unproven reserves and uncertain investment climate. As the contracts did not impose any strict set of accounting principles on company record-keeping, the companies found themselves able to allocate depreciation costs much as they liked, and up to the full 40 per cent 'cost' portion of production. This was a significant concession to them, allowing accelerated recovery of capital costs. The feature of these contracts that proved especially attractive for the smaller companies, on whom initial acceptance of the production-sharing contract form depended, was the virtual guarantee that all costs could be recovered from production so long as oil was found in the area of operation. As Indonesian oil-fields are relatively short-lived, companies place a high priority on recovering their capital expenditures. Ibnu Sutowo seemed to recognise that this was an important consideration in encouraging investment, as the 40 per cent 'cost' oil provision was never changed, while the 'profit' oil split was revised in later contracts and signature and production bonuses were introduced.

When therefore in 1976 Pertamina proposed, among other things, to abolish the 40 per cent 'cost' oil provision, replacing it with more normal depreciation procedures, the companies protested vigorously, making it clear that this was not acceptable. The principal fear of the companies was that, under the original proposals, more stringent accounting methods would require them to depreciate capital expenditure over a much longer period of between eleven and nineteen years, with preproduction cost recovery stretching out even further up to a possible 30 years. Under the revised terms that were finally agreed, the government compromised by dividing the companies into two groups according to their reserves and previous levels of production. Those in Group I, with proven reserves of less than 300 million barrels, had an estimated economic production life from their contract area of seven or less years, and would be allowed to recover capital expenditure over seven years; while companies in Group II, with larger reserves whose estimated remaining production life exceeded seven years, would have to spread recovery over fourteen years. Furthermore, under an additional incentives programme introduced in February 1977, companies could depreciate capital investment for new oilfields over seven years, irrespective of their size.[31]

There were two significant features of the new depreciation procedures. First, cost recovery was to be on a double declining-balance basis, which allowed for an accelerated pay-out in the earlier years of production. As companies were classified on the basis of production life from only their proven reserves and previous production, the majority of companies, 20 out of the 26 then operating,[32] were effectively placed in Group I, as only 12 of the 52 production-sharing contract areas had reached commercial production at the time of renegotiation.[33] And to grant them depreciation on a double declining balance for as short a period as seven years was to concede an extremely rapid initial recovery.[34] It should also be noted that the classification of companies was somewhat wayward, as it took no account of later additions to proven reserves as companies reached production or of further increases in existing production, both of which might radically alter their operating position.

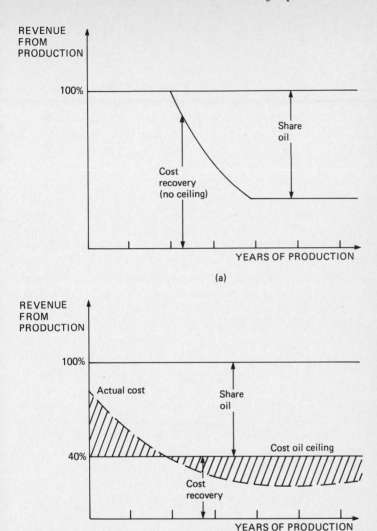

Fig. 2. (a) Cost recovery under current production-sharing terms. (b) Cost recovery under previous production-sharing terms. Source: Indonesia, Pertamina, *The Production Sharing Contract: Current Status* (Jakarta: 1980), p. 14 (adapted).

Secondly, companies could theoretically recover costs out of the whole of production, and were no longer restricted to 40 per cent. It is unclear as to the extent to which companies benefited from the removal of this restriction. It would appear, though, that the major companies with established production found that 'generally acceptable accounting practice'[35] built limitations into cost recovery which significantly reduced the percentage of production recoverable against operating costs. On the other hand, companies with smaller operations or at the beginning of commercial production were able to recover well over 40 per cent of production against costs. Indeed, in several contracts, for example with Indonesia Cities Service in East Java and with Mobil Oil over Liquefied Natural Gas in Arun, North Sumatra, cost oil recovery reached the theoretical limit of 100 per cent, as Pertamina was believed to have received no revenue during the initial stages of production.

There were indications that Pertamina found that it did not possess the supervisory resources to administer the new terms effectively, and that the companies found them less restrictive than they had first thought. As one oil-company executive remarked, 'This makes the cost recovery more palatable as you can stick a lot of costs into your first year claim . . . The revenue stream is now higher because of higher oil prices . . . It makes it even better still.'[36]

While cost-recovery terms under the standard production-sharing contract were thought of as generous, yet the foreign company was still limited to 40 per cent of production. This meant that the Indonesian side received revenues right from the commencement of production, even though the company's total costs had not yet been covered. This was a significant improvement over the profit-tax system where, in the early stages of the extractive operation, the host government received no revenues, apart perhaps from a modest royalty payment. Indeed, in ensuring that the host government received a financial return irrespective of profitability, the standard production-sharing contract was more effective than a royalty provision. Under the revised terms, however, this advantage of production sharing over tax or royalty arrangements is nullified, as Pertamina only receives income after capital costs have been paid and if profitability is achieved. Indeed the arrangement no longer involves a division of production unless and until such a stage is reached.

It may be suspected that, in this case, depreciation has been used for a purpose beyond simply that of allowing for the using up of capital assets; and that it now represents at least in part a positive investment incentive to the foreign company, enabling it to postpone taxes at low production levels. This manipulation of depreciation to grant investment incentives has always been inherent in the production-sharing contract form. As oil deposits in Indonesia are relatively short-lived, the depreciation rate will have to shorten the presumed economic life of capital assets so that the company can write these off before terminating production. But the revised terms did ensure that even though the companies were allowed a higher depreciation at the commencement of production, the government side would make up for this in later years. This might be considered as equivalent to levying a lower tax rate on company operations initially, and recouping foregone revenues by imposing a higher tax later.

It is generally supposed that investment decisions are only slightly influenced by tax factors, and hence governments should be wary of applying depreciation as a financial incentive. The Indonesian experience in petroleum, however, suggests that the large capital expenditure required in extractive operations can make the method of depreciation an extremely important influence affecting company decisions.

A further distinction is sometimes made in accounting practice between depreciation for fixed tangible capital assets and amortisation and depletion expenses. Amortisation in mineral agreements takes account of expenditure on intangible assets, including development costs required to bring the resource deposit into production, while depletion covers exploration and development costs prior to attaining economic production.[37] It may be seen that when depletion is directly related to preproduction cost recovery, it forms no more than a part of amortisation.

Under the concession system, amortisation costs were treated as part of general expenses and could therefore be expensed directly. Contracts of work differentiated between depletion expenses, termed 'preproduction costs', and amortisation, described as 'intangible costs of exploration and development operations'. The former, as has been seen, was treated separately, while the latter was again included within general costs, hence separate from depreciation, and therefore written off immediately.

Production-sharing contracts also limited depreciation to physical capital assets; amortisation was therefore included in operating costs, while depletion as a separate allowance was eliminated.[38] This removal of the depletion charge was in line with trends in other oil-producing countries. In the standard contract, operating costs were expensed without limit up to the 40 per cent 'cost' portion of production, with unlimited loss carry-forward to succeeding years when costs exceeded the value of this part of production. The revised production-sharing contract form abolished this limit, allowing all non-capital costs to be expensed in the year of expenditure up to the maximum value of production. Unrecovered non-capital costs were carried forward and expensed in subsequent years on a straight-line basis following the same time periods used for depreciation recovery, but the companies were allowed to make an additional eight per cent interest charge. Allowing amortisation as a currently deductible expense may be recognised as a financial incentive, as it inflates operating costs, thus reducing income on which taxes are levied.

BALANCING HOST- AND HOME-COUNTRY INTERESTS

When a company conducts mining operations abroad, although it may be free to negotiate financial provisions with its host-country government, both it and the host government have to reconcile these terms with the interests and requirements of the home government in which the company is incorporated. The issues involved relate primarily to taxation and the need to harmonise the financial stipulations laid down in different tax codes, so as to enable the company to retain the maximum possible revenue and not be financially penalised.

The issue of local incorporation of the extractive enterprise may have financial implications if the company is entitled to claim tax deductions from its home government. Thus American oil companies operating abroad were for a long time allowed to deduct amortisation payments, comprising intangible exploration, development and drilling costs, from their income in the United States, even when these costs were incurred outside the country. They could also deduct depletion costs on a percentage basis, when they depended on production from the extractive operation for a return on their capital investment.[39] These claims were forfeited if the entity actually engaged in the extractive operation concerned was not a US company. Hence American firms tended to resist local incorporation for their affiliates abroad, even where local regulations have required this, as they would then have lost those home tax advantages which depended on their operating as a branch of the parent company.

Indonesian regulations appear to require the local incorporation of foreign investors. The 1967 law on foreign capital investment states that 'an enterprise . . . which is operated wholly or for the greater part in Indonesia as a separate business unit, must be a legal entity organised under Indonesian Law and have its domicile in Indonesia'.[40] Production-sharing contracts circumvent this requirement, presumably on the grounds that, formally at least, the foreign company acts merely as a contractor to Pertamina, being engaged to execute the petroleum-extractive operation on behalf of the latter. The presence of the foreign company is therefore implicitly transient, and it is clearly described as being organised and existing under extra-territorial jurisdiction, being required only to appoint an authorised representative with an office in Jakarta. The later joint-participation agreements are in the form of unincorporated contractual joint ventures, thereby also allowing the foreign partner to retain home tax benefits where these exist, as it directly owns its share of production. The partnership is not established as a joint-stock company under local law, and hence does not form a domestic corporate entity.

The problem of local incorporation had been encountered earlier under the concession system, though the issue then centred on United-States-government support of American companies trying to gain licences from a colonial government which discriminated in favour of Dutch-owned firms. Only after the passing of the American 1920 General Leasing Act, which restricted Dutch firms in the United States by denying public land leases to foreign companies whose home governments discriminated against American companies, and after further diplomatic effort, did the colonial authorities take a more liberal attitude over the awarding of concessions.

Reconciling the interests of the home-country tax code with the foreign company's contract in the host country may limit possible choices in the formulation of contracts. Terms may have to be phrased so as not to contravene legal requirements laid down by external fiscal authorities, in order that the company be not subject to double taxation from both host and home governments on its operational profits. This issue is sometimes settled by inter-governmental treaty.

Difficulty over rival tax claims arose in May 1976 when the US Internal Revenue Service (IRS) revised its tax allowances granted to American oil companies operating abroad under production-sharing contracts. The IRS instruction was given in the context of a contract which Mobil Oil proposed to enter into with Pertamina, at a time before a double-taxation treaty between Indonesia and the United States had been agreed upon. It proposed treating the Indonesian tax payments of American production-sharing con-tractors, which were included in Pertamina's share of production, as a royalty rather than a tax, thereby disqualifying the companies from obtaining a foreign tax credit on that portion of production taken by Pertamina, and subjecting them to double taxation.

The IRS based its ruling on the following grounds: first, Perta-mina's share of production provided the Indonesian government's only revenue from the extractive operation, with no separately pay-able royalty as recompense for the expending of petroleum reserves which appertain to it. Secondly, cost deductions were confined to a fixed percentage of output, thus artificially predetermining oper-ating profits on which taxes were based. In this way, the Indonesian government could exact taxes from the company regardless of actual profitability. Finally, the income from each production-sharing contract held by the same company was calculated and taxed separately, and the company could not offset costs on any particular operation against its overall profitability. Taxes were therefore not levied on the company as a whole, but rather from each individual extractive operation.[41]

The similarity between the payments procedure under production-sharing and royalty payments, resulting from the guarantee to the Indonesian side of some minimum payment so long as production occurred, was noted earlier. The IRS had, how-ever, previously allowed the companies to credit Pertamina's pay-ments to the Indonesian treasury on their behalf, in lieu of Indonesian income tax, against US tax obligations. The stringent conditions subsequently imposed as to what constituted a tax pay-ment to a foreign government had two implications for the foreign-company–host-government relationship. First, the procedure for levying taxes would have to be reformulated so as to base it directly on the receipt of income by the company, considered overall as a single tax-paying entity, any other financial charge such as a royalty payment being independently levied. And secondly, the unique manner in which operating costs were recovered under production sharing would have to be abandoned in favour of an approach which defined the company's tax base along more conventional lines.

The revised post-1976 form of the production-sharing contract satisfied the IRS requirements as follows. First, the contract provided for a pre-tax profit split from net production of 65.91:34.09 in Pertamina's favour, with the company's share remaining fully taxable, as Pertamina's share was clearly exclusive of income tax charges. In this sense, the corporate and dividend taxes that were subsequently levied were imposed directly on operating profits, and this part of the company's payment was therefore charged to the Indonesian government. In effect, these direct taxes constituted 56 per cent of total crude-oil production (less cost recovery), Pertamina claiming a further 29 per cent (the balance of the earlier agreed Indonesian share of 85 per cent), leaving the company with 15 per cent. Furthermore, these operating profits were definitely recognisable as such because company income was determined on the basis of actual sales prices, instead of being dependent on any artificial price or extraneous calculation.

Secondly, that part of the Indonesian production share separate from the tax payments which the foreign company was required to make and which was paid to Pertamina, may be taken to constitute a royalty payment. The Indonesian government was therefore compensated for the extraction of nationally-owned mineral assets, and at a rate commensurate with their value, as payment was made out of net production. This royalty payment was determined separately from income-tax charges, and the amounts paid under both were clearly calculated independently of each other.

Thirdly, the extractive operations within Indonesia of each company were considered as a whole in computing taxable income. The cost of operations in any one contract area could therefore be used to offset income from other contract areas, for the purpose of defining the base on which corporate and dividend taxes were applied. And in calculating these taxes, income and expenditure arising from any other activities of the company within Indonesia would also be consolidated with the net income from its entire extractive programme.

Finally, the new contract form completely revised the procedure for cost recovery, as described earlier, removing the 40 per cent 'cost' oil restriction. In reckoning its taxable income, the company could deduct, without limitation, all expenses incurred, with only certain restrictions imposed by the depreciation method used on the recovery of capital expenditure. Thus the income base for calculating tax charges was determined in a more orthodox fashion.

The changes which this dispute engendered all served to weaken both the principle of production sharing and the status of Pertamina. Although the Indonesian government side stated at the time that the difference involved only a matter of terminology,[42] yet the issue required more than a change of format, as it could only be resolved by devising what amounted to a new tax procedure for foreign petroleum companies.

TAX INCENTIVES AS PART OF A FINANCIAL PACKAGE

The financial issues to be considered in arriving at an agreement for a petroleum-extractive operation are ineluctably complex. Provisions have to be devised not only to secure a financial reward for the government from the company's operations, but also to try to influence the latter's behaviour through a package of financial measures which attempt to apportion benefits and costs between the two parties, so as to reflect their relative bargaining powers, general attitudes and institutional considerations outside the bilateral relationship. The financial package that results will almost certainly be complicated, with individual measures devised to satisfy specific requirements on both sides. This discussion of financial provisions has so far concentrated on measures which exact costs from the foreign company. But in putting together a complicated package, the host government may require other kinds of financial provisions in order to induce foreign investment or to help choose between different foreign companies. This brings into consideration the controversial question of tax incentives. The use of percentage depletion and accelerated depreciation as investment incentives has been discussed. Other kinds of incentives include the provision of tax holidays and the granting of investment credits.

The use of tax holidays, in which the foreign firm is exempted from tax obligations for a fixed period, is not encountered in Indonesian petroleum agreements. More complex tax-rebate arrangements have, however, been designed to encourage particular operational activity from the companies. Thus, when exploration activity by production-sharing contract holders trailed off following the difficult contract renegotiations of 1976, Pertamina found it necessary to put together an incentive package in February 1977, with the intention of stimulating exploration out of its depressed state in order to maintain overall production.

These incentives resulted in a reduction in the government 'take' from the extractive operation, and were therefore equivalent to a tax reduction for the firm. As they were aimed at stimulating exploration and hence production, they were largely directed toward benefiting new producers, with production either from new oil-fields or from the further development of existing contract areas. One aspect of the new incentives, which allowed for capital depreciation for new oil production over seven years regardless of field size, has been mentioned.

The package had two other features. First, all companies would be allowed to charge the prevailing market price on that part of their production share which they were required to supply to the domestic market (and on which they had previously only been able to charge a nominal fee above their costs). This concession ran for five years, and the additional proceeds received by the company were intended to help finance further exploration or well development within its area of operation. (This condition was at first stipulated explicitly, but in April the requirement was liberalised, being rephrased as an 'understanding' that the funds would be so used if there were an opportunity to do so.[43]) Second, an investment credit was granted to those companies faced with developing new oil-fields in areas where initial costs were high, either onshore in remote regions more than 30 miles from a possible terminal or transshipment point, or offshore in water with a depth of over 300 feet. (This condition was similarly relaxed the following April, being extended to cover all new field development and full-scale secondary recovery projects within existing fields.) The credit amounted to 20 per cent of the capital investment cost for setting up production facilities, and was taken by subtracting petroleum equal in value to the appropriate amount from gross production, before dividing the 'profit' oil with Pertamina. This expense deduction was separate from and in addition to that gained from depreciation.

In May 1977, companies operating under contracts of work also received a financial incentive equivalent to a tax rebate, which was granted for a period of five years on production from new wells or from secondary recovery techniques applied to existing wells within their area of operations. Their contracts entitled them to take over the government's share of production, which they paid for on the basis of f.o.b. realised prices, and on their 'new' production they were allowed on this payment to deduct US$0.50 per barrel from the value of this petroleum.

Under these circumstances, the host government has to ask if the investment credit or other financial incentives granted to the companies does indeed induce the desired behaviour from the latter. It is therefore worth noting that the companies' response, in terms of increased exploration and additional production, remained sluggish, even as many of them took advantage of the new conditions. There was only a marginal increase through 1977 in the number of new wells drilled, and no increase in the number of active exploration rigs. Exploration activity only began to pick up in 1978 after the Indonesian government had finally resolved its dispute with the US Internal Revenue Service over methods of taxation.

It is therefore reasonable to question if tax rebates are of value to the host country, bearing in mind the cost in forgone revenue. Empirical research in other fields does indicate that special financial incentives are not generally of fundamental importance in the investment decisions of companies. They are therefore unlikely to have a significant effect on the flow of investment, and, in the extreme situation, companies may well act no differently, irrespective of financial incentives. This would appear to have been the case for the financial incentive offered to companies operating under contracts of work. Only Caltex signed an agreement to initiate new exploration and secondary recovery in exchange for the financial rebate. Stanvac did not take it up, presumably because it had no plans for secondary recovery projects.

Tax concessions may be made more effective if a direct connection can be established between the incentive offered and the activity to be encouraged. Of the various measures comprising the incentive package offered to production-sharing contractors, only the investment credit was directly tied to the company's activities, originally recognising the need to help companies finance the higher initial costs and greater capital expenditure required to develop production in difficult work areas. And later, though liberalised, it still funded and hence required additional exploration and development work by the company. On the other hand, companies were permitted to use their additional income from the price allowance on their domestic allocation of production in any way they saw fit, if they could find no opportunity for further exploration. And the concession on depreciation could be taken advantage of by companies who would in its absence have acted in just the same way in developing new production.

Financial incentives do of course possess a certain symbolic value, and the incentive package may have taken on this attribute in showing that the country desired foreign investment in its petroleum industry, thus repairing the strained relations between companies and government which had resulted from the difficult contract renegotiations of 1976. It may also be noted that the incentives offered were phrased so as not to affect the tax payments of the oil companies, which formed an entirely separate transaction within the format of both work contracts and production-sharing contracts. This is an important consideration when the home-government tax policy of the company concerned is taken into account, for a tax rebate may well be of no advantage to the host government nor to the company if the latter's home government increases the company's tax liability by reducing its foreign tax credit up to the amount of the forgone taxes.

The contract agreed upon by foreign company and host government may well contain a complex package of financial provisions which have been tailored to fit an individual situation. Production-sharing contracts are individualised by requiring companies to pay a signature bonus payment at the commencement of exploration, and various production bonuses when oil production from the contract area reaches certain stipulated levels. These payments are additional to the payment of 'profit' oil to Pertamina following the division of production, as they cannot be recovered from operating costs.

The system of signature and production bonuses works in much the same manner as an auction. The amounts to be paid are not fixed, and provision is made for bonus bidding, with companies competing for the same contract being invited to offer amounts which they are prepared to pay under the various bonus headings. These bids will presumably be motivated by additional non-financial considerations, especially the fear that rival companies may pre-empt a potentially attractive production source. Although the company offering the highest bonus payments significantly increases its chances of winning the contract, the sums offered are considered to be more of an inducement than a decisive consideration, as other factors also have to be taken into account in choosing between companies. Thus, although bonus payments vary considerably in amount between different production-sharing contracts, there is no clear-cut reason accounting for these differences.

The bonus system provides for a series of one-time payments which can constitute a welcome contribution to Indonesia's foreign exchange receipts. Though the amounts paid, when considered overall, have been quite substantial, they do not seem to significantly affect company calculations of operational profitability. On the other hand, it may be argued that these payments expend financial resources which the company might otherwise use for immediate exploration and development of the contract area granted to it, thus delaying the commencement of commercial production and therefore as well the government's own benefits from the extractive operation. Furthermore, it is not certain that the best choice of company for a given contract area is made under such a system, if the differences between the bonus bids of various companies depend in the main on their perceptions of the risk involved.[44] The system does, however, provide a convenient way of raising additional revenue from the marginal financial considerations of companies, when rates of payment have already been standardised in a general contract form.

It is clear from the above discussion that the contractual terms of different agreements or the effects of changes in any particular arrangement are not easily comparable, as an assortment of very different financial provisions has to be taken into account. When alternative assumptions about prices and costs or future trends in reinvestment or debt financing have to be considered as well, these calculations take on even greater complexity as the results of various hypothetical situations are worked out. But while thorough analysis of alternative financial flows makes for clarity of judgment in negotiating a work agreement, comparisons become yet more difficult when the non-financial requirements of economic development provisions, with their non-quantifiable results, are considered. It is to this topic that the discussion turns next.

4. PROVISIONS FOR DEVELOPMENT AND NATIONAL CONTROL

Integrating the contribution of the petroleum sector with general plans for economic development has become a matter of growing concern to producer governments in charge of significant petroleum industries. In examining the terms of Indonesian oil agreements, we are here concerned with those provisions which are aimed at compelling the foreign company to engage in activities which directly benefit the wider national economy. In so doing, the government's attempts at asserting its authority over the extractive process through various control and supervisory measures will also be assessed.

Despite the notable increases in the world price of crude oil since 1973, producer countries have not necessarily believed that they have profited from the rise in value of their resources to a commensurate extent in terms of material benefits for their domestic society and economy. What host governments have wanted goes beyond seeking still higher prices for petroleum products or improved terms of trade between raw material prices and the prices of imported manufactured goods. They require a broader range of benefits, not necessarily quantifiable in financial terms, which derive from extractive operations within their economies. Such attendant benefits are by no means a novelty. Many producer governments have, for some time already, taken various limited measures aimed at widening and increasing the contribution to development made by foreign petroleum companies. The record of such efforts is a mixed one, however, for the nature of petroleum extraction is such that by itself it contributes little to the general process of economic development. Its effects are confined to spatially limited social and economic enclaves.

In their efforts to harness this investment to provide a more wide-ranging economic contribution, most host governments have sought logically to engage the foreign company in a broad range of activities which generate external benefits. The object has been to promote linkages between the extractive operation and the wider economy, and thus force the company to extend itself beyond its own restricted area of interest. But the effectiveness of such efforts to extend the contribution of petroleum production beyond increases in government revenue and foreign exchange remains open to question. There is no consensus of opinion on the subject.

The conventional economic argument is that the extractive operation may be taken by itself to constitute an engine for growth, whose economic activity can, if properly channelled, stimulate other sectors of the national economy and hence induce a broad-based development. Even though the foreign company is motivated exclusively by its own interests, the host country is assumed to benefit, to the extent that the welfare functions of company and host country are interdependent and compatible. This understanding is of course simply an extension of the premise, advanced by proponents of a free-enterprise system, that, given proper conditions, the individual striving for private gain contributes inevitably to the collective benefit of society.

In the case of foreign investment in petroleum extraction, the activity generated by the foreign company mobilises indigenous resources both directly, as inputs into the extractive operation, and indirectly, by stimulating the provision of complementary services. In its turn it also improves these local factors of production by disseminating technological and organisational skills. Thus the operation produces various 'externalities' which increase local productivity, but for which the foreign company cannot charge a payment in return. So even if the extractive venture operates within an economic enclave, beneficial effects will result which spill over operational limits and will, over the period of operation, almost certainly come to assume a significant economic magnitude.

Critics of foreign extractive investment on the other hand stress its 'enclave' nature and question its ability to stimulate growth over the wider economy. Some even argue that the effects of such investment actually work to retard local economic development, as the foreign company is concerned only with exporting the extracted production, and accordingly fixes its attention firmly abroad while attenuating its domestic interests. Moreover, extreme critics of the phenomenon of foreign resource investment regard the developmental stimulus generated as fundamentally harmful, introducing the wrong type of technology. And by appropriating local productive factors to serve a capital-intensive overseas-oriented enterprise, broad-based rural development is stifled by distorting the domestic economic structure. The effects of such investment are therefore judged to be detrimental to the interests of stable long-term development; and this has led, in Indonesia's case, to the charge of 'show-case' development against the Soeharto régime.

Regardless of the validity of such criticism, it does seem plausible, given the nature of 'enclave' development with capital-intensive production processes isolated from the surrounding economy, that mineral extractive operations will encounter difficulty in attempting to foster and develop links with local economic life. And, especially if the surrounding economic environment proves unreceptive, the promise of the developmental impulse transmitted by these links in stimulating general development can easily be overrated.

Host governments with mineral extractive companies operating within their countries have nevertheless thought it desirable to implement policies, either through the general body of law or within individual agreements, to ensure that such investment begins to contribute to government revenue as soon as possible after the commencement of operations, and that it will provide economic benefits in addition to such financial contributions. No matter what the form of agreement may be, most foreign companies engaged in petroleum extraction have therefore found themselves undertaking to engage in a range of development activities not directly related to their primary concern.

ESTABLISHING EXTERNAL CONNECTIONS WITH THE
WIDER ECONOMY

The development of linkages between the petroleum extractive operation and the wider economy is necessary if the economy is to realise advantages that are external to the project itself. The possible ways in which such linkages can be established may be divided into two groups.

First, the domestic economic environment may benefit from

extending linkages backwards by drawing local inputs into the extractive operation. The economic activity generated may be directed to encourage a pattern of demand which critically expands the market for goods and services, and which in turn provides opportunities for the development of domestic industry and agriculture. The operation itself may also be employed as a means of training workers which, if they can subsequently be employed elsewhere, would result in an improvement in the general level of skills within the host country. In addition, the project may require the development of infrastructure within the area of operations, which may be used to support other economic activities beyond the requirements of the operation.

Second, linkages may be extended forwards by focusing on the output of the immediate extractive operation. Extending the production process domestically prior to exporting the output affords an opportunity to develop processing industries which, if they can add significantly to export value, may provide an important contribution to national income and foreign-exchange earnings, as well as expanding employment. The raw material output may also be diverted to domestic use, where in the case of petroleum it can, if appropriately priced, provide a cheap source of energy to stimulate a wide range of local economic activity. This course of action does, however, carry the long-term danger of distorting the domestic economic structure, if a significant portion of the local economy comes to depend on artificially priced energy.

These specific linkages will be considered in turn. Within the Indonesian context, examples of all types of linkages may be found to a greater or lesser degree. And, on the face of it, Indonesia is no exception to the general disposition of host countries to tie the operations of the foreign oil company to the domestic economy.

By seeking to induce the foreign firm to purchase the products it needs locally instead of importing all its requirements, the host government aims to provide a new market for domestic industry and agriculture. Such government pressures work in two ways. Either local businesses may start up to supply the necessary inputs, with the foreign firm often directly assisting their development, or the firm brings along its own suppliers from abroad who then in turn establish themselves in their own right as investors in the host country.

Contracts of work first introduced a requirement obliging the foreign company to 'give priority to utilisation of goods produced domestically' so long as 'all other conditions, including design, quality, price and delivery date . . . [were] equal'. The company was also required to 'cooperate in the encouragement of the production and manufacture within Indonesia of goods, equipment, materials and supplies of a type and quality which are needed in the country and which will assist in the conduct of the operations'.[1] This linkage requirement was clearly aimed at establishing local businesses to supply the extractive operation. The company undertook to use qualified Indonesian contractors to the maximum extent possible, and in turn agreed to assist Indonesian entrepreneurs in the development of their enterprises. Such measures were held by the contract to be in the national interest as they promoted the growth of the domestic economic and social structure.

It has been difficult, however, for the government to ensure that foreign companies have adhered to such a loosely worded provision. The company undertook to purchase its needs locally only if these could be met in every respect to a comparable standard, but no method of comparison was set out. A simple limitation on the price the firm would have to pay for the local product would, it seems, be required. This price limitation could be related to the c.i.f. price of the imported product or equated with its local price, where this was available. If necessary, a further safeguard could also be inserted to ensure that the quality and rate of delivery of the local product would be comparable to its imported equivalent.

In effect, the company was unlikely to substantially integrate its operation with the wider economy, beyond stimulating production of various local consumer goods and services. It may be noted that contracts would appear to have such limited objectives primarily in mind. Agricultural products for the consumption of the work force were for instance mentioned in the contract as a specific example of the type of enterprise the provision was intended to encourage.[2] More direct inputs into the extractive process would be difficult to procure domestically, owing to the level of technological sophistication required in their manufacture and as insufficient skills have been available within the country to create industries for supplying such products. Moreover, Indonesian government officials have conceded that any attempt to set up specialised support facilities for oil rig construction or technical servicing would require considerable numbers of skilled workers and specialised capital equipment, and would constitute a misdirection of the country's limited developmental resources.

Such a linkage provision was absent from the initial production-sharing contracts, though it re-appeared in an abbreviated form in contracts signed after 1969, requiring the foreign company to 'give preference to such goods and services which are produced in Indonesia or rendered by Indonesian nationals, provided such goods and services are offered at equally advantageous conditions with regard to quality, price, availability at the time and in the quantities required'.[3]

This clause, again ambiguously phrased, has not, however, been regarded as an injunction to the companies to support indigenous business activity. Rather it has been construed by Pertamina to justify the arrogation of supply-procurement decisions for the extractive operation from the companies concerned to itself. Pertamina has used this right to help establish a network of foreign sub-contractual suppliers, with foreign companies setting up within the country to supply technical services to the main contractors directly responsible for the extractive process. In taking a positive role to set up this backward linkage, Pertamina was fully cognisant of the inadequacy of the former measures under contracts of work, as it attempted to move beyond these earlier efforts aimed just at encouraging local businesses, to emphasise an expansion in the range of foreign investment activity as well. The latter approach has, however, brought other problems in its train.

Though the companies have been obliged to defer to Pertamina in the choice of sub-contractual suppliers, they have quite naturally resented nominated sub-contractors being imposed on them, especially in cases where the principal contractor had been accustomed to working regularly with what it regarded as its own suppliers. The companies could point out that the clause under which Pertamina warranted its involvement in controlling this aspect of their operations, did not specifically authorise the latter to assume such a potentially monopolistic power.

The Indonesian government for its part also has an interest in this issue, as it too has been concerned to obtain the local incorporation[4] of foreign service companies. A licensing system was introduced in 1972 to achieve this end. It had the effect of subjecting all service companies engaged in operations within the country to the governmental tax-levying authority, so that they could not evade Indonesian tax payments on their support activities for extractive operations, even where these were sited outside Indonesian territorial waters.

Despite the problems engendered by Pertamina's attempt to decide companies' sources of supply for them and the resultant emphasis on additional foreign investment, the relevant clause in many production-sharing contracts remains comparable to its contract of work equivalent in obligating the company to give preference to local goods and services as long as these are similar in quality and availability. Hence many contracts still attempt to establish a direct linkage with the local market for services and industrial products. In the production-sharing case, however, there is more involved in establishing this local economic link.

The contractual right of Pertamina to use equipment imported by the foreign company, as this becomes its property, has been mentioned. This singular feature of the production-sharing contract allows Pertamina's use of equipment, to which it gains title, only after consultation with the company. This proviso ensures that the latter is not hampered in the performance of its own operative functions. If Pertamina is regarded in its other role, as a local oil-producing company in its own right operating in onshore production areas, then this provision may also be seen to encourage linkage between the foreign investor and local economic activity, with the foreign oil company helping to support local petroleum production through the provision of a measure of technical equipment.

A second backward linkage may be set up to increase employment opportunities and provide training which would enlarge the pool of skilled labour available to the host country. This would help to accomplish developmental objectives which have been of particular concern in the development plans of the Indonesian government. It has indeed been a long-standing feature of the terms under which foreign investors have been required to operate, to include at the minimum some reference to their intentions to meet specified objectives of local employment and job training. For example, the concession system in 1930 laid down the rudimentary requirement that three-quarters of the company's work-force on the site of its extractive operation should be Dutch subjects.[5]

This requirement was expanded upon by contracts of work after 1963, which set out conditions for the engagement of local employees so as to constitute an incentive for the company to set up a training programme. The jobs available were classified into seven categories based on the relative skills required: unskilled labour, skilled labour, clerical, administrative, professional, technical, and managerial. And the government side stipulated that within eight years of the contract date, at least 75 per cent of all positions in each grade were to be held by Indonesian citizens. To meet this injunction, the company undertook to organise a comprehensive programme for training personnel through active operations and in educational institutions both in Indonesia and abroad. This programme was subject to review from the government side. The contract included a saving proviso for the company, obliging it to comply with the set employment quotas only if in its view there were sufficient Indonesian citizens available with acceptable qualifications.

In setting a time-table that required progress in turning over jobs to local personnel, this provision might have been expected to work well in compelling training. But the safeguard allowing the company the right to assess the availability of qualified personnel may be regarded as unsatisfactory in ensuring an ongoing pattern of training over the life of the company's operations, especially as the company was not required to submit to the government any reasons for exceptions in meeting employment targets. The adequacy of its training programme would presumably have had to be justified when set out for government review. And the companies themselves do claim to have made considerable efforts in this regard, with their interest in education and training being by no means confined to programmes which are of direct benefit to their operations. Indeed contracts of work may fairly be regarded as instrumental in instituting regular training as an integral part of company operations, thereby breaking the earlier pattern of Indonesian nationals being used largely as manual workers.[6]

Such a detailed time-table for the recruitment and training of Indonesians was, however, dropped when new production-sharing contracts began to be introduced in the late 1960s. Under the terms of these contracts, the foreign firm was still obliged to 'employ qualified Indonesian personnel in its operations' and, once commercial production commenced, to 'undertake the schooling and training of Indonesian personnel for labour and staff positions including administrative and executive management positions' at its own expense. At the same time, the company was further required to 'consider with Pertamina a programme of assistance for training of Pertamina's personnel',[7] this scheme being funded on a mutually agreed basis.

Pertamina claims to attach particular importance to the issue of Indonesianisation, the employment of local nationals to replace foreign expatriates, as it is seen as a source of training which increases the pool of skills available both to Pertamina and to the country generally. But a certain degree of ambiguity may be discerned in its attitude towards this requirement. Production-sharing contracts may stipulate general commitments by the foreign company to engage Indonesian nationals, to organise a training programme in order to provide skilled manpower, and possibly even to assist in Pertamina's training of its own staff. Yet all these commitments set no clear-cut target which could provide a yardstick to assess the company's compliance with the government's dicta in this regard. Moreover, the equivocal nature of the contract provision has generated disagreements over definition, timing and enforcement.

To begin with, production-sharing contractors have found themselves left almost entirely in control of their personnel policies, being virtually free to employ and train their own staff as they pleased, despite the declared intentions of Pertamina to set far more ambitious goals for Indonesianisation than had been achieved under contracts of work. The government increased its supervisory function in 1972 when, to reinforce contractual provisions, the Directorate General of Oil and Natural Gas issued a decree formalising the procedure under which oil companies employed foreign personnel. This decree compelled the firms to submit a schedule annually on their use of expatriate employees, delineating this requirement within their overall operational needs, and to detail the efforts being made to replace these expatriates with qualified Indonesian staff.

The 1972 decree prepared the ground for the imposition in January 1975 of a government-set time-table requiring progress for the Indonesianisation of petroleum company staff. The schedule that was introduced established job categories according to the level of skills presumed required, and set deadlines for achieving the transfer of jobs to local workers. Management-level functions were divided into three main groups: executive and senior technical and operational posts remained open for an unspecified period to foreign expatriates; junior technical posts were to be transferred to Indonesian staff over a period of three to five years; and all supervisory and administrative posts had to be Indonesianised over two to four years. Lower-level non-management functions were divided into skilled labour and clerical service groups, with the former transferable to Indonesians over one to two years, while the latter category was entirely closed to foreign staff. Thus progressively faster rates of turnover were set up for jobs requiring decreasing levels of skills, instead of a blanket requirement as in the contracts of work, and an attempt was made to match the opening of job categories to foreign expatriates with the availability of suitably qualified Indonesian nationals. Any delay in achieving the required transfer of staff was to be penalised by the imposition of a monthly fine, set initially at US$100, for each expatriate employed beyond the specified time-frame.

In the implementation of this time-table, Pertamina took upon itself not only to decide if a particular job should be Indonesianised as was required by the schedule, but also to determine if expatriate candidates for intended appointments were suitably qualified for their assigned jobs. The assumption of these powers by Pertamina immediately brought it into dispute with the companies who regarded such decisions as an interference with their staffing policy, a matter which was wholly their responsibility. They further deemed Pertamina's actions as seriously hampering their operations through the premature curtailment of expatriate supervisory personnel. The situation was further aggravated by the indistinct definition and arbitrary demarcation of jobs within the timetable, with various work functions of the company's operation being inappropriately juxtaposed.

Pertamina for its part saw a strict implementation of the Indonesianisation policy as necessary in the context of its overall role as manager of the petroleum sector. For management was taken to include the ability to carry out necessary operations by itself without relying on foreign assistance. The process was therefore not just quantitative in nature by employing more Indonesians, but also qualitative, involving their training and promotion within the companies. On this issue Pertamina regarded the companies as being indifferent if not indeed apathetic, and therefore needing a certain amount of pressure to initiate training and replacement programmes. Pertamina itself has in turn been pressed on this matter by a variety of government agencies, such as the Ministry of Mines and Energy and the Ministry of Manpower, both of whom have control over the use of foreign manpower by Pertamina's production-sharing contractors, and by various parliamentary committees concerned with the implementation of the Indonesianisation policy. Such political pressure groups as the latter, without specialised knowledge of the oil industry, may not be able to fully appreciate the operational problems faced by foreign companies in attempting to meet the government's time-limits.

While the companies claim that they do indeed try to meet these deadlines, they are not prepared to jeopardise the security and efficiency of their field operations by employing inadequately qualified or inadequately experienced Indonesians. They have therefore made attempts to extend the work permits of their foreign staff beyond the stated limits; and where this has failed they have even privately conceded their readiness to pay the government-imposed financial penalty. The issue is basically one of a trade-off between the safety and efficacy of the extractive operation and rigid compliance with the requirements of the time-table. The companies maintain that the former can only be ensured if their posts are Indonesianised in accordance with schedules drawn up by themselves even if these training programmes fall short of set deadlines, and that this compromise should be accepted by Pertamina. This has in fact been the result, with Pertamina maintaining that most oil companies have made satisfactory efforts to employ Indonesians, while the companies have not managed to meet the objectives laid down by the government. But while Pertamina may show a measure of flexibility on this matter, it still has tightened its supervision of company training efforts, delegating representatives to visit training programmes, and requiring the companies to show a detailed individual training plan for the replacement of each expatriate post before renewing the foreign employee's work permit for the post under consideration.

The question remains, to what extent have companies Indonesianised their staff? With the introduction of a time-table for Indonesianisation, the number of foreign expatriates employed by the oil companies began to drop, thus apparently indicating that jobs were being turned over to Indonesians even if not at the rate stipulated by the schedule.[8] However, the figures conceal two important facts. First, although the level of expatriate employment fell from 1976, this fall coincided with a slow-down in petroleum exploration when the number of oil companies operating in the country, and hence of expatriate posts available, was reduced.[9] And secondly, Indonesianisation seems to have progressed furthest in filling what are regarded as 'soft' administrative jobs. Thus the change in the level of expatriate employment at the all-important technical level has been even less significant. It should be noted here that the time-table did in fact set stringent requirements especially for the replacement of technical staff engaged in maintenance functions. If companies most obviously fell furthest short of their Indonesianisation objectives in this area, this was only a consequence of the limited availability of Indonesian technicians qualified to service operational equipment, and of the unrealistic period of time allotted in the schedule for the training of such personnel.

The assertion by the companies that there is a serious shortage of qualified Indonesians has led to the widespread practice of companies 'raiding' each other for skilled local staff to supplement their own training output. Initially this practice caused difficulties, especially for established companies like Caltex, which had a long-standing training programme and hence a pool of experienced Indonesian personnel from which other companies attempted to 'poach' staff. Caltex eventually had to seek an injunction from Pertamina in order to prevent the latter's production-sharing contractors from recruiting Caltex personnel. The problem has now particularly affected smaller companies, unable to provide extensive training facilities, which thereby face problems in meeting Pertamina's requirements. They find the loss of trained local staff especially difficult to make good.

It might be thought that a possible solution to this problem would lie in Pertamina having some control over its contractors' Indonesian employees so as to be able to curb to a certain extent their movement between companies within the petroleum industry. In 1972, Pertamina did in fact attempt to require the companies to secure its approval for all appointments, promotions and transfers of local staff, advancing this proposal on the ground that it was better able to handle the companies' Indonesian employees through its own internal screening and disciplinary mechanism.

The companies, however, unanimously refused to comply with this requirement, regarding it as an intrusion into their managerial authority, which was at stake if they were not able in the last resort to decide their own personnel policies. They viewed it too as an indirect means of expediting possible future nationalisation. And they also feared lest their employees be subject to divided loyalties as a consequence. Indeed, they reported that their own Indonesian staff were themselves opposed to having what was termed 'Pertamina status' conferred on them.

When therefore Pertamina attempted to resolve the issue through a typically Indonesian compromise, whereby all foreign-company local employees signed a 'letter of engagement' for Pertamina while in practice the companies themselves remained free to employ and promote staff without reference to Pertamina, this proposal too was rejected by the companies. Though Pertamina refrained from pursuing the matter further, the issue remains a highly sensitive one, and it has been referred to over the years by Indonesian officials.

Finally it is pertinent to question the value of this particular linkage with employment in the Indonesian context. The capital intensity of the Indonesian oil sector (the value of capital invested in the industry for each full-time worker employed) was estimated in a 1975 study at US$33,000:1.[10] This may be compared to a capital intensity figure of $6,599:1 for foreign investment projects in general (excluding investment in the petroleum sector) over a period from 1967 to 1975, and a corresponding figure of $3,740:1 for domestic investment projects.[11] The disparity in investment requirements widens further as additional investment in the petroleum industry in subsequent years is taken into account. A figure of approximately $94,000:1 may be proposed for capital intensity in the oil sector up to the beginning of 1980.[12]

If the creation and maintenance of jobs in the petroleum industry requires substantial capital investment, it is not surprising that its contribution to overall employment is very limited. Indeed the proportion of the labour force employed in the whole mining and quarrying sector is only 0.2 per cent, a figure that has not risen since 1965.[13] Productive employment in the mining sector has therefore done no more than keep pace with the growth of the labour force. In this respect, the Indonesian employment configuration is similar to that of other countries. The mean employment in mineral extraction is generally low even within the group of less-developed countries, because extraction and refining methods are extremely capital-intensive.

It is for this reason that the kind of technology used by the foreign investor has become an additional employment-related concern for host governments. Extensive unemployment has prompted governments to appeal for the use of labour-intensive production methods where practicable, so as to mitigate the problem. Their concern has been expressed even where the area of operation, as is often the case in mineral extraction, is remote and sparsely populated. With a labour force of some 45.6 million, the Indonesian government is no exception to this general concern, and it has explicitly called for capital investment policy to be 'aimed at stimulating labour-intensive projects', with foreign investment policy to promote the 'utilisation of more Indonesian labour'.[14]

Mining firms have tended to respond to such government pressure by claiming that there is no feasible alternative to capital-intensive technology in extractive operations. They point out in any case that whatever Indonesian government intentions, its policies often encourage the substitution of capital for labour, rather than the reverse. The granting of duty exemption for the import of capital equipment and of investment credits,[15] whatever the beneficial effect in encouraging investment, do give an edge to the use of machinery at the expense of labour by firms facing a choice of production methods. Company arguments are, however, not necessarily entirely valid. They have for instance criticised overtime rates and dismissal procedures, which form part of the minimal protection afforded to local workers by Indonesian labour law, in justifying their adoption of labour substitution policies.

The extent of the concern which the Indonesian government has shown towards the employment linkage in oil-extractive operations might be thought excessive bearing in mind its limited possible contribution to overall employment. The use of capital-intensive techniques in the industry does, however, provide an opportunity to set up a training programme for turning out skilled labour and managerial and professional staff which are in acutely short supply in Indonesia. In the long term, such trained manpower could well find employment in other areas of the industry, leaving employment opportunities to be created from the spread effects of generated growth in the wider economy.

A third backward linkage may well come about indirectly through the infrastructure built and services provided by the extractive enterprise. The transport and power facilities constructed by the foreign company for its own use are often capable, if made available for other purposes, of stimulating economic activity and serving the general community in the region where the company is operating. Host governments, recognising this wider potential, have increasingly come to insist that company facilities be made generally available. And mineral contracts often include provisions granting the host government rights of access to and use of company-built infrastructure, on terms that avoid disrupting the company's own operations. When no longer required by the company for its own use, the contracts provide for these facilities to be transferred to government ownership and control.

Specific provisions to this effect are conspicuously absent from Indonesian petroleum agreements. The concession system even entitled concession holders to be compensated in the event that transport facilities constructed within their operational area impeded the execution of their work. Contracts of work introduced a requirement calling only for a general commitment from the company to 'give full consideration to the aspirations and welfare of the people of the Republic of Indonesia and to the economic development of the nation', to 'cooperate with the Government in promoting the growth and development of the Indonesian economic and social structure', and to 'study the possibility of further activities . . . which might assist in promoting the growth and industrialisation of the Indonesian economy'.[16] This exhortation, though lengthy, clearly avoided compelling the foreign company to undertake specific commitments or to concede particular rights over infrastructure use.

Such an undertaking was omitted from production-sharing contracts, though, instead, equipment imported by the company did become the property of Pertamina. This ownership, however, was limited in its practical effect, as Pertamina was entitled to use this equipment only after consultation with the company, and only to the extent that company operations were not interfered with. Furthermore, the provision limited its definition of 'equipment' in this context only to 'movable' assets, and specifically excluded such fixed in-place items as supply, power and communication systems, facilities which might reasonably be considered of especial importance in the application of company resources to benefit the regional economy.

Nevertheless, petroleum companies operating in Indonesia have seen the development of this linkage of their own volition as being in their interests in maintaining a good public relations image. Such activity is most marked for companies with onshore extractive operations, and longer-established companies have naturally built up a more extensive network of activities. Thus the steady development of the Minas oil-field in Central Sumatra from the 1950s by Caltex in a region with originally almost no economic infrastructure has transformed the local economy through access to transportation facilities built by the company. The company infrastructure has been used for quite different purposes, enabling other industries, such as timber production, crop cultivation and even tourism, to start up. The opening up of remote areas also has an important effect on population location as people from other regions are drawn into the immediate area in increasing numbers either to be directly involved in the extractive operation, to render support services, or to be engaged in other employment made possible by the generally higher level of economic activity. Caltex's activities have extended beyond making its facilities available for other uses to catering directly for third-party users. Thus education and medical facilities to serve the region were funded and constructed by the company, and accommodation and transportation provided for government needs. So despite the fact that the Indonesian government may not have taken a more aggressive approach towards infrastructure development, it has been helped where it has lacked the financial and administrative resources to extend services into such remote areas. And through the incorporation of such company activities, its plans for regional development have therefore been augmented.

Turning to the establishment of forward linkages, the setting up of processing facilities is often a significant consideration in host-government attitudes towards foreign investment in mineral extraction. Determining whether or not a decision to invest in domestic processing of the mineral production represents a feasible and rational economic choice is a matter which can only be decided by an analysis of the relevant benefits and costs. Discrepancies over the outcome arise where the government views such net benefits in social terms, including gains to the economy and society which are external to the project itself, while the private investor is concerned only with a more narrow calculation of his individual costs and benefits. If the host government decides to proceed with an approach aimed at encouraging the construction of processing facilities, it therefore may well have to ensure that such a project would be practicable in terms of company profitability and that the company may be relied upon to establish the requisite facilities.

Such a governmental concern was not evident under the concession system. The mining laws which governed company operations were not concerned with refining crude production. Nor did contracts of work contain any specific provision for the establishment of processing facilities, though the company was required in a general way to be prepared to consider undertaking other activities in the petroleum sector. The first few production-sharing contracts did introduce a provision whereby the company undertook to consider reaching a further agreement, on terms which would be mutually agreeable, under which it would engage specifically in the local processing of its crude-oil production from the contract area. This requirement was soon expanded upon in order to seek a more explicit commitment from the foreign company. Production-sharing contracts from 1968 have usually included a standardised clause under which companies were required to refine a fixed proportion of their petroleum production locally upon achieving a stipulated level of production, and to construct the necessary refining capacity for that purpose should none be available. The requisite proportion was generally set at ten per cent of the company's share of crude oil after deduction of the 'cost' element of production, with this processing requirement being conditional on a rate of production from the extractive operation which gave the company an entitlement of at least 100,000 barrels per day from the division of the 'profit' oil component of production. The provision, however, was effective only if both parties to the agreement judged the necessary investment to be an economical venture, thus safeguarding the company. It was furthermore allowed, in place of helping to set up local refining facilities, to invest an equivalent amount in another petroleum processing or petrochemical project instead. A few contracts have attempted to carry this reinvestment requirement further by compelling the foreign company to invest a fixed percentage of its local profits in basic industries which, in the opinion of both the company and Pertamina, would generate general economic growth across the national economy.

Contract terms under production sharing therefore recognise that the government's prime concern here is to ensure the foreign company's commitment to construct processing facilities, while reassuring the latter that it retains sufficient flexibility over its future course of action so as not to be forced to undertake an unprofitable venture. An unambiguous approach such as this, relying on the terms of the contract itself, may be attempted where there is little likelihood of company non-compliance; a company in the field of petroleum extraction usually having its reputation plus a substantial amount of investment capital at stake. Both sides agree to the establishment of processing facilities at a verifiable point when crude-oil production reaches a fixed level, so failure on the part of the company to comply with its commitment may be seen to constitute a clear breach of contract. On the other hand, the agreement does not specifically require the company to engage in further processing at that point but allows it to assess the feasibility of constructing the necessary plant and to retain the option of an alternative investment, more viable from the private viewpoint, in its place.

With, however, an agreement that provides neither the certainty that processing facilities will be built nor clear penalties for the company in the event that they are not, it would appear that the Indonesian government does not place a high priority on the setting up of such plants in its actual negotiation of petroleum production-sharing contracts. The processing requirement does not form a major component of the arrangement, being subsumed under a general section at the end of the standard contract. More importantly, none of the financial terms in the contract appear to have been devised with either the recognition or the encouragement of the future processing of production in mind. And were the requirement to be invoked, it would affect only an extremely small proportion of total output from the contract area.

Indeed domestic refining had a poor record for a long time, though it has more recently improved. The percentage of Indonesian crude-oil production processed in domestic refineries actually fell over a ten-year period from 39.2 per cent in 1964 to 18.3 per cent in 1974, and by 1978 had fallen even further to

17.3 per cent. In real terms, the physical output of local refineries, which totalled 64 million barrels of processed petroleum products in 1964, rose only to 86 and 94.5 million barrels respectively in the corresponding years 1974 and 1978. The 1979 oil price rises and consequent domestic petroleum shortages did however spur the Indonesian government to increase its refining capacity. It undertook, on its own initiative, three major refinery expansions at Dumai in Central Sumatra, Balikpapan in East Kalimantan and Cilacap in South Java. These projects were directly funded by the government and built by foreign contractors on a turnkey basis.[17] The construction of an intended additional oil refinery had, however, to be rephased in 1983, as a fall in raw material prices and hence export earnings obliged the government to limit its foreign currency expenditure. Nevertheless, the refinery expansions which were completed raised refining output to 146 million barrels by 1984, a figure which could be doubled once teething problems have been overcome and the plants become fully operational.

All refineries operating in Indonesia have been managed by Pertamina since January 1970. They are located close to producing oil-fields and are therefore source- rather than market-oriented, being closely tied to local output. Production still caters largely for the domestic market, as Pertamina's insistence on managing refining operations makes it difficult for Indonesian refineries to compete with the established supply networks of the major oil companies in finding markets abroad for petroleum products. Nevertheless, the increases in refining capacity have helped Indonesia to cut down its imports of refined oil products, which have reduced overall oil revenues, and therefore improved its balance-of-payments position.[18] Finally, it should be noted that the importance of the Indonesian petrochemical industry is marginal in terms of consumption of domestic petroleum production, its major component consisting of a polypropylene plant at Plaju in South Sumatra. Here again, government plans to expand petrochemical production had to be trimmed in 1983, with the rescheduling of both an intended major petrochemical complex at Aceh, North Sumatra, and a further aromatics plant at Plaju.

If a criterion of the effectiveness of the financial terms in a contract is the incorporation of enforceable standards, this applies equally to the contract's non-financial aspects. But such standards are even harder to define in the latter case, a course contingent on a vague and non-binding agreement in the future as to its economic viability, which provides no meaningful yardstick to measure the accomplishment of processing intentions.

In the last resort, the establishment of processing facilities depends to a great extent on the interests of the foreign company, even though the provisions of its contract can play a part in determining what those interests might be. A company with adequate refining capacity would have no reason to construct new facilities. Petroleum companies in any case generally prefer to refine their crude production closer to consuming markets and in areas where refining is subject to minimal governmental controls. The use of intermediate 'swing' refinery centres, located midway between various crude petroleum sources and a number of different consuming markets, offers large firms greater flexibility to alter their crude intake and product disposal patterns to suit changing circumstances, thus simplifying shipping and marketing problems. Furthermore, the company may also have to face high tariff barriers on processed petroleum products in some countries developing their own refining industries, a situation which may arise for other export products as well.

The prospective establishment of processing facilities is therefore a complicated issue to negotiate, when neither the government recognises the difficulties faced by the company in exporting processed products, nor the company recognises the social benefits to the host economy of local processing. Planning difficulties are further compounded where there are substantial uncertainties over the flow of future production from the contract area. With insufficient information available at the time of signing the contract, an agreement to carry out a formal feasibility study at a set future date would appear to be necessary. Such an agreement should also ideally contain a careful specification of standards, reflecting the host government's concern with stimulating economic development, supplementing free market notions of profit maximisation. And it may be further combined with the financial inducement of tax incentives conditional on the setting up of processing facilities.

The company may of course be required to offer a part of its output to any other company prepared to establish processing facilities. The objective would be to allow another agency to set up local processing in Indonesia if the producing company itself is not prepared to act. However, an economically-run refining plant may require more than just a portion of any one company's output. This brings into consideration the second type of forward linkage, the local use of the raw material output; for all petroleum companies in Indonesia, operating under both contracts of work and production-sharing contracts, are required under the terms of their contracts to supply a part of their crude-oil production to help meet the needs of the Indonesian domestic market. The petroleum allocated under this domestic supply provision is required to be made available to Pertamina at designated refineries in Indonesia. It thus provides a guaranteed source of supply for refining facilities operated by Pertamina, which is obtained from all foreign oil producers operating in the country.

Contracts of work required the oil company to supply petroleum in proportion to its share of total national production. The exact quantity to be made available was that percentage of the company's gross crude-oil production from its contract area equivalent to its percentage share of total Indonesian production, so long as this quantity was not greater than either the same proportional share of the total domestic consumption requirement for petroleum or a quarter of the company's gross crude-oil production.[19]

The early production-sharing contracts either did not contain a domestic supply provision or included a clause phrased in elliptical terms requiring the company to 'fulfil its obligation towards the supply of the domestic market'. In the latter case, this stipulation was qualified by an assurance that the company was 'not required to supply more than the proportion of its total Indonesian production to the entire Indonesian production of all petroleum companies'.[20] It would therefore appear that the company's supply liability was calculated along similar lines to that of the contract of work.

The company's position under production sharing was gradually clarified, and from mid 1968, production-sharing contracts included a uniform clause obliging the company, once commercial production was attained, to supply the domestic market with a portion of its share from the division of the 'profit' oil component of production. This allocation was to be determined annually in the following manner:

(i) multiply the total quantity of crude oil to be supplied [i.e. the overall Indonesian consumption requirement for petroleum] . . . by a fraction, the numerator of which is the total quantity of crude oil produced from the contract area and the denominator is the entire Indonesian production of crude oil of all petroleum companies; (ii) compute twenty-five per cent . . . of the total quantity of crude oil produced from the contract area; (iii) multiply the lowest quantity computed [from] either (i) or (ii) by a fraction, the numerator of which is the quantity of crude oil to which [the company] is entitled [this being the company's share of the 'profit' oil] . . . and the denominator is the total quantity of crude oil allocable [*sic*] [to both Pertamina and the company after the deduction of the 'cost' oil component of production] . . . The quantity of crude oil computed under (iii) shall be the maximum quantity to be supplied by [the company].[21]

Production-sharing contracts therefore require the company to allot for domestic use a quantity of crude oil, in proportion to its percentage share from the division of the 'profit' oil element of production, taken from that percentage of the total national domestic consumption requirement equivalent to the percentage share of the contract area's gross production to the total of Indonesian crude-oil production; and provided that this proportion of the domestic consumption requirement does not exceed the limit imposed by 25 per cent of gross production from the contract area. It should be noted that whereas contracts of work calculated the domestic supply allocation 'off the top' from the operation's overall output, production-sharing contracts calculated this requirement as a proportion of the company's 'profit' oil share, which therefore reduced its real absolute value. Furthermore, Pertamina's own crude oil production is included within the 'Indonesian production . . . of all petroleum companies' referred to in the calculation of the company's domestic supply liability, thus reducing this obligation even further.

The calculation of the domestic supply requirement is therefore somewhat complex under both the contract-of-work and production-sharing systems. It may be said, though, that the proportion of production each company supplies varies according to its own output level, and it decreases as overall Indonesian oil production increases. For the pro-rata crude oil under both work-contract and production-sharing arrangements, Pertamina reimburses all company costs, including transportation and delivery charges, in addition to paying a nominal fee of US$0.20 per barrel. This requirement effectively skews the actual profit split from production in Pertamina's favour, and also helps supply heavily subsidised oil to meet local demand, a politically astute move on the part of the government. But Pertamina claims it to be more than that, in that it is symbolic in its view of ownership of oil resources by the people who directly benefit through access to petroleum at a concessional price. In turn it requires the foreign company to consider the welfare of the local population. This argument is a curious one, because if the oil is not owned by the foreign companies there is no reason for Pertamina to compensate them for it. Similarly it contradicts the claim in production-sharing contracts which lays down that title to its share of petroleum only passes to the company at the point of export.

In any case, the Indonesian side does not necessarily take its full entitlement of crude oil, the requisite quantity varying according to the extent of demand in the local petroleum market. Companies generally tender about 20 per cent of their share from the apportionment of 'profit' oil for domestic use.[22] Nevertheless, company income from the sale of their domestic allocation of petroleum can only be regarded as negligible in comparison to their earnings from the rest of their crude oil entitlement. As part of an incentive package introduced in February 1977 intended to stimulate further exploration and production, Pertamina therefore allowed all production-sharing contractors to charge the prevailing Indonesian market price on their domestic allocation of petroleum for a period of five years. This temporarily rescinded the concessive aspect of the provision, while continuing to retain a guaranteed intake of local crude oil for domestic refineries.

RESTRICTING THE ECONOMIC CONTRIBUTION OF THE FOREIGN COMPANY

While it might be thought that financial concerns pose the greater difficulties in formulating the terms governing the foreign-company–host-government relationship, managing the broader range of non-financial activity which may be required of the foreign company can prove an equally intractable affair for the host government. There may be areas where there is an inherent coincidence of interests between the two sides, but the problem remains one of reconciling the firm's private interests with the government's social responsibilities where these come into conflict. Even if private costs may be traded off against social benefits, there is no implicit connection between the two, given the imponderable nature of the latter, arising from difficulties of quantification. The host government's attitude in negotiations with foreign investors therefore tends to place a higher priority on the more easily measurable gains from tax levies, where the benefits are immediately tangible and more readily apprehended by the local population.

Difficulties in assessing non-financial benefits are further exacerbated by another consideration. The greater the contribution made by the foreign company to developmental objectives, the more it will come to intrude into functions normally carried out by the national government, thus presenting what may be perceived as a threat to that government's sovereignty. Communications facilities such as road and telex links or social amenities like schools and hospitals which are built and even run by a foreign entity may have a separate existence difficult for the government to control and may show up the limitations of the government's own developmental projects. And even where this is not the case, the emphasis placed by national governments on their governmental prerogatives and the fragile, and hence jealously guarded, sense of national identity evident in many less-developed countries can easily evoke suspicion if not hostility towards the foreign investor's extra-operational activities.

The Indonesian government is as much aware of its sovereign status as any other host government. Indeed it has shown an ambivalent attitude towards various linkage possibilities which might maximise the contribution of foreign companies to the local economy. This stance demonstrates that the Indonesian government is, if anything, even more circumspect in its perception of challenges posed by the ingress of foreign entities into areas of responsibility which it properly regards as its own. For it, the issue is not so much one of compelling the foreign company to implement programmes which have a broader impact on general development, as of ensuring a proper respect by the foreign investor of its concept of national sovereignty.

This concern is especially clear in the petroleum sector, where the Indonesian government has actually taken care to limit the 'visibility' of foreign oil companies, which are by their nature particularly conspicuous. It has confined them largely to offshore contract areas, reserving their onshore participation to joint agreements with Pertamina, where possible. Their contractor relationship with Pertamina has been used by the latter to shield them from domestic social forces, Pertamina securing required facilities and supplies for foreign oil companies and liaising on their behalf with different government departments.

While the country's formal development plans have been quite open in stating explicitly that the petroleum sector has an important role to play in economic development, they have in turn also come to rely on oil-sector income for over half of export income, domestic revenue and public investment. Thus in 1979, President Soeharto could remark, in the context of income to finance the Third Five-Year Development Plan that, 'Revenues from oil corporation tax remain the biggest source compared with other revenues. They kept on increasing annually, due to expanded production, increased export and international price hike of crude oil . . . This . . . includes revenues from LNG, which, thank God, we have started early in dealing with it [*sic*].'[23] This heavy dependence on oil-sector income remains despite current weak oil prices, which have forced the government to seek much higher non-oil tax revenues and to pursue a more broadly based investment policy. Yet the use of oil revenues to improve Indonesian productive capacity and to promote desired social objectives has been the designated responsibility of Pertamina, rather than of the companies. Pertamina thus extended its activities into collateral areas, endeavouring to increase the secondary effects of oil development within the Indonesian economy.

Through its size and, for a long time, multifarious interests and semi-autonomous status, Pertamina effectively managed to contain the presence of the foreign companies, and to provide a buffer between them and the Indonesian polity with its undercurrents of latent distrust toward foreign entities. It has sought and continues to seek to involve the oil companies in meeting broad development targets by channelling their efforts through its own organisational infrastructure. Thus any contribution by the petroleum sector to economic development is given a Pertamina imprint.

The companies have for the most part been quite prepared to operate through Pertamina, realising the advantages to be gained from maintaining a low profile in such a sensitive public environment. Furthermore, on a practical level, reducing their dealings with government departments minimises, so far as is possible, the constant need to manoeuvre among diverse local interests and cope with bureaucratic inefficiency and petty corruption. Pertamina, for its part, in its drive to increase the multiplier effects from oil extraction through expanding its own subcontracting capacity, has had to take into account the business considerations surrounding its decision to expand into a particular economic activity. Choosing such a course from among other competing options may be necessary if, as is usually the case, the market is not large enough to support more than one local operation. Prevailing upon the companies themselves to engage in oil-support activities by setting up local operations would therefore not be justified by considerations of economic efficiency. And if Pertamina were to give preferential status to one foreign company, that would confer a near-monopoly status at little cost to the latter, while pre-empting other foreign competitors.

The Indonesian government has therefore been constrained from further expanding the types of linkage discussed earlier. It has not gone out of its way to develop new methods of compelling foreign companies to assist its development programmes directly, preferring to retain clear control of its own development efforts and to be seen to do so.

MANAGING THE EXTRACTIVE OPERATION

If the Indonesian government has been disinclined to press for greater direct participation by petroleum companies in developing some, though not all, of the possible linkages from their extractive operations, it has, in the production-sharing contract, introduced one novel feature which has served as a vehicle for governmental efforts to compel the companies to assist, in an indirect fashion, the country's general development. The production-sharing contract incorporated a clause vesting Pertamina, the state company, with sole responsibility for managing the extractive operation. This represented a radical departure from preceding contract forms, where the company retained full management rights over the process of extraction.

The management clause might be regarded as serving to distance the foreign company, acting as a contractor to the state enterprise, from those broader decision-making considerations which would impinge on local political interests, confining its attention to purely economic and technical matters. But while the management clause in production-sharing contracts has been used to limit the wider role of foreign companies, it had a more important practical objective, that of involving Pertamina in all stages of oil-company operations. And so it provided an educational opportunity for the Indonesian side to study oil-company activities in detail, in this way assisting in the transfer of managerial and technological expertise.

This clause was termed a 'masterpiece of ambiguity' when first introduced.[24] While the companies wished to define the article more clearly, Pertamina tried deliberately to keep it vague. The principal concern of the oil companies lay in the loss of control over their operations implicit in giving Pertamina prerogative rights in management decisions. This fear was quite apart from additional considerations that the clause would provide a legal pretext for subsequent attempts at nationalisation, or that other host governments might regard it as a suitable precedent for inclusion in their own contractual arrangements. The point of conflict arose basically from the implicit separation of the investment function, with its concomitant risk-taking requirement, from the managerial function, with its responsibility to ensure the proper utilisation of the capital invested. Ibnu Sutowo always glossed over this basic difference in elaborating his views on the clause, saying that it had to be seen in the context of a situation where both parties had a common interest, and should therefore be conceived of as indicating a partnership. Within an agreed overall work programme, difficulties posed by the extractive operation were reduced to problems which were technical in nature, and therefore more readily resolved. But he conceded the need to maintain good relations with Pertamina's contractors, and was later to remark, 'We refrained ourselves from interference with [company] efforts into greater details [*sic*], as this might hamper the progress of their operations.'[25]

In actual practice, therefore, government control has been more theoretical than real. As Pertamina is itself aware that it is in no position to overrule the companies because of its technological and managerial deficiencies, Indonesian representation or even nominal control can be expected to generate little influence over decision-making. Indonesian officials themselves admit that Pertamina is in no position to match the greater resources which the companies are able to deploy. It therefore cannot, in such a situation, make effective decisions on behalf of the companies. Rather it has to limit its management role to reviewing company decisions, requesting clarification of and justification for the course of action pursued by the latter, such an approach indicating the educational potential of the management clause.

Foreign oil companies are meant to submit various reports to and to discuss all major policy decisions with the Foreign Contractors Coordinating Body (BKKA),[26] a division of Pertamina. This is where Pertamina's management is supposed to assert itself, and the company–state enterprise relationship at this interface is meant to provide the learning process which would benefit the Indonesian side.

The key contractual provision through which supervision takes place is the requirement obliging the foreign company to submit annually to Pertamina a work programme and a budget, setting out its intended operational activities for the coming year for the latter's approval. Pertamina is allowed to propose revisions to specific details in the company's submissions, though these intended revisions have to be approved by the company before being carried through. Other clauses further limit Pertamina's managerial latitude, by providing the company with an escape mechanism to undertake unilateral changes to its work programme should it judge such changes to be required, and requiring Pertamina to give the company an assurance that its approval of the latter's work programme would not be so delayed as to hamper the efficacious implementation of company operations.

It is difficult to assess the extent to which company operations in the petroleum industry have been affected by Pertamina's nominal control. Pertamina states that in exercising its management function through reviewing work programmes and budgets, it is required to approve basic details of geological and geophysical exploration schemes, drilling operations and time-tables, rig contracts and all service subcontracts, and personnel and training policies. Once commercial production commences, companies have bi-monthly (originally monthly) operational meetings with the BKKA where their department managers provide a review of their departmental activities for the preceding two-month period, and the companies are meant to settle their differences with Pertamina.

In practice, however, the companies have claimed that these requirements on the part of Pertamina are largely formalities with marginal operational influence, and that they are free in effect to make their own decisions. One oil-company executive recalled that Pertamina seemed initially to be more interested in obtaining information and advice on how companies operated, including answers to such basic questions as how budget decisions were made and costs computed, what criteria companies used to determine profitability and the commercial viability of a given venture, and how companies operated within the petroleum industry, while on the other hand subjecting managerial programmes to an extremely cursory review.[27] The management clause has not provided an opportunity to manage, but rather a chance to sit in on the companies' management process insofar as the companies have been prevailed upon to allow it. On the other side of the relationship, a former member of Pertamina estimated that it took six years from the signing of the first contract before Pertamina was able to even properly evaluate a company budget. Approval of budgets and work programmes was therefore originally a highly tenuous procedure. And even later, as company operations could not be held up so as to allow Pertamina the length of time necessary to carry out a thorough examination, Pertamina found itself able to verify only those aspects of company submissions which it had the capability of gauging immediately. It should also be noted that IIAPCO, which signed the first production-sharing contract in 1966, had the previous year rejected out of hand a proposed contract with Permigan, one of the three state oil companies then functioning, when the latter took a more literal, if perhaps impractical, view of its intended management prerogatives.

Pertamina claims that the operational meetings fulfil a useful function as a forum in which it can discuss operational problems with the companies. It would appear, however, that the companies are less than candid in presenting their problems within the context of a formal meeting, and that the resulting discussion does not lead to any joint resolution of different opinions. This situation results despite Pertamina's contractual power to compel the company to revise its work programme if Pertamina reaches a contrary conclusion, on the basis of the data submitted, as to the viability of the project concerned.[28] Work programmes and budgets are generally approved with little dispute. They may occasionally be queried by Pertamina, even over some detailed point, but only minor alterations are requested to which companies can still appeal against, generally with success.

Since the mid 1970s, Pertamina has acquired a certain technical proficiency which has been translated into more stringent control. But the companies claim that this is no more effective. Thus a proposal by the BKKA in 1979 to revise the procedure for approving budget accounts had to be withdrawn when the companies claimed it would induce unacceptable delay. This proposal would have required the oil companies to file four separate submissions for each item (as an intended purchase, then as an approved purchase, then again immediately after importation of the equipment, and finally when submitting the annual operating account), therefore unduly holding up the acquisition of necessary equipment to the point of obstructing the company's execution of its project.

The companies complain that often inefficient bureaucratic procedures now characterise their relations with Pertamina and cause unnecessary delays in implementing decisions. The majority of its staff with whom they have to deal adopt a rigid posture and insist on going through lengthy procedures which have little practical value.

Pertamina's increased technical competence has arisen gradually over the years during which production-sharing contracts have been operating. Its staff have seen from submitted reports how operational decisions on exploration surveys, field development, budgeting and the like are arrived at by the various companies acting as contractors to it. The question remains, why has this acquired ability not been translated into more efficient supervision of these companies? The answer may lie in part with Pertamina's own internal structure and style of management, where an emphasis on bureaucratic procedure and a traditionally authoritarian leadership style has led to compliance with regulatory procedures and emphasis on a regard for authority. Management under the production-sharing system requires, at least formally, the superimposition of Pertamina's management on the oil companies' management of their extractive operations. And Pertamina's attempts to apply the same internal managerial style and practices of work in exercising its management function externally fit uncomfortably into the companies' own accepted operational methods, and indeed are not conducive to achieving the effective discharge of the latter's duties.

Companies therefore complain of encountering inflexibility from Pertamina staff at the level where their relationship with Pertamina functions in practice. They find pending decisions channelled through over-elaborate determinant procedures, often an inability to reach an operational decision which the companies can proceed to implement, and a refusal to think through the possibly adverse consequences of a particular decree. The companies tend to set such difficulties against greater required profit margins, and bureaucratic delays are just factored into the time horizons envisaged for the project in question. So, as they claim, the resulting losses are generally borne in effect by the Indonesian side.

The difficulties of coordinating Pertamina's and the companies' management are compounded by the lack of any clear statement from Pertamina as to the form such a relationship should take and the procedures that ought to be followed in carrying it through. While speeches by Pertamina officials stress that management is in the hands of Pertamina, as laid down in the contracts, and appeal vaguely to the 'spirit of production sharing', there has been no attempt to formally define the nature of this management relationship. And government attempts to reassure the companies that their interests will be accommodated, should insoluble problems arise in their operational relationship with Pertamina, have been sceptically received.

But effective supervision of the companies through the management clause also remains a function of the total amount of resources available for Pertamina to deploy in terms of finance and skilled managerial and technical staff. And Pertamina appears fully aware that, despite its improved capabilities, it does not possess such supervisory resources in sufficient quantity to achieve the aim of full managerial control over all areas of the extractive operation which it seeks. Its authority to approve company decisions must hence remain a somewhat token one. For if it cannot match the technical competence of the companies, it hence cannot critically analyse the cost-benefit terms of company budgets or attempt to alter decisions reached in company work programmes. Pertamina therefore still concentrates its attention on the educational aspect of the management clause, seeking to further expand the process by which technology transfer takes place. In this respect the new form of joint participation contract could prove a better vehicle for the transfer of practical information, as the extractive project will require operational work in the field by both Pertamina and the foreign company's staff.

As for the access which the management clause was supposed to provide to company information, this was afforded by a provision within the production-sharing contract specifically requiring the foreign company to deliver to Pertamina transcripts of all original data collected and reports compiled from the extractive operation. Pertamina's right to receive this information was reinforced by having title to all such data conferred on it. And Pertamina in turn gave an assurance that it would preserve the confidentiality of submitted data, which would not be divulged to other parties without prior consultation with the company concerned.

This submission-of-information clause has, however, also been of limited benefit, as the information companies submit is only their most basic data which they also transmit to their head offices overseas for evaluation. Pertamina lacks a scientific ability comparable to that possessed by the companies to analyse this raw primary data, a particularly critical handicap as it does not receive copies of the companies' secondary reports which result from their evaluation, and which form the basis on which companies make their operational decisions. Furthermore, the value of those facts which are disclosed is further reduced as many companies reportedly delay their submissions for as long as possible. Pertamina, though, does try to ensure that information is made available as and when the company obtains it.

The companies for their part maintain that they are under no obligation to pass on any information which is derivative in nature, hence their retaining head-office reports. This reluctance of the companies to keep Pertamina informed may of course be ascribed simply to a natural desire not to strengthen the latter's hand, which might encourage it to unilaterally revise company work programmes. But there is also a certain uneasiness on the part of at least some companies that confidential information in Pertamina's possession could be revealed to other interested parties. In this respect it should be noted that even the safeguard incorporated in production-sharing contracts, obliging Pertamina to retain submitted data, provides no cast-iron guarantee against information leaks. For Pertamina is contractually bound only to discuss with the company affected any intention on its part to let out information, and is not compelled to accede to the company's wishes in this respect. The contracts do also require Pertamina to pass to the companies any pertinent information held by the government side on the operational area and its environs, though the companies claim that the value of such information tends usually to be over-rated.

The ambiguity inherent in the management clause might be regarded as a reflection of the government's weakness in its dealings with the companies. But it should be noted that the clause grants potentially immense powers of control to Pertamina, even if these have so far not been fully utilised. It cannot therefore be dismissed out of hand as merely a symbolic transfer of management rights to the host-government side, devised in order to disarm local critics and placate nationalistic sentiment against the exploitation of domestic natural resources by foreign interests. Even at that level, it is not inapt to maintain that the management clause fulfils a useful purpose in creating the appearance of national control over national resources, a claim always stressed in speeches and statements by Pertamina officials. Lowering company visibility provides a certain assurance to the companies that their position in the country is tenable, and that they are unlikely to face a disputatious domestic environment which might spur unilateral Indonesian attempts to nationalise their local operations, an underlying fear of at least some companies. The companies have in any case fewer formal rights to relinquish publicly and their de facto privileges are more easily preserved, at present and at least for the foreseeable future, through implicit agreement with their Indonesian administrative counterparts in Pertamina and the government. The latter readily recognise their own inability to take over complete management of the companies' activities. But, in the long term, the management clause provides for the possibility of more far-reaching changes in the company–government relationship as the Indonesian side builds up its own administrative and technical capability. The Indonesians will have no cause to abrogate contract terms, should conditions change, in order to exert greater control over resource extraction. They already hold the legal means to effect the transfer of petroleum extraction from the foreign companies to indigenous management.

THE RATE OF EXTRACTION AND ITS IMPLICATIONS

Concern over the wider implications of foreign investment in mineral extraction also has a temporal dimension. The host government's concern to maximise the advantages to its domestic economy must take as an important consideration the time required by the extractive operation to reach commercial profitability, and hence to yield income and other benefits, and the rate at which these benefits accrue. This rate is an obvious function of the geophysical characteristics of the mineral deposit, which determine the relative ease with which it may be mined. Such a factor is not patently within the purview of government policy, and so host governments run the danger of paying insufficient attention to it. Yet there are two further contributory determinants of the rate of extraction which depend on government negotiation with foreign companies. For the nature of the company chosen by the government and the strict regulation of its operational performance can critically affect the speed at which benefits are obtained. A host government with extensive mineral deposits and an economy with a limited capacity to absorb the income from their development, might regard the conservation of these resources as an attractive policy option. Yet other governments, including the Indonesian government, attach great importance to earning immediate income from the mineral operation, and therefore wish to ensure that they begin to benefit from the extractive process as soon as possible.

From the company's point of view, while it may wish to exert control over a resource deposit and hence be prepared to enter into an extractive agreement with the host government, this desired control need not necessarily include any intention to exploit the mineral resource. The company's motives may be purely speculative, or it may be concerned to maintain high prices through restricting output, or else it may wish merely to establish a presence in a particular geographic region to pre-empt rival firms or to ensure that competitors do not acquire a mineral source which might prove cheaper to operate than existing sources.

The host government has no assurance that a foreign company seeking a contract for mineral extraction does in fact intend to work the deposit. It therefore has to ensure that it chooses a company which has a primary interest in resource development, and the correct identification of such companies must form an important criterion of the process of selection, alongside other measures of company suitability. The study of company reports to establish their reserves position and sales requirements would aid the screening process. Thus a petroleum company with extensive downstream processing facilities may be keen to establish a corresponding position upstream, or a company with guaranteed access to certain regional markets may be anxious to seek secure sources of crude-oil supply. In general, the larger oil 'majors' with their more extensive global positions are likely to be motivated by more complex considerations. So when the Indonesian government moved in the mid 1960s to open up offshore areas for petroleum exploration under production-sharing contracts, its deliberate choice of smaller 'independent' oil companies, instead of the oil 'majors', reflected an awareness that the smaller firms, as new entrants into the industry, placed a high priority on securing petroleum sources for exploiting to the fullest extent possible.

Another course of action which the host government might pursue would be to insert enforceable safeguards into the contract, which can also provide ascertainable standards by which to monitor the company's commitment to develop the mineral deposit. The agreement could include a schedule setting out levels of expenditure and production targets over the life of the operation which the company has to meet, and also require the accomplishment of certain functions having a bearing on the company's productive performance. For the Indonesian petroleum industry, while under the concession system the company retained the right to exclusively determine its rate of production, contracts of work introduced, and production-sharing contracts also included, specified minimum annual expenditure requirements for the initial contract years and a provision to progressively reduce the size of the contract area. The effectiveness of these conditions in guaranteeing performance may however be questioned, as they appear insufficiently specific in compelling the company to carry out exploration and production activities at some determinate level.

It may be argued that no useful purpose is served in setting more detailed performance standards if there is no adequate means of ensuring that these standards are then met. The government's difficulty is further compounded as, during the negotiating stage, when the contract is being drawn up and prior to detailed survey work being carried out on the contract area, it cannot usually forecast precisely what levels of investment and expenditure would be consistent with reasonable exploration and development activity on the part of the company. Even without comprehensive data, however, greater care by the government to incorporate a firm requirement within the contract that the foreign company commit itself to certain minimum annual expenditures would help enforce its terms of operation, together with a proviso for some form of financial penalty or the termination of the contract should these expenditure levels not be reached.

If the emphasis in drawing up such a safeguard clause should be placed on obtaining a guarantee from the company of an agreed minimum commitment, then the terms of Indonesian work contracts and production-sharing contracts do allow the company considerable leeway to determine its rate of work. Under both systems, the company is permitted, should its annual expenditure exceed the minimum stipulated in its contract, to offset the excess amount against its required minimum payments in subsequent years. In addition, work contracts and some production-sharing contracts allow the company, should it spend less than the contractually specified amount, to make up the shortfall in the following years.

Furthermore while it is obviously advisable to restrict those expenditures that the company is permitted to charge against its minimum payment requirements, there is no such clear limitation in either work or production-sharing contracts. If the aim of the provision is to ensure the company's contract performance, only those costs resulting directly from the exploration effort should qualify, and it is most important to exclude any general expenses which may have no connection with the particular extractive operation. Yet work contracts allow the company to charge overhead expenses. And most production-sharing contracts allow all operating costs to be taken into account,[29] these operating costs being defined so as to include a proportion of the company's general and administrative expenses.

The value of the area-reduction clause in work and production-sharing contracts would lie in limiting the amount of time granted to the company to carry out survey and exploration work. While the terms of this mandatory relinquishment provision vary between contracts, they usually require the company to surrender specified portions of its contract area at certain fixed intervals, so that it eventually retains somewhere between 10,000 to 15,000 square kilometres, or somewhat less than half of the original area, by the tenth year of operation. It has been estimated that four to six years is generally adequate to meet exploration requirements,[30] and, if so, the period of time allotted in Indonesian oil contracts for this purpose is probably excessive.

Establishing the date on which these requirements become effective may also help to speed up the company's time-table. While some mineral contracts take effect from the commencement of production, most, including Indonesian oil contracts, take their effective starting point from the date of ratification or governmental approval of the contract. As production may not begin till after a considerable period of time has elapsed from the actual signing of the contract, the latter course is preferable where the government is concerned that the operation should achieve commercial production as soon as possible.

As for the portion of the contract area finally remaining, production-sharing contracts provide for relinquishing only those parts of it where the company does not submit an exploration programme for two consecutive years, and only after agreement by both company and government that the resumption of exploration at some point in the future is not feasible. This might be regarded as unsatisfactory from the point of view of efficient usage of the contract area, as relinquished acreage, which would otherwise be neglected, can be and usually is tendered out to other companies. Such relinquished areas have therefore also to be of a suitable size and shape for petroleum operations to be carried out within them.

The issue of establishing appropriate rates of production is, however, not as straightforward as it might at first seem. The host government's interest need not necessarily lie with maximising production. In currently prevailing conditions of oversupply or depressed prices, prudent policy might dictate reducing output and conserving resources. An additional consideration has been to keep within production quotas imposed by the Organisation of Petroleum Exporting Countries (OPEC), of which Indonesia is a member, and to comply with required production cuts. For onshore production, there are also issues of environmental protection and the rights of indigenous residents to consider. Such protective provisions have a long history in Indonesia. The concession system specified an extensive series of guarantees to enable local residents to be compensated for any damage to land or property, and to allow them to continue traditional practices and activities by keeping mineral development clear of religious sites and areas of economic importance to them. The company was also obliged to comply with supervised safety requirements in its working methods, and to help restore the ground of the contract area to its original condition after the termination of the operation. The Indonesian government's Law No. 44 of 1960 which currently governs oil production also includes similar restrictions. Companies operating under contracts of work are required to carry out their operations in a 'good' technical manner and in accordance with internationally accepted engineering and economic practices. Production-sharing contracts include a clause obliging the company to implement its work programme 'in a workmanlike manner and by appropriate scientific methods . . . [to] take the necessary precautions for protection of navigation and fishing and . . . [to] prevent extensive pollution of the sea or rivers'.[31]

While these contractual provisions are laudable in the concern displayed for the social and ecological impact of the extractive operation, they do not appear sufficiently precise to compel companies to seriously consider the broader implications of their work. Requiring the companies to engage independent consultants to monitor and report on this issue, and incorporating detailed stipulations within contracts on appropriate methods of mineral extraction, may help secure a greater response from the companies. But in its desire to ensure the proper protection of local society against the damaging effects of oil-related activities, the government has to consider the extent to which the benefits from environmental protection, which need not necessarily be monetarily quantifiable, exceed the costs incurred. Such a trade-off is not easily made, especially when there is a pressing need for income.

Whatever measures the Indonesian government has introduced to obtain the direct contribution of foreign oil companies to the country's overall development, whether it be through establishing linkages between the extractive operation and the domestic economy or asserting direct control over company functions, the government has seen its achievements in this regard limited by its finite administrative and technical resources, regardless of whatever rights it may have arrogated to itself. It also has reservations about such direct company involvement where this may appear to impinge on its sovereign status.

Nevertheless, in dealing with the oil companies the Indonesian government may be expected to show greater concern over issues related to the general development of its society and economy. Just as new assumptions of financial benefit have led the government to demand changes in its relationship with the foreign companies, so too has an increased emphasis on developmental concerns, as the government's perspective is equally altered. Such attempts to revise contracts are never easily resolved, and the problems arising from them form the next issue to be dealt with.

5. PROBLEMS OF NEGOTIATION AND CONTRACTUAL CHANGE

DISPUTE SETTLEMENT WITHIN AN EVOLVING PROCESS
OF CONTRACT RELATIONS

After having examined the division of financial benefits within Indonesian oil contracts, their development provisions and the authority which the government attempts to assert over the extractive process, it has still to be asked how valid these terms are likely to remain. It is therefore important in examining the formal contract to assess how both parties are likely to respond to its terms over the long run, how adherence to existing terms can be maintained, and what is likely to lead to changes in the contractual relationship. Such issues of contractual change and negotiation are addressed in this chapter.

If the negotiating framework surrounding the petroleum-extractive operation is regarded as part of a dynamic process, in which a changing pattern of government–company relations gives rise to shifts in the bargaining positions of both sides, it would then seem inevitable that dissatisfaction over the governing set of contract terms will arise. Pressure for an improvement of terms from governments keen to maximise their returns from oil extraction has resulted not only from the extensive changes over the long term in the global environment of the international oil industry; nor can it be ascribed solely to any specific local development which might have strengthened the host government's bargaining hand. Quite apart from these factors, pressure for change is inherent in the nature and development of the extractive operation as it moves from one stage of activity to another.

In general, as the process of extraction moves from its initial exploratory phase to production of the petroleum reserves, the relative bargaining strengths of both parties shift significantly at the point where petroleum is discovered in commercial quantities. Prior to reaching that point, the government's position is usually comparatively weak, although its bargaining hand may be strengthened if basic geological information of a favourable nature already exists and there are a number of prospective oil producers interested in securing contracts. However, the moment these broad indications of the existence of commercially viable petroleum deposits become crystallised into certainty following further exploratory and feasibility studies, then the perceived commercial risk of the venture falls sharply, and the previously agreed returns to the oil company may well seem unjustifiably generous to the host government. On the other hand, so long as substantial funds are still needed to finance the development of the resource, the government may have to be extremely circumspect in negotiating a revision of terms. It will need to maintain a reputation for political and financial probity so as to assure foreign lenders that their investments and the loans which they have committed are secure. Only after the operation has matured and foreign capital is no longer required can the government feel itself free to impose revised terms on the company. But it can do so only so long as it does not require the latter's managerial and technical expertise or sales outlets, and with the further qualification that it can consider a particular project in isolation from other foreign investment operations within its territory, a condition which can seldom be fully met in practice.

The argument between the two sides may therefore be basically characterised as a contention over the risk of the enterprise. Who should carry this risk and how it should be rewarded may be decided in the initial bargaining process, but changes in the perception of risk over the life of the operation will introduce an element of uncertainty and hence tension. This uncertainty may be compounded if both sides expect at the beginning that any terms agreed upon may be renegotiated at a later stage. The company would reasonably expect that its investment in a project fraught with risk will be rewarded by a share of the rents (the return to factors of production, labour or capital, above that required to employ them for that particular purpose) which arise from developing the petroleum reserves, should they be discovered. Expectations that the government will move to capture a greater share of rents for itself can only render the process of negotiation more difficult, as the division of rents is decided upon ultimately by the two sides' relative bargaining strengths, which will not remain unchanged over time.

The host government's overall position should also be considered, it being engaged in negotiating and supervising a series of ongoing extractive ventures. It may be argued then that the additional rents which it may be able to secure from one operation, through revision of contract terms after an investment has been made by the foreign company, may make other companies more reluctant to invest in other areas or lead them to demand stiffer and more watertight terms from a government perceived as unreliable. Companies tend to stress the sanctity of contracts, which they regard as a fundamental principle underlying their participation in the extractive operation.[1] Host governments would, however, argue that foreign investors have consistently respected contracts because these have been negotiated under circumstances so obviously favourable to themselves. And with the establishment of a more equitable bargaining context, it is only to be expected that host governments should attempt to revise contractual relationships.

It is important, therefore, in examining the formal contract to assess how both parties are likely to respond to its terms in the long run, how adherence to existing terms can be maintained and what is likely to lead to changes in the contractual relationship. In any event, conflict between host government and foreign company that is readily resolved within a commercial context only indicates the satisfactory working of an existing arrangement. Conflict becomes significant when the debate over terms escalates towards breaking point, for then it almost invariably becomes charged with a highly politicised content.

Given the complexity of host-government and foreign-company considerations, disputes over contract terms are always a likely possibility and may occur over a wide variety of issues. Yet they are essentially of two kinds. Disputes may be concerned either with the interpretation of agreed contract terms or with the suitability of the terms themselves. Within the Indonesian petroleum industry, this distinction is an important one in devising practical procedures for bridging gaps between the two negotiating sides. For while work and production-sharing contracts include a means of recourse to arbitration for resolving arguments over the interpretation or enforcement of existing terms, there are no provisions to deal with possible situations where the terms of the contract as seen by either side fail to reflect an improved relative bargaining position. Instances of disputes over interpretation have been referred to earlier. We are concerned here chiefly with the other type of disagreement, that is, over the actual terms of the contract.

The problem is not just that the legal arrangements for dealing with disputes over terms have not been well worked out. This is not an area where resort to litigation or the interpretation of law is of major relevance. While the company–government relationship as expressed through production-sharing agreements may have the status of a negotiated contract between two parties, contract disputes inevitably assume a significance with which few legal comparisons can be drawn with common problems of breach of contract. This significance does not derive specifically from any special legislative legitimisation of the contract, but rather from the scale of its importance in the shifting balance-of-advantage considerations of both parties and the high financial stakes involved. In this respect, there is a dearth of useful precedents to serve as legal reference points.

The vast majority of contract disputes in the mineral extractive industries has indeed been settled by direct negotiation between the parties, sometimes involving in addition the foreign company's home government. Relations between the contending sides may be so delicate that an overt resort to arbitration might even result in heightening the controversy and impairing the prospects of continuing a reasonable working relationship. It may also be argued that the arbitration mechanism is formulated to deal only with the sort of disagreements peripheral to the essential concerns dividing foreign company from host government, and hence most serious contract disputes have not found their way to arbitration. Yet a firm agreement to submit disputes to arbitration does help to provide a sense of security for an intending investor that an opportunity exists for it to resort to third-party decision-making. Agreements within the Indonesian petroleum industry have therefore come to include a provision to submit disputes arising in the course of the venture to some form of external judgment. These formal arrangements will be discussed first so as to give some perspective to the following discussion of conflict resolution within an extra-legal context.

RESOLVING DISPUTES THROUGH ARBITRATION

Arbitration mechanisms have traditionally been regarded as the prime means for resolving arguments over the terms of an extractive operation. The concession system, as it operated up until 1960, allowed the concessionaire a right of appeal only to the Governor General during the colonial period, or, after independence, to the Indonesian Supreme Court. Appeals were allowed not only over compliance with the mining law, but also over 'a refusal of permission to transfer a licence . . . and of dispositions containing amendments of the conditions made in a licence decree or refusal of an amendment of the conditions as requested'.[2] The circumstances for lodging an appeal were therefore correspondingly broad, dealing not only with interpretation of the mining law, but also allowing for differences over terms which were no longer acceptable to either party to the contract. But the settlement mechanism was not set out explicitly, though its final decision was declared to be irrevocable. Thus any sense of security induced by the broad terms of reference would have been largely unjustified.

A formal arbitration procedure was first introduced in the succeeding contract-of-work system. This provided for recourse to arbitration, referring any dispute to an independent board whose composition would be determined by a free choice of both parties, to settle 'any dispute . . . concerning anything related to [the] contract or the operations . . . including opinions that a party is in default in performance of its obligations'.[3] The method of arbitration was set out in a manner calculated to ensure its functioning so long as one side to the dispute in question was determined to bring the issue to arbitration; though of course both sides would have, by signing the contract, agreed in advance to arbitration in principle, arbitration being thus a consensual procedure. And again the terms of reference allowed for disputes of a fairly varied character to be submitted.

The scope of disputes eligible for submission to arbitration was narrowed in the following production-sharing contract system to 'disputes . . . arising between the parties regarding the interpretation and performance of any of the clauses of this contract'.[4] It was therefore made explicit that problems arising either from terms that were no longer acceptable to one of the parties or from conditions not envisaged when agreement was originally reached would not be dealt with by arbitration. While arbitration might have some use in settling differences of opinion over the interpretation of contract terms, this limiting phrase clearly bars arbitration as a means of dealing with more serious disputes. In consequence, companies have not been especially predisposed to resort to arbitration in their dealings with the Indonesian government.

Two further points have to be made. First, the mechanism of arbitration may appear unnecessarily cumbersome for dealing with those minor differences which continually arise in the working of the extractive operation over the interpretation of contract terms. A quick solution to such lesser problems by some more expeditious process can help ease the operational relationship between the parties. Arbitration on the other hand requires strict adherence to a set of procedures designed to ensure a measure of equity in dealing with competing claims. If flexible enough to be employed over a wide range of problems, it might be unjustifiably time- and resource-consuming in coping with smaller disputes. Contracts of work require the two sides to try to reach mutual agreement through conciliation before proceeding to arbitration. Production-sharing contracts set out a process of consultation whereby both parties meet regularly to discuss operational problems and try to resolve any differences which arise. Neither attempts to differentiate between those problems of a legal nature involving matters of opinion which might be submitted to arbitration, and disputes turning on questions of fact which might be dealt with by a more streamlined procedure. In any case, companies have generally claimed that the government, in its administration of contracts, has been inclined to issue decisions as administrative fiats regardless of consequence, taking the attitude that matters of detail are its own concern and therefore should not be liable to any external authority with overriding powers.

Secondly, many contracts between Latin American governments and foreign companies operating concessions in that region include a clause termed the 'Calvo Clause', under which the foreign company explicitly renounces the protection or assistance of its home government over its operation of the contract. The object here is to ensure that any disputes shall be referred to local courts of law and to exclude the jurisdiction of international arbitral tribunals. The legality of the Calvo Clause remains dubious, however, for while it may be proper for the host government to insist on the complete jurisdiction of local tribunals, it cannot expect to deny the right of other states to protect their nationals abroad. In this respect, while the Indonesian case does not go that far, it does allow recourse to local courts of law to back up, rather than to replace, as the Calvo Clause attempts to do, the arbitration mechanism laid out in oil-company contracts. Contracts of work allow either party to submit the issue being disputed to Indonesian courts should the arbitration procedure fail. And production-sharing contracts lay down that the dispute should be referred to local courts in the event that a decision cannot be reached through arbitration.

To try to exclude arbitration would be difficult, given the mistrust of foreign companies of the fairness of the local judiciary when dealing with disputes between them and the host government or its agencies. Companies will in consequence tend to seek to have provision for arbitration explicitly included in their contracts so as to circumvent the necessity of working their way through local courts. But the inclusion of a clause providing for local adjudication to reinforce arbitration proceedings in the manner of Indonesian oil contracts might help spur the arbitrators to reach some mutually agreeable decision, if only from being aware that the aggrieved side could take the unresolved issue to even more unwieldy legal proceedings. And foreign companies might also be encouraged to try more seriously to settle disputes before arbitration is involved. In any case, even though Indonesian oil contracts provide for arbitration involving the possible intervention of non-national parties, they also clearly state that the contractual relationship is governed by Indonesian law. It would therefore seem that not much leeway is left to legal interpretation, whether done by arbitrator or local judge, except on matters which infringe international law.

FORMAL ADJUSTMENT OF THE CONTRACTUAL
RELATIONSHIP

While arbitration or other legal procedures may be unable to cope with disputes over contract provisions where the structure of the entire relationship is called into question, the continual need for renegotiation over the life of the contract suggests the desirability of some sort of interactional process being institutionalised within the contract. This process might provide a basis for regulating change, without attempting to define precisely the future course of the relationship.

It would be reasonable if both sides recognised at the outset the distinctive nature of their contract agreement from most commercial transactions. This distinctiveness arises from the contract's extreme complexity, with many details affected by major uncertainties before the venture commences, the diverse range of issues it covers, and its possible extension over a long period. Given the likelihood of change under those circumstances, it would be prudent to include provisions within the contract which help facilitate those changes that are predictable. This line of reasoning has however led to such provisions tending to focus on specific items, rather than providing a general framework for smooth renegotiation. Within Indonesian oil contracts, provisions for change appear sporadically and have tended to be specific, though not exclusively fiscal, a wide variety of issues being susceptible to possible revision.

The clause in contracts providing for the periodic reduction of the operational area acts as a provision for change negotiated beforehand. The issue of control over surface area may provide a potential cause of friction if the company wishes to hold on to a larger area than it is able to develop, either to pre-empt competing firms or as a reserve for future production. The government, though, could well have other intentions as to the desired rate of exploitation. Possible differences here may thus be avoided through having the rate of relinquishment set out in advance.

Of more far-reaching importance has been the inclusion in many contracts since 1969 of a clause providing for a phasing-in of local equity ownership upon the discovery of commercially viable quantities of petroleum. This reflects the shifting balance of advantage between the two parties at its most significant point of transition, allowing the local investor, either in the form of a private participant or a government entity, to avoid the operation's initial risk, investing capital only upon the confirmation of the project's profitability. It is difficult to programme a future shift in equity ownership within the contract as both sides cannot predict their future bargaining strength, and the equity the company has been obliged to offer has amounted to no more than ten per cent of its contractual participation. Yet a token shift in ownership falling

short of a full take-over may still help to stem political dissatisfaction arising from a long-term foreign presence. And the local gain
in financial benefits can still be significant given the scale of the
extractive operation.

There is, however, a problem of valuation, given that the
company has to be paid for the share of its contractual participation that is taken over. Initially the basis for valuation was set at
the higher figure of either the average cost to the original shareholders or the value determined by an external authority, who was
to be a security analyst of the New York Stock Exchange. The offer
price was soon changed to the local participant's percentage share
of the foreign company's operating costs and its various bonus and
compensation payments made as agreed to Pertamina. Setting the
payment at original cost as was first done would clearly result in
undervaluing the assets to be transferred, as it neither provides for
any discounted later value of the extractive operation, which would
appreciate significantly given confirmation of its commercial
profitability, nor allows for the erosion of inflation on the value of
the original cost. And the alternative of obtaining an outside evaluation is unsatisfactorily vague, leaving open the question of what
criteria the security analyst should apply. Stipulating the basis for
valuation at actual operating costs plus the various payments made
by the company up to the time of transfer would mean basing the
sales price on book value. This, however, would still not fairly
reflect the commercial worth of the assets to be transferred, given
that assets entered in the company's books would be valued at their
historical cost, which does not recognise their later appreciation in
value. (The company could of course update book value by revalu-
ing its assets, but the Indonesian contract provision refers to actual
costs incurred historically.)

However valuation is determined, the method and rate of payment would obviously also be important in the financial considerations of both sides. Initially, the local participant was obliged to
pay in cash which was convertible into foreign currency. This was
soon changed to allow the participant the option of paying out of
half of his production entitlement instead; though if he chose to do
so, he would have to pay one-and-a-half times the originally
required amount. This higher sales price was set in order to allow
for the considerably longer duration of payment, the local party
being able to postpone his obligation through not commencing

payment until the beginning of commercial production, and even then being able to stretch payments out over a period of time.

Such a method of payment parallels the procedure for compensation commonly employed in changes of ownership, whether programmed in the contract or unplanned through nationalisation, where the government pays for the transferred assets out of future dividends. Indeed the considerations made above would also apply in situations where the foreign company was faced either with a partial or full nationalisation of its assets, or where it wished to withdraw from the country and therefore had to dispose of its property, because it no longer felt that the future of its local operations was viable.

The latter position was one in which Royal Dutch Shell found itself in 1965 with its existing operations yielding insufficient production to feed its local refineries, the prospect of a continued long-term production decline, and a hostile political climate, with the fear that its property might be confiscated in the future. Shell therefore negotiated the sale of its Indonesian assets to Permina, one of the three state oil companies then functioning. The basis of valuation agreed on was interesting for several reasons.

To begin with, valuation was to be based on book value, and hence referred only to surface installations within the contract area (such property as refineries, oil-field equipment, pipelines and so on, which would comprise the company's tangible assets). Though both sides accepted this basis of valuation, Permina also agreed to make an additional payment, termed a 'good-will' allowance, as compensation for the petroleum deposits 'in the ground', so as to indemnify Shell against its loss of future earnings. The textual construction was necessitated by Permina being unable to recognise overtly that Shell had any claim over petroleum reserves, when the Indonesian constitution laid down that the country's mineral reserves were 'controlled by the state', to whom by implication they belonged. The company would be expected to favour any evaluative standard that provides for compensation above book value, and the additional 'good-will' allowance acts to discount the stream of earnings that would accrue to Shell if it continued to retain ownership.

Though Permina committed itself to paying something in excess of book value, it did on the other hand also manage to secure an acceptance by Shell that the sales price would have to take into account the limited capacity to pay of the Indonesian government at that time. The Indonesian side hence secured recognition by the company that it would forgo any attempt to obtain compensation up to the full value of its loss for the transferred assets. Shell agreed to partial compensation set much closer to book value than it had originally wished.[5]

Payment was fixed at US$110 million, of which ten per cent would be made as a down payment in cash, the remainder being paid over a period of five years from the sale of petroleum (as valued by a joint committee) and with interest set at ten per cent per annum on the outstanding balance. As a surety against default, Shell was given exclusive entitlement to all proceeds from petroleum sales until each annual payment was concluded. This guarantee was readily enforceable, as Shell still controlled the marketing outlets abroad for petroleum from its former Indonesian operations. This control over export production provided Shell with a measure of oligopsony influence, as it would be difficult for Permina to find alternative buyers, there existing at the time substantial excess global productive capacity of petroleum. Furthermore, the guarantee also ensured that Shell had a continued interest in the maintenance of production from the assets given up and would therefore assist in the orderly transfer of control. For if production failed to keep pace with projected output, Shell would be unlikely to obtain payment by turning to what was then a government on the brink of financial insolvency.

If changing circumstances tend to lead to contract revisions, it might be thought that some specific provision for the periodic review of contract terms would help minimise friction and facilitate a process of orderly change. Such clauses have been included in some petroleum contracts in other countries, though generally the terms of reference of the clause limit revision to 'most favoured nation' considerations. In other words, only those provisions that have subsequently been accepted by the foreign company in another country may be substituted for existing contract terms, if these provisions are more favourable to the host government than those incorporated within the contract.

Such a review provision may facilitate a subsequent opening of renegotiations by legitimising the possibility of later contract revisions. From one point of view, companies might consider it within their interests to guard against what is after all a very likely possibility. They may therefore choose to agree to such a provision while seeking to maximise the protection of their interests by fixing in advance limits on the types of contract provisions that will be subject to review and the time periods required to elapse before initiating the review process. Indonesian production-sharing contracts provide for a process of consultation which is limited to considering the practical conduct of petroleum operations to ensure its conformity with existing contract terms. It would seem possible to broaden the scope of this consultative process to include a periodic review of the appropriateness of the original terms. Petroleum companies operating in Indonesia have generally, however, adamantly emphasised the integrity of their contract agreements. Given such an attitude, they have consequently opposed the idea that their contracts should even mention the possibility of revision. Production-sharing contracts in fact embody a clause stipulating explicitly that their terms should not be modified or abrogated except by mutual consent of both parties. It is questionable if such a clause strengthens the legal force of contract provisions as, in any case, under ordinary rules of law, contracts can be altered only with the joint agreement of the parties involved. Indeed there is some room for doubt as to the legal validity of such a clause.

Pertamina has since let it be known that all production-sharing contracts should offer the same basic terms.[6] This would imply the application of a provision paralleling 'most favoured nation' treatment, allowing for some sort of 'most favoured company' consideration. It would presumably provide for the substitution of terms and conditions reached in later contracts for other terms agreed in earlier contracts, and this would apply in whichever direction, whether more or less favourable to the government, the difference between the terms went. Pertamina's stated intention was to treat all parties equally and to promote uniformity across different agreements, but it has not yet managed to spell out its proposals, much less attempt to apply them.

The problem remains that with foreign companies working under widely varying operational conditions, contracts have become more individual in character, for provisions have to be tailored to suit specific conditions so as to ensure optimal government revenues and the maintenance of a conducive exploration and development climate. It is therefore almost impossible to consider any single provision in isolation from the rest of the contract.

And to attempt to readjust one provision in this complex structure, without taking into account the other parts of the agreement, would simply defeat the whole purpose of negotiation. From the point of view of the host government, such a provision is not only inhibitory, in discouraging it from negotiating with other companies specific terms that are less favourable than those of previous agreements (which may be required to operate on a smaller or less valuable deposit); it is also potentially dangerous, for without an efficient administration the government may not realise in the process of contract negotiations that it has automatically initiated a revision of an earlier agreement. The companies were also unenthusiastic about the Indonesian proposal, realising that a worsening of terms in later contracts would necessarily lead to a similar deterioration in terms for all other contract-holders.

THE NEED TO FACILITATE CHANGE

With the advent of Indonesia's independence in 1949, a petroleum industry was inherited wherein the conditions under which foreign companies were allowed to operate derived from their unimpaired ownership rights over their concession areas. These companies should have realised that such privileges especially would be regarded as contrary to the government's newly acquired sovereign status. Dissatisfaction over foreign ownership and exploitation of such basic national resources as petroleum had formed part of the nationalist demand for independence, expressed in the idea that the Republic should exert direct control over its own resources, of which oil was regarded as especially vital. In 1950 a committee was set up to study the oil and mining laws enacted in other countries with a view to preparing new legislation, but the resulting law regulating petroleum development did not come into effect till October 1960. In the interim period, oil companies operated under conditions that were somewhat confused.

The origin of the 'let alone' agreements under which oil companies operated lay in the temporary contracts reached by them with the Dutch colonial government in 1948, governing their return to Indonesia. Under these contracts, the companies undertook to rehabilitate their production facilities. In return for doing so, they were permitted to retain all foreign exchange earnings from the ensuing production, so long as they provided the necessary additional foreign exchange from their own overseas financial sources to cover the substantial investment envisaged.[7]

The petroleum companies were seemingly protected by the 1949 Round Table Agreements, in which the Indonesian government agreed to recognise all previous concessions and licences granted and to honour the 1948 agreements. Yet the companies were hampered by persistent interruptions to their work which derived from two main sources. There was first no consensus of political opinion on the future status of the oil companies. Extreme nationalist groupings as well as the Indonesian Communist Party wished to force nationalisation of the oil companies, while other political groups within the government felt that the companies' interests should not be prejudiced, in order to attract further foreign investment. Secondly, strong pressures for regional autonomy built up through the 1950s which resulted in increasing political instability and posed serious problems for a government attempting to assert centralised control over the oil industry. The companies' situation was therefore an anomalous one. While on the one hand their presence was welcome, at least formally, and the continued retention of their assets assured, yet their position remained insecure with domestic political forces in contention over the local control of oil-fields, and with arbitrary interventions in the companies' management of their operations.

The government's inability to resolve these issues led to prevarication. A parliamentary resolution was passed in 1951 prohibiting the granting of new leases, thus effectively confining companies to existing areas. This freeze on expansion, while originally intended to last for three months, continued in effect for ten years. The colonial mining laws remained in force during this period, thus formally ensuring the continuation of existing operational arrangements between companies and government. Yet the problem of contract renegotiation arose as early as the beginning of the 1950s, when new terms had to be agreed upon for the disposition of foreign exchange earnings as the earlier ad hoc agreements of 1948 began to run out. As the government had no clear policy for its oil industry, these negotiations were conducted in a rather dilatory fashion. Thus though Stanvac's original foreign exchange agreement expired at the end of 1951, negotiations were protracted until March 1954 when a succeeding arrangement was agreed upon. As a study of the company noted:

The progress of negotiations was complicated by changes of government during the course of the discussions. The government could draw on only a very few Indonesians with special knowledge of the petroleum industry to fill decision-making positions. As a result, the company would spend much time and effort in acquainting a group of government officials with the salient features of the Indonesian petroleum industry and the economics of Stanvac's position in it. Then, the government would change; new personalities, both at the cabinet level and below, would become concerned with petroleum policy, and the process would be started all over again.[8]

Such an attitude resulted, however, from a misconception of the government's position, and did not apportion sufficient weight to the constraints limiting government policy. The government's considerations were rather more complex, as the negotiating position it adopted had to respond at least in part to the shifting and inconstant political character of the country. Yet despite the frequent turnover of governments at that time, attitudes toward foreign investment remained consistently favourable among office-holders. It was the increasing hostility of political groups outside the immediate government which necessitated an apparently tougher negotiating attitude being taken towards the companies. And this attitude persisted, for with each change of government the new administration had to establish its nationalist credentials afresh. The extra-parliamentary opposition had no clear idea of the economic organisation which it wished to impose on the petroleum sector, having only a vague concept of domestic cooperation within an autarkical structure, the practical implications of which were not worked out. The problem with the whole issue of oil-company negotiations was that it became tied up with these differing domestic attitudes.

In the course of negotiations, the companies were unable to obtain an unambiguous commitment from the Indonesian government supporting their continued presence. A new oil and mining law was reportedly prepared by the end of 1956, but internal political difficulties prevented any legislative action on the matter. And the 1958 regional rebellion further complicated governmental bargaining over oil revenues, as one of the claims of the separatist forces, especially in South Sumatra, was that local provinces did not benefit in due proportion to their exports.

The enactment of Law No. 44 in 1960 set out a legal framework for the mining of oil and natural gas. It did not, though, provide any clear guidelines for company investment, failing to lay down exactly what contractual relationship foreign companies should have within the Indonesian petroleum industry. This deliberate obfuscation derived from a need to leave the terms of the Law open to varying interpretations so as to accommodate differences of opinion on the question of foreign company investment which might lead to future shifts in policy. The Law did, however, alter the formal position of the foreign companies, they being obliged to give up their concessionary status and to seek new work contracts with state companies. It further attempted to pressure the companies over the requisite renegotiation of their terms of operation by abrogating their then existing rights after an unspecified period of time. And though it granted them priority in negotiating new working arrangements within their existing operational areas, it did not guarantee that they would necessarily be accepted as contractors under the new Law. Problems of reaching accord were glossed over with the statement that the companies would still be able to operate under terms which satisfied them. Nevertheless, negotiations with the three established oil companies were prolonged till 1963, after the Indonesian government had reached a 'work contract' agreement based on the new Law with another foreign company wishing to embark on petroleum operations in Indonesia.

In an effort to secure agreement, the Indonesian government set a deadline for the completion of negotiations, an exercise in brinkmanship which was matched by the companies giving notice that they were prepared to suspend oil exports if a satisfactory agreement was not reached. Accord was finally secured in June 1963, largely through the companies realising that their new 'contractor' status as proposed by the Indonesian side was not in reality so very different from their previous 'concessionaire' one, but also after their having secured a number of important financial concessions from the government.[9] In addition, further pressure was placed on the companies by the United States government which felt compelled to intervene in the final stage of negotiations in an attempt to secure a compromise; as it feared that, if the country's economic problems were aggravated, this would push Indonesia further into the communist sphere of influence.

These difficulties encountered with the negotiation of contracts of work in the early 1960s were not met with when production-sharing contracts were introduced in the latter half of the 1960s. To begin with, these contracts were taken up by new companies, therefore not involving any renegotiation of previous terms, so the companies had no existing interests to defend. Furthermore, the companies the Indonesian government chose to negotiate with were either of Japanese origin or were subsidiaries of North American 'independent' companies. Hence they were different from the 'major' oil companies which hitherto had dominated the Indonesian petroleum industry. The Japanese were seeking to diversify their country's oil supply sources away from the Middle East, their perception of vulnerability having been sharpened by the 1967 War. And the oil 'independents' were encountering difficulty in obtaining oil leases or concessions in an international industry then dominated by the 'major' companies. Despite the poor history of relations between governments and foreign oil companies in Indonesia, the advent of the Soeharto régime in 1966 had encouraged the foreign companies, as the government demonstrated an increasing ability to secure political stability and, to a lesser extent, economic stability. In any case, the offshore areas being opened for exploration under the new terms allowed the companies to maintain a lower domestic profile, with less reliance on local labour and on the local economic infrastructure, thus minimising the possibility of political controversy.

Though it was feared at the time that a number of the companies operating under production-sharing terms had neither the financial resources nor the technical expertise to fully exploit the contract areas granted to them, some of these companies did subcontract part of their interests to larger, more experienced companies. In this way, the Indonesian side secured acceptance by foreign oil companies of its new production-sharing terms which were at least nominally stringent, choosing to conduct negotiations initially with relatively unknown companies in the hope that this would then bring in larger companies on similar terms.

The question of renegotiating these production-sharing agreements first came up following the 1973 Middle East War. Pertamina managed to introduce new demands into its contracts to reflect the higher post-1973 price of oil, after relatively amicable discussions with the oil companies. The companies recognised that these financial amendments did no more than bring the Indonesian division of profits into line with changes in the Middle East, and, if not introduced, would only have rendered them liable for higher taxes levied by their own home governments. Thus the new profit split of 85:15 in Pertamina's favour applied only above a set base price, below which the original contract terms remained in force. This neatly made the point that the companies' profit expectations when agreeing to their original contracts would be met only insofar as prices remained unchanged (though allowing for inflation); the move to renegotiate contract terms being motivated solely by a desire to gain a larger share of that portion of net profits deriving from the windfall effect of the higher oil price. For the same reason, the Indonesian government decided not to insist on a reduction in the 40 per cent limit to the 'cost' component of production which had been advocated by some sections of public opinion.

The climate of contract renegotiation changed drastically following Pertamina's attempt to unilaterally impose new financial terms on the oil companies in 1976. The background to this move is complex, involving Pertamina's financial overcommitments as a result of overspending on its own development projects, and government pledges to both meet the interest on and eventually repay Pertamina's debts and also allocate alternative funds to cover its national development requirements.[10] As a result, the Indonesian government determined to take another look at oil company contracts. The first sign of this intention came when President Soeharto presented the 1976/77 budget to the Indonesian House of Representatives in January 1976. He described the 'bitter experience' of the Pertamina affair and proposed a 7.6 per cent increase in corporate oil taxes, which would give an estimated additional revenue of US$280 million.[11]

The government then moved to demand an enhanced profit from companies operating under older contracts of work, requesting an additional levy of $1 per barrel of production. The government based its claim on World Bank figures showing that Caltex, the principal work-contract holder, was earning a net profit of some $2.35 per barrel, with estimated total revenues of approximately $700 million. The company argued in return that a high profit margin upstream was necessary to counterbalance its less profitable marketing activities downstream. Agreement was reached only after the government had implicitly threatened a resort to unilateral decree. It did however partially concede the companies' case, allowing them to offset transport costs to consuming markets against the proposed surcharge. This left a net charge estimated at an average $0.85 per barrel;[12] and on some long-distance sales to the United States East coast, the companies paid a charge of only $0.20 per barrel.[13]

When Pertamina began negotiations with its production-sharing contractors on amending their contracts, these talks also became deadlocked. Although the Indonesian side had originally issued no specific proposals, they were believed to be intending to impose a surcharge of $2.50 per barrel on the companies' share of 'profit' oil from production, and possibly as well to cut the companies' cost recovery allowance from a maximum of 40 per cent of production to 25 per cent.[14] This plan was dropped when the companies argued that, at the then current costs and prices, the surcharge would not only eliminate any profit from the 'profit' oil split, but also shear their returns back into the 'cost' component of production (which was after all intended as an allowance against operational expenditure).

Pertamina therefore rephrased the new terms it wished to impose. These comprised two basic demands: raising the 'profit' oil split to an overall 85:15 in Pertamina's favour, and abolishing the 40 per cent 'cost' oil provision, capital costs being depreciated instead, following more conventional accounting principles. There was apparently little objection to the former request, company opposition focusing instead on the latter demand.[15] Negotiations were carried out with the companies on an individual basis. By the set deadline of 31 July 1976, all but one of them had acceded to the Indonesian directive. But after openly objecting to the imposition, this one too fell into line by the extended deadline of 15 August 1976.

Under the superseded 40 per cent depreciation allowance, most companies recovered their pre-production costs in two-and-a-half to four years, while the new depreciation procedure as finally agreed obliged the major companies to spread capital cost recovery over fourteen years. Yet it also recognised the need for an early or 'high front end' recovery from production of both exploration and initial capital expenditure. Thus companies were allowed to depreciate capital expenditure by a double declining-balance method, and non-capital costs could be expensed without limit. The viability of this cost-recovery procedure was nevertheless disputed, the companies claiming cash flow problems which prevented them from recycling investment into continued exploration.

It is difficult to assess the validity of this argument, though the new terms would obviously affect the companies to differing degrees depending on the stage of their operations and the conditions characteristic of their operational area. In general, it would be expected that the companies within major producing areas, with substantial invested capital, would endeavour to protect existing investments as far as possible; while companies in contract areas without commercial discoveries or production would more readily reduce intended investment. The behaviour of those contractors either on the threshold of commercial production or with only more limited production, would therefore be decisive in determining the nature of the companies' general response. In the event their reaction was to drastically reduce all field development, on the ground that the higher costs resulting from a later recovery of expenditure had rendered potential production uneconomic. Meanwhile non-producing contract holders, as expected, virtually halted exploration activity. It became apparent that while the Indonesian government may have opted for maximum current cash flows obtainable from oil operators, it was risking a long-term reduction in production and profits.

The main attraction of the old-style production-sharing system had been the cost-recovery entitlement. This benefit allowed oil companies, especially smaller ones with limited funds, to finance a continued high level of exploration and re-investment, the pattern of numerous relatively small oil discoveries requiring this cycle to sustain output. So the recalcitrance of the companies did appear justified. And the Indonesian side was seen to have gone too far in its redrafting of contracts, the new provisions on depreciation being especially deleterious.

Pertamina seemed to accept these arguments, for a note of contrition crept into its statements on the renegotiation dispute. The then President-Director of Pertamina, Piet Haryono, admitted the need to offer further inducements for oil exploration, expressed his appreciation to the companies for their 'understanding of the situation', and stated that while the companies may have felt that the new terms had been imposed on them, this had not been Pertamina's intention.[16] Indonesian officials outside Pertamina were sufficiently concerned to organise a meeting in January 1977 between President Soeharto and executives from the affected oil companies. The meeting was held in order to assure foreign contractors that their presence in Indonesia was appreciated, and that the issue of further exploration incentives was being actively studied. President Soeharto pledged Indonesia's continued cooperation in the exploitation of its petroleum reserves, and promised consideration of company proposals.

Pertamina consequently initiated a further exploration incentives programme in February 1977, revising its proposed depreciation procedures in favour of the companies, including a concession on the companies' domestic supply requirement, and providing an investment credit to be deductible for tax purposes. The following May, contract-of-work holders also received a tax concession on additional investment. As formulated, these terms were clearly aimed at that decisive group of companies in between non-production and full-scale production. They were intended to accelerate exploration and speed development of promising contract areas, by allowing companies to recoup their initial expenditure within a much shorter time period. The companies' response was therefore interesting, for there was no significant increase in field exploration.

The renegotiation dispute between Pertamina and the companies had meanwhile been complicated by the fortuitous coincidence of an American IRS ruling in May 1976, which treated Pertamina's portion of the 'profit' split from production sharing as a royalty and not a tax. It hence disallowed American companies from claiming a foreign tax credit and rendered them liable to double taxation. This issue had been pressing the companies even further. The IRS had granted them a one-year reprieve to negotiate new contracts, and the then Indonesian Minister of Mines and Energy, Mohammad Sadli, reassured them that the Indonesian government would endeavour to have the IRS decision reversed, moving quickly as well to secure American legal advice in the drafting of new contract terms. Yet the Indonesian side delayed issuing its new proposals to counter the IRS ruling, as its attention was caught up in securing acceptance of its new terms on depreciation and a revised profit split. When finally presented in November 1976, the revised terminology still proved unacceptable to the IRS. Further revisions by the Indonesian side were finally accepted in May 1978, when the IRS agreed to treat the value of production committed to the Indonesian government in lieu of income tax as deductible for United States tax purposes.

In the interim period, the largely American production-sharing contractors became increasingly concerned at the prospect of having to pay huge increases in taxes to the US government from their Indonesian operations, their worries over the approaching IRS deadline even leading some of them to submit alternative proposals of their own to the IRS. What is significant, though, in the context of the renegotiation dispute between Pertamina and the foreign oil companies is that a substantial increase in programmed drilling occurred only from early 1978, when a favourable decision by the IRS was already anticipated. It therefore does appear that the impending swingeing increase in the companies' overall tax burdens, which would result from an inability to claim US tax write-offs on their Indonesian payments, was more decisive in their investment plans than the companies were prepared to admit.

Even more important than the changes in contract terms was the change that resulted in the environment surrounding the foreign-company–state-enterprise relationship. Formerly a high level of trust had existed between the two sides. Pertamina realised that its concept of production sharing could only be developed because of the willingness of the smaller companies to enter a new form of cooperative agreement, while the companies understood that Pertamina would not actually exercise its management rights to the detriment of their activities.

It is believed, though, that Pertamina's move, which amounted to a unilateral abrogation of existing company contracts, was initiated by Bappenas, the National Development Planning Agency, on the basis of a confidential World Bank report. This report contrasted Indonesia's relatively unfavourable 'take' from petroleum companies with other producer governments in the Middle East, and Pertamina's own objections to having to implement the Bappenas initiative were overruled by the government.[17] If this interpretation of the Indonesian action is correct, however, the resultant dispute, caused at least in part by the inflexibility of the Indonesian side, may have been intensified by the consequences of the crisis caused by Pertamina's over-expansion into non-oil-related activities. For as the government moved to regain control over Pertamina, the adamant manner in which decisions affecting Pertamina's oil company contractors were implemented may possibly have been the result of government officials asserting their newly acquired control over the policy of the formerly largely self-governing state corporation. The companies were left unsure who was ultimately responsible for Indonesian petroleum policy.[18] They also complained that the proposed changes had been presented to them as an ultimatum. For their part, government spokesmen adopted an unyielding attitude, publicly announcing that the companies would be required to 'submit'.[19] Minister Sadli did later concede that the changes at Pertamina had adversely affected the Indonesian negotiating attitude, and that the government had since come to learn a great deal about the characteristics of the Indonesian petroleum industry.

As pointed out earlier, production-sharing contracts are little different in practice from more usual work contracts, though they embody major symbolic differences which obscure their substantive similarities and fulfil a political function in providing both an appearance of equality and a framework within which the Indonesian side can work to bring this desired equality closer. The spirit motivating production sharing was therefore one of cooperation, and if this remained more ideal than real, it nevertheless inhibited both sides from indulging in behaviour which might be deemed obstreperous or unreasonable by the other. Thus conflict was minimised and a more peaceful operational setting provided than would normally be found in other oil-producing countries. The manner in which company contracts were abrogated, and the use of confrontation and brinkmanship tactics to secure the acceptance of proposed amendments, brought about a permanent change in this environment.

From the companies' point of view, there is a widespread feeling of aggrievement and a commonly held view that if, as is all too likely, the Indonesian government runs into further financial difficulties in the future, it may return to pursuing a similar course of action. The companies' own position is, however, a not entirely valid one. They have always stressed the sanctity of contract terms despite the vast changes in their governmental relationships elsewhere in the oil-producing world. They also continue to underestimate the government's determination to exercise a larger proportion of its latent powers under production-sharing agreements, as Pertamina gradually acquires the ability to carry out its management functions more effectively. And this leads to difficult managerial problems when imposed deadlines on various stipulations approach, and accusations by Pertamina of a breach of good faith if these are not met.

The companies appear to find it difficult to understand Pertamina's and in general the Indonesian approach to managing its relationship with them, with its stress on reticence and an imprecision of terms to cover possible differences, its abhorrence of direct confrontation with the companies themselves, and its own authoritarian and bureaucratic style of decision-making. If they are to achieve a manageable relationship with Pertamina, the companies will therefore have to adjust their behaviour patterns so as to better fit in with Indonesian norms. And they will need to alter their own values and standards in doing so, realising that these changes do not necessarily carry the same significance as they would in a more familiar operational environment.

The government's position has been that the contract abrogations of 1976 constituted an ad hoc and never-to-be-repeated event, to meet the unique difficulties caused by Pertamina's financial crisis. Certainly the concessions it had to make, and the realisation that it had overplayed its hand, make a repetition of these events unlikely. Pertamina was forced to face the fact that the smaller oil companies, on which it relies to a large extent, have a more narrow financial margin to absorb changes in their operational conditions. It may also be noted that the dispute over oil-company contracts occurred at a time when the Indonesian government was preoccupied both with its military invasion of East Timor and the run-up to general elections in 1977. Although there was no direct link with these two events, they may have heightened pressures on the government to assert its nationalist credentials as well as worsening its financial problems, thus making a more compromising attitude less tenable.

The lingering caution of the companies was evident from their investment commitments. Although exploration activity did pick up after 1978, it is significant that the major oil companies only resumed signing new exploration contracts with Pertamina from the end of 1979 onwards. New investment up till then came only from smaller companies with a more restricted choice of investment alternatives. The companies were presumably encouraged by the oil-price escalations of 1979 (and also political unrest in Iran and the Middle East), which brought substantial windfall profits in their train and increased Indonesia's attractiveness as a country in which to search for oil. The corollary to this motive, though, would imply that the expansion in the Indonesian petroleum industry from 1980 was at least partly the result of a factor having no connection with Indonesian policy towards the oil companies.

Indeed, in their dealings with Pertamina the companies continue to remain hypersensitive to the ramifications of any negotiating difficulty encountered and to question the reliability of the Indonesian side. This attitude has been most notable in the negotiations to convert the Caltex contract of work,[20] which expired at the end of 1983, into a production-sharing agreement. Both sides had agreed on this course in 1971, outlining a model contract which set different profit ratios for existing production and for 'new' output requiring substantial further investment. But in 1981, Pertamina proposed a complex formula which, while in effect also dividing production into 'old oil' and 'new oil' components, would treat only the latter under standard production-sharing terms. The 'old oil' component would come instead under Pertamina's control, presumably in the belief that there was no need for continued assistance from Caltex in extractive operations where transfer of technology had taken place over several decades. Pertamina would take over production from existing well-heads, with Caltex responsible for secondary recovery operations which would be handled in a normal production-sharing fashion. The Indonesian proposal was actually not as unfavourable to Caltex as may at first appear, for production from the present contract area can only be maintained through an extensive secondary recovery programme; and should this be embarked upon, the 'new oil' component would come to comprise the major portion of production.[21]

Caltex, however, took the view that the agreement reached in 1971 clearly envisaged applying normal production-sharing terms to the whole of its onshore production (though it was prepared to consider revising the profit ratios which were reached then, given that the profit split in standard contracts had changed significantly in 1976). And it claimed to regard any attempt to alter that basic understanding as a renegation by the Indonesian side of a previously agreed commitment. While accepting that it has accrued substantial profits from its onshore operations, continuing to produce without further risk, Caltex pointed out that the envisaged secondary recovery needed to maintain production would require an extremely large capital investment.

In the event, a standard production-sharing arrangement was eventually agreed upon in late 1983, though the 'profit' component of production was divided at a new rate of 88:12 in Indonesia's favour. Despite continued assurances from the new President-Director of Pertamina, Judo Sumbono, that foreign-company agreements would not be tampered with, the course of this disagreement with Caltex was viewed with mounting unease by Pertamina's other foreign contractors, they fearing that it might presage another major change in policy similar to the 1976 abrogation of their contracts. It would seem though that Pertamina does consider Caltex to be a unique case, with much of its investment amortised and with operating fields whose reserves have been clearly defined. Given this realisation, it would be highly unlikely for Pertamina to try to impose the new profit split agreed with Caltex on other production-sharing contract holders. Nor is it likely to attempt to do so for new contracts, given that it has been obliged to substantially lower its signature bonus demands in order to stimulate interest in new contract areas from foreign oil companies.

The companies' fear, however, was enhanced by another dispute in August 1981, when Pertamina ordered Atlantic Richfield to cease operations in a field off North-east Kalimantan on the grounds that the field was not commercially viable.[22] In this case, Pertamina applied a new definition of 'commercial' production, requiring that revenue equivalent to 51 per cent of estimated production should fall due to itself. Given the company's exploration costs over the previous ten years, which were to be offset against production, together with Pertamina's estimate of field reserves, this criterion could not be met. This decision was the first instance of Pertamina exercising its overriding management powers to terminate a still continuable contract operation. The dispute was quietly resolved in July 1982, and Atlantic Richfield was allowed to resume production till its costs were recovered, before relinquishing the concession. But should companies be thereby discouraged from spending more on exploration, it would lower the incentive to explore smaller marginal fields where most of the yet undiscovered oil in Indonesia is believed to lie.

What the companies failed to consider was that Indonesia had parliamentary elections in May 1982 and a presidential election in

March 1983; and that in pre-election periods criticism against the government's policy of working with foreign investors tends to arise, particularly over activities which deplete natural resources. Thus opinions questioning the wisdom of the 1971 Caltex agreement and calling for a 'better deal' for Indonesia were voiced, one union leader even advocating nationalisation. Hence the Indonesian side found itself under the pressure of domestic public opinion to at least be seen to be fighting for the best possible deal, and to appear to come out of the negotiations victorious. For political reasons, Pertamina was therefore compelled to adopt an unyielding negotiating stance, though this did not preclude a realistic settlement acceptable to the companies. Such realism would certainly be required, given Indonesia's continued need to work with foreign companies in its petroleum industry.

It may also be argued that in its continuing effort to find the contractual formula that will maximise both exploration rates and returns from production, Pertamina may occasionally find that it has overstepped the limits of what is possible at any given point in time. And such an error of judgment would be more likely to occur in a period of transition such as that following the assumption to office of a new managerial team under Judo Sumbono in April 1981.

Pertamina has successfully managed to negotiate new contracts on reasonably favourable terms with the oil companies. It has emphasised maintaining a large number of oil contractors, in its own words keeping 'a lot of players on the board',[23] the sheer diversity allowing it to deal forcefully with any one individual company. And it has managed to achieve better terms for itself by playing off potential contractors against each other, making them compete for instance over signature and production bonuses, and keeping a short list of bids to be used in individual negotiations as a third-party ploy.

It needs, therefore, to devise similarly successful procedures for renegotiations of agreements, institutionalising change as it were within the contract itself. This would serve to reduce the bitterness that has accompanied demands for revision, and help to provide a means for each side to understand the other's position. Minister Sadli recognised this fundamental weakness of the basic production-sharing format when he attributed the difficulties of contract renegotiation to the absence of any clause in production-sharing contracts dealing with adjustment to change.[24]

The future shape of the foreign-company–host-government relationship thus depends very much on the approach of both sides. If companies and government can develop a better sense of empathy for each other's motives and position, and so reconcile nationalistic aspirations with recognition of the need for foreign investment, then the present system of production sharing in the Indonesian petroleum industry may continue to have utility as an arrangement for binding such diverse interests together. When first introduced, this system, despite its failings, did represent an original and interesting attempt to shift the balance of advantage from the companies to the government side, and it provided a workable relationship within which the process of oil extraction could proceed unimpeded. For it to remain so, it has to be viewed by the participants involved not as a fixed set of terms to be invoked in times of dispute, but as a means for instituting a continual discussion of differences which will in turn modify the formal relationship as circumstances and conditions of operation change. It may even be possible in the drafting of future contracts to identify from experience those provisions most likely to become the subject of dispute. Differences over contract terms in the Indonesian petroleum industry may indeed have been settled without recourse to conflict resolution clauses. But allowing for the possibility of change within oil contracts would be very likely to reduce the ill-feeling attendant on attempts at contract revision, and would limit the pervasive fear of possible disruption.

Allowing for conflict resolution does not invalidate the need for both sides to recognise that conflict would be most probable if the agreement is viewed as confirming an existing relationship, given that the conditions appropriate to its original terms are not immutable. Here the attitude of the foreign company is critical. For although the days of gunboat diplomacy may be over, the company still has recourse to other measures aimed at protecting its interests. The company may for instance take out insurance against political risk to protect itself from such possibilities as civil unrest, expropriation, or the imposition of governmental injunctions preventing it from freely converting currency or transferring profits abroad. Or it may institute litigation in the law courts of other countries where the host government with whom it is contending holds assets or maintains commercial interests, in an effort to seize these assets or have them legally impounded in order to obtain compensation from the host government in question.

The latter approach was taken by a major creditor in the wake of the Pertamina crisis of 1975, when the latter's financial difficulties prevented it from meeting payments on its hire-purchase charters of a number of oil supertankers. The creditor, acting through several affiliated companies, lodged a series of lawsuits in various countries, seeking to attach a wide range of Pertamina's assets. The first claim was filed in New York in July 1976, where Pertamina's initial defence was to allege that the deals reached were improper and did not result from commercial transactions at arm's length. Pertamina also maintained that Ibnu Sutowo, its former President-Director, had no authority to enter by himself into shipping contracts. Pertamina further claimed that its assets should not be seized because it was an agency of the Indonesian government, in effect asserting the protection of sovereign immunity, a doctrine which questions the ability of a court to wield jurisdiction over a government or a governmental body and to judge the legality of some action of a foreign sovereign state. This argument was not accepted by the American court on the grounds that the transactions involved were commercial and not public acts, Pertamina carrying on as if it were a private business company. And the court issued orders of attachment impounding a number of Pertamina vessels. The course of the dispute was complex, with further protracted litigation. Both sides eventually negotiated an out-of-court settlement in August 1977, under which Pertamina surrendered the disputed tankers and made a part-payment. In return, the contracts were cancelled and Pertamina released from further financial obligations.

Foreign companies are therefore not entirely helpless in that they are able to resist unfavourable actions by host governments. Yet the legal remedies open to them are clearly measures of last resort to be applied only in extreme cases. Most governmental attempts to alter contract terms would have to be countered by other means, the companies ultimately having to rely on the host government's need for their continued presence. The government's negotiating posture has therefore to be considered. For the host government may well be able to influence the shape and substance of the settlement reached, depending on its own negotiating skills, the efficiency of its administration, and the technical, financial and managerial resources available to it. The relevant organisational structure on the government side and its approach to negotiation will hence be examined.

6. ORGANISATIONAL STRUCTURE AND THE NEGOTIATING PROCESS

The governmental organisation and domestic structure set limits to the types of contract which a host government may set out to secure. The host government has to know what arrangements are possible to achieve and would be practicable in effect when bargaining with foreign companies. The governmental configuration, so far as it affects foreign oil companies, is therefore examined here. But in the Indonesian case, a further consideration comes into the picture. For in dealing with the oil companies, the government came to find that its principal weakness has been its ineffective authority, which derived from the autonomous status of the governmental body charged with responsibility for petroleum concerns. The problem of the state oil company's accountability to the central government therefore requires special attention, an issue of especial relevance to host governments which delegate responsibility for mineral affairs to organs not under direct government control. Finally, given such confines, any settlement which may be arrived at will also reflect the ability of the government side to negotiate effectively and to employ to maximum advantage those resources available to it. So beyond the government's formal configuration, its approaches to negotiation will have to be dealt with for a complete understanding of the host government's situation.

It is often the case for host governments that the skilled personnel and technical and financial resources necessary to effectively negotiate and administer contracts are not available in sufficient number. Moreover, poor organisation has often meant that the host government does not even utilise efficiently its limited capacities. One way of overcoming these difficulties is to hire the

159

requisite expertise from outside the country. But foreign advisers, if unfamiliar with the particular social, political and economic concerns shaping the host government's policy and only superficially acquainted with the host country's social norms and culture, cannot be an effective substitute for a capable indigenous negotiating body. Indeed, calling in foreign expertise may even be harmful in the long run if it hinders the development of local expertise.

Such a line of argument was adopted within Indonesia to justify building a negotiating structure through national experience, with only minimal dependence on foreign advice. Indeed, state participation in the Indonesian petroleum industry has a long history, dating back to 1921 when the Netherlands Indies Oil Company was incorporated as a joint partnership between Shell and the Dutch colonial government, the latter providing half the financial capital but remaining a passive partner in the company's extractive ventures. State intervention by successive independent Indonesian governments developed in a haphazard fashion through the interaction of diverse political groups acting both within and outside the government and its bureaucracy.

After the enactment in 1960 of Law No. 44, which required petroleum policy to be implemented only by state enterprises, the government had to decide on the number and identity of state oil enterprises that would be formed. While there were proponents of the idea that only one national oil company should be created, the country's political development resulted in three national companies, Permina, Pertamin and Permigan being established in 1961. These represented a balance of control among the dominant political forces of the day, respectively the army, the government under Sukarno, and the Indonesian Communist Party. Each state enterprise had one major foreign oil company working for it: Stanvac with Permina, Caltex with Pertamin and Shell with Permigan. But as the triangular political structure which underpinned this arrangement became increasingly unstable, so the relative standing of the different state enterprises was affected. Permigan was dissolved after the allegedly communist-instigated coup of October 1965, and its assets taken over by the government. And in 1968, Permina and Pertamin were merged to form Pertamina, thus creating a single state oil company. This merger reflected political conditions in post-1965 Indonesia, where, with a new military régime in power, the balancing policies pursued under Sukarno were dispensed with.

The governmental structure concerned with the implementation of petroleum policy altered therefore according to the fortunes of the country's political groupings. As one group, favourably disposed towards foreign investment, consolidated its power, a parallel transformation occurred in the petroleum sector. And a unified structure capable of implementing consistent integrated policies towards foreign oil companies was made possible.

A host government's ability to deal effectively with foreign companies clearly depends on its having such a stable negotiating framework. The government can delegate virtually complete authority to a single state enterprise to conclude agreements with foreign investors for the extraction of petroleum. This state enterprise is then able to act independently of other government agencies, who may have different concerns and possibly rival priorities, in setting contracts with foreign companies, thus ensuring consistency of purpose. And the host government's difficulty in finding people with a knowledge of the technical aspects of petroleum extraction and conversant with oil company operational techniques, is minimised. All such skilled personnel as are available can be concentrated within one organisation. In the Indonesian context, it has been easier to attract highly qualified people to work for a state enterprise such as Pertamina, which can offer larger salaries, better working conditions and a higher social status than can the civil service in general. Furthermore, it is easier to assure continuity of personnel under these conditions, thus accumulating expertise and familiarity with the concerns of private companies.

Such considerations underlay the Indonesian government's decision to establish Pertamina as its sole state oil enterprise. Pertamina is itself managed by a headquarters organisation consisting of a President-Director with six supporting directorates dealing with oil exploration and production, petroleum processing, domestic supply of petroleum, general affairs, financial affairs, and shipping and telecommunications, each directorate overseeing a number of operating divisions or subdirectorates (see fig. 3). The state company's varied responsibilities as indicated by the functions of its different directorates, which cover the provision of

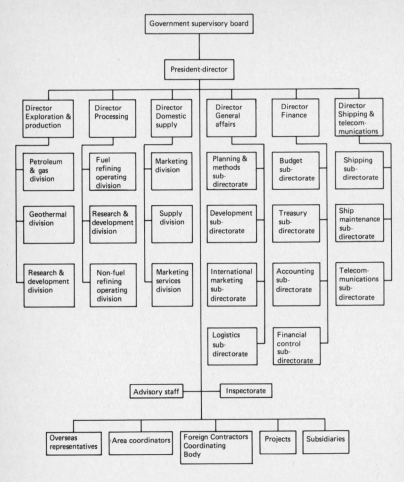

Fig. 3. Pertamina: organisation chart. Source: Indonesia, Pertamina, *Pertamina Today: A Review of Indonesia's Petroleum Industry* (Jakarta: 1979).

supporting services for oil-company operations, and domestic downstream activities as well as its own petroleum production, enable it to become better acquainted with those technical and financial issues of especial concern to foreign oil companies. A separate office, the Foreign Contractors Coordinating Body, deals specifically with foreign-company relations, thus providing a focus for the development of negotiating expertise.

A governmental organisation wielding wide-ranging powers and exclusively concerned with the implementation of petroleum policy towards foreign oil companies, does however have a potential disadvantage in its very independence. For it is difficult for the host government to strike the right balance between granting its subordinate body sufficient autonomy to allow it to operate with sufficient flexibility and to enable it to function in a creative and nonbureaucratic manner; while yet retaining effective control over the latter's operations to ensure that it respects the government's ultimate authority and remains accountable to the government for its actions. This dilemma had to be faced by the Indonesian government in determining Pertamina's position within the country's oil industry.

Pertamina's management board, consisting of the President-Director and the heads of the six directorates, is accountable to two governmental bodies. Responsibility for Pertamina within the government is vested in a Council of Government Commissioners (DKPP),[1] formed to represent the government's interests under the provisions of Law No. 8 of 1971, which was enacted to define Pertamina's scope of operations. The DKPP is chaired by the Minister of Mines and Energy, and comprises the Minister of Finance as vice-chairman and the Head of the National Planning Board as a third permanent member, together with two additional temporary members who are currently the Minister of State for Research and Technology and the Head of the State Secretariat. It functions as an integral part of Pertamina, supervising the state company's activities and setting policy for Pertamina's management to implement. The two additional members are appointed at the discretion of the President, who need not make any appointment should he so wish. And the two current members were appointed to the DKPP after the March 1983 Presidential election, replacing the Defence Minister and the Industry Minister. While the DKPP needs to be fairly representative of government ministries with a relevant interest in Pertamina if it is to properly fulfil its supervisory role, the changes represented a particular tightening of Presidential control over Pertamina's functioning, the State Secretary (Sudharmono) being a close associate and the Research Minister (Habibie) a protégé of President Soeharto.

Indonesian government policy within the petroleum sector is determined in broad outline by the Ministry of Mines and Energy, to which Pertamina is also responsible. Within the Ministry, a Directorate-General for Oil and Gas (Migas)[2] has primary responsibility for petroleum and energy policy. The supervisory role of Migas as it affects Pertamina's relations with foreign companies, is, however, mainly concerned with ensuring that these companies comply with the relevant Indonesian laws dealing with operational matters such as land use, foreign-exchange regulations, import and export restrictions, and work-site safety requirements.

While on paper the government maintains an effective control over Pertamina's activities, this control did not always ensue in practice. When Pertamina was headed by General Ibnu Sutowo, the formal authority exerted by the DKPP and Migas was overridden by the strong entrepreneurial character of Pertamina's management; and the close personal links between Sutowo and President Soeharto circumvented the DKPP's and the Ministry of Mines and Energy's own direct responsibility to the President. This situation, with no clearly defined limits to the powers of Pertamina's authority and with ambiguous lines of control extending from superior-ranking bodies within the governmental structure, led through gross mismanagement to the de facto bankruptcy of Pertamina in 1975. And this predicament caused serious strains in the government's relations with foreign oil companies. As Pertamina's financial crisis was engendered by its autonomous status, the issue of accountability, with its implications for the effective functioning of Pertamina as the government's principal policy-implementing agent in the petroleum sector, has to be considered in greater detail before going on to discuss the actual process of negotiating contracts.

THE PROBLEM OF ACCOUNTABILITY

The problems which Pertamina's functioning have posed for the Indonesian government derive from a range of topics which cannot be adequately encompassed by the term 'corruption'. These concerns do indeed cover the use of Pertamina's profits for various irregular political and social purposes, and the personal benefit obtained from company activities by various officials from both inside and outside Pertamina. However, they range wider to encompass, for example, the question of the commercial viability

of Pertamina's policies and the integration of Pertamina's operations with national economic development plans. Attempts to
investigate such matters lead to a nebulous realm because of their
controversial and politically sensitive nature. Numerous allegations of improper conduct contrast with little hard evidence of
guilt and no proper accounting for the validity of these charges.

The report in 1970 of the Commission of Four, specially
appointed to investigate the problem of corruption in Indonesia,
dwelt at length on Pertamina and constituted the first formal
inquiry into the latter's activities. However the report failed to deal
adequately with Pertamina's lack of accountability, a situation
aggravated by the idiosyncratic control exercised by its President-
Director, Ibnu Sutowo. This problem of inadequate accountability
was the crucial cause of Pertamina's later difficulties. For so long as
Pertamina remained in effect amenable to no authority other than
that of President Soeharto, unless and until he chose to exercise his
prerogative, Pertamina was able to act without any need to justify
its actions to any jurisdiction. The Commission questioned Pertamina's organisational irregularities; but did not take the issue a
stage further by attempting to identify a clear borderline between
Pertamina's legitimate and its improper functions, or by querying
a situation in which a state company, whose primary area of
responsibility was the country's petroleum industry, was engaging
in a diverse range of other economic activities.

The report did manage to make a substantial criticism of Pertamina by pinpointing its financial irresponsibility: its failure to pay
corporate taxes and other dues as required to the government, its
secretion of foreign exchange through various illegal manoeuvres,
and other operational practices which enabled it to evade formal
government control. The Commission therefore concluded that
the government should exercise more intensive financial control
over Pertamina, proposing that a Board of Commissioners be
established to superintend Pertamina's board of directors, and that
Pertamina's budget and accounts be subject to close scrutiny by the
Ministry of Finance.

These proposals helped to shape the law on Pertamina passed in
September 1971, which set up the DKPP as a supervisory body
from whom Pertamina was obliged to seek approval for its work
programme, budget and annual accounts.[3] This enhanced supervision, however, failed to achieve any practical effect, and

Pertamina encountered little hindrance in carrying on its individualistic manner of operation. The DKPP met infrequently, and its lack of technical expertise prevented it from properly evaluating Pertamina's various projects; while an objective appraisal of Pertamina's accounts would properly have required an independent audit carried out by an agent from outside the government.

It is difficult to assess to what extent Sutowo was sanctioned or even encouraged to proceed on his autonomous path in managing the Indonesian oil industry. In his previous capacity as head of Permina, one of Pertamina's predecessor state oil companies which was linked to the Indonesian army, Sutowo had from the beginning provided an important source of funds for the military. After October 1965, through helping to meet the army's financial needs, he aided the consolidation in power of the Soeharto régime. It would seem, therefore, that effective governmental control over Pertamina was not possible, given the informal understanding apparently reached between Sutowo and various members of the Soeharto régime. This agreement granted the former independence of action as a quid pro quo for providing a source of 'extra-budgetary' funds benefiting the latter. And this trade-off worked in a manner which encouraged Sutowo to engage in a wide variety of projects with only peripheral relevance to the oil industry. These activities served to deflect official criticism from the state company. So long as the impetus of the different projects could be maintained, enabling political figures within the military establishment to claim credit for and to benefit from them, no one in the government could be expected to be especially eager to scrutinise the state company's procedures. Indeed the peripheral activities Sutowo was encouraged to undertake included development projects specially delegated to Pertamina by President Soeharto, which Sutowo proved able to finance and to implement. Furthermore these activities generated a host of smaller benefits to the advantage of local communities, such as schools, medical clinics, roads and other economic infrastructure; and these items too had a semi-political purpose in enhancing the image of the ruling régime.

Criticism of Pertamina from outside the governmental establishment was inhibited by the belief that many of the projects undertaken, though not subject to cost-accounting or feasibility studies, were fundamentally worthwhile. So in the interest of their com-

pletion, it was therefore better to give Sutowo a degree of operational latitude rather than place him under tight ministerial control or within rigid bureaucratic constraints. Sutowo reinforced
these feelings by fostering an image of himself as one of Indonesia's
few successful entrepreneurs whose ad hoc managerial methods
worked best outside conventional government channels.

This is not the place to detail the range of Pertamina's operations.[4] These activities may be broadly divided into two not
readily separable categories: operations which directly support the
process of petroleum extraction, and other activities with at best
only a tangential connection to the petroleum sector. Sutowo himself claimed that 'if we want the oil business to increase the state
income in a direct way, we must attempt to ensure that the money
used for the development of oil resources is mostly spent in
Indonesia. One of Pertamina's objectives is to see that services
needed for the exploitation, production, processing, as well as
transportation of oil are mostly available in Indonesia.'[5]

Such a motive would ostensibly support the first group of
projects, with the object of building Pertamina into a vertically
integrated business entity, covering all phases of petroleum production from exploration and development to production, processing and marketing. These operations included Pertamina's
shipping fleet, which comprised both ocean-going tankers and
inter-island transport vessels, its aircraft and helicopter fleet, its
telecommunications network, service and equipment supply
centres, and its refineries, fertiliser and other petrochemical
plants. But Sutowo's professed justification for his state company's
expansion would not vindicate the second group of projects which
took in such diverse activities as real estate investment, insurance,
the industry and tourist components of the development scheme
for Batam Island, the Krakatau steel works, the South Sumatra rice
estate, and an extensive construction programme encompassing
office buildings, residences, hotels and restaurants. These ventures
were undertaken because Pertamina came to be regarded as a focus
of growth for economic activities outside the petroleum field, and
they turned the company into a large multifarious conglomerate.

To finance these heterogeneous interests, Pertamina did have
considerable financial resources at its disposal from its production-
sharing contractors, from refining and the domestic marketing of
petroleum, and from its own crude-oil production. But as the

company expanded, these resources proved quite inadequate to finance the huge investments that were needed. And as Pertamina outstripped the government's control, so the potential scope for misjudgment by its financial management grew. The problem was aggravated by the extravagant manner in which these projects were implemented, with no regard for their validity or cost-effectiveness.

Examples of the various ways in which Pertamina's profligacy manifested itself may readily be given. A propensity towards new experimental technology was revealed in such projects as a floating fertiliser factory for the production of ammonia and urea from off-shore oil and natural gas production, a plan of dubious feasibility which had eventually to be abandoned. The development of Batam Island, lying 12 miles south of Singapore, into a logistics and operational base for oil exploration and development formed part of Pertamina's attempt to encourage foreign oil companies to base their Indonesian operations within the country. But it was over-ambitiously extended into a 'demonstration project' to create a major new industrial and commercial centre. Pertamina embarked on a massive investment programme following a study prepared by American and Japanese consultants. However, it proved difficult to engage the participation of foreign companies, apart from some oil-related business, and various projects were either abandoned, suspended, or reached only a semi-operable status. The government was forced to intervene, reducing the scale of the whole project and cutting back Pertamina's involvement in it.

The Krakatau Steel Works at Cilegon in West Java was the largest and most controversial of the non-oil-related projects, providing the most striking example of mismanagement. Undertaken originally by the Soviet Union for the Sukarno régime, the project was abandoned as uneconomic; but in 1971, President Soeharto directed Sutowo to reactivate the scheme. This Sutowo not only proceeded to do, but he further expanded the scope of the project, adding a second stage which quadrupled the plant's intended capacity, and expending an estimated sum of around US$1,250 million in the process.[6] A government investigation commissioned in 1975 uncovered extensive prima facie evidence of corruption, revealing gross over-pricing in the contracts signed by Pertamina with payment schedules based on the passage of time without reference to progress of work. The government eventually decided to cut its losses and substantially reduced the scale of the operation, though this did not dispel the existing doubts as to the project's ultimate viability. As for the Palembang Rice Estate project in South Sumatra, this was a scheme to develop 20,000 hectares of swamp-land into a large farm for the production of high-yield rice, grandiosely promoted as being intended to provide a formula for making Indonesia self-sufficient in rice. It too had to be drastically curtailed to more realistic proportions and eventually transferred to the jurisdiction of the Ministry of Agriculture.

In order to undertake these diverse projects, Pertamina began to borrow on an increasing scale in international financial markets. The Indonesian government, under pressure from the International Monetary Fund to assert greater control over the company's burgeoning activities, decreed in October 1972 that Pertamina would have to seek government approval through the DKPP for all loans of one to fifteen years duration. The understanding behind the limits imposed was that Pertamina's functioning should not be unnecessarily restricted; and it should therefore be left free to obtain loans covering less than a year for the purpose of providing short-term working capital and loans extending over fifteen years to finance long-term development. But this regulation only led Pertamina increasingly to borrow short-term at high interest rates (it being more difficult to raise long-term credit) so as to avoid having to go through government channels.[7] Repayments on its long-term investments were then met by rolling short-term loans over continually, refinancing maturing liabilities through new borrowing.

This intricate debt pattern could not be sustained indefinitely. In September 1974, Pertamina suffered a 'liquidity squeeze' when several banks refused to reschedule repayments which were due. A consortium of creditors eventually agreed to extend a new loan to cover what was then thought to be a temporary difficulty. Then in February and March 1975, Pertamina failed to meet two further repayments. An American bank[8] brought the problem to public notice by threatening action to attach certain of Pertamina's properties. A technical default was, however, avoided when Bank Indonesia, the country's central bank, moved in to pay off the two loans and to guarantee all the state company's short-term debts.

In order to preserve the country's investment climate and its own credit rating with the international financial community, the government had to publicly acknowledge its intent to honour all justifiable Pertamina commitments and to take specific measures to solve Pertamina's financial problems. A government-initiated external audit calculated Pertamina's overall debts at US$10,600 million, of which the government paid off part and entered into negotiations to reschedule, reduce or cancel the remainder. Pertamina's internal organisation was recast to provide a clearer division of functions, more direct lines of managerial and budgetary control, a centralised accounting system and an inspectorate to monitor the company's finances. Its non-oil-related activities were for the most part either cancelled or scaled down, and were largely removed from its control.

Sutowo was eventually dismissed in March 1976, and replaced by Piet Haryono, a former Director-General of the Budget in the Ministry of Finance. The government, however, refrained from holding Sutowo accountable for Pertamina's mismanagement. It feared such a course of action could lead to public criticism of the army's 'dual function', a central tenet of the Indonesian armed forces, justifying their role in the country's civilian life. And it was also anxious to avoid any public trial which might reveal evidence embarrassing to other people within the Indonesian establishment who were implicated in Pertamina's expansionist activities. A major rescue operation by the international banking community helped avert the state company's imminent financial collapse. Immediate loan packages were extended by two banking consortia and assurances given by the Inter-Governmental Group on Indonesia (IGGI), the principal channel of governmental foreign aid to the country, that further requests for aid would be favourably considered.

One noteworthy consequence of Pertamina's financial crisis was its implications for Indonesia's relations with foreign oil companies. It led to the protracted effort to impose new terms of operation on them in 1976, in an attempt to increase revenues in order to pay off the debts incurred. In this regard, Pertamina's weakened status contributed to the tougher more inflexible Indonesian attitude displayed during those negotiations, which engendered much ill-feeling on the part of the companies. Moreover, there was general scepticism within Indonesia over Pertamina's claim that it had already managed to extract the best possible terms from the companies. Minister of Mines Sadli declared that while Pertamina remained responsible for preserving good relations with its foreign oil contractors, the central government would have to pay greater attention to the details of Pertamina's production-sharing arrangements, and to intervene in contract negotiations even to the point of deciding on contract terms, because these terms would significantly affect the government's own financing.[9]

A number of broader points for consideration presented themselves in the wake of the Pertamina crisis. It would not, however, appear that the Indonesian government, despite the remedial measures which it undertook, fully managed to resolve them.

To begin with, it might seem that a need existed for greater disclosure of governmental affairs both within and without government circles. For as the crisis showed, Pertamina was able to proceed with its financially reckless policies because only a small group of officials, not all of whom were completely disinterested participants, had adequate information to properly evaluate its policies. In addition, the informal relationship between Sutowo and President Soeharto bypassed those officials in Bappenas, the Finance Ministry and the Central Bank who should have been monitoring Pertamina's activities. And given the confidential nature of the Indonesian power structure, the lack of public information left public groups outside the ruling establishment without hard facts with which to query official policies. While the government has not felt able to introduce more open public accountability to curb the excessive autonomy of individual state enterprises and government agencies, it has attempted at least to institute checks and balances within the bureaucracy and to exercise a broad control over Pertamina's investment activities and financial situation.

The Central Bank, Bank Indonesia, took over the administration of oil revenues from Pertamina's own accounting system, with payments to Pertamina nominally passing into Pertamina accounts for quarterly transfer to the government, as previously, but with the Central Bank having withdrawal rights. On the basis of its monitoring of petroleum shipments, Bank Indonesia was therefore able to secure the government's share of the proceeds. The new arrangement represented an improvement on the previous procedure, whereby receipts from Pertamina's own oil exports went into Pertamina accounts abroad, wherever the oil was sold. And it was Pertamina's responsibility to pass on revenues from production-sharing income to the government every quarter. It was only on

income from contract-of-work producers that Bank Indonesia
always had automatic withdrawal rights.

The government also placed restrictions on borrowing by Pertamina, requiring new loans to be centralised under the aegis of Bank
Indonesia and the Ministry of Finance. Haryono himself pledged
not to bring Pertamina into the capital market for short- and long-
term loans but to obtain them instead through the Finance
Ministry.[10] The government measure clearly imposed an effective
curb on Pertamina's foreign borrowing, though it has to be asked
why the DKPP was not also made responsible for this control function so as to ensure that the government as a whole had an effective
knowledge of Pertamina's financial policies.

Indeed while the supervisory role of the DKPP was strengthened,
its structure remained unchanged. Pertamina was, however,
ordered to submit monthly statements and other reports at predetermined intervals to the DKPP, which it had always been
required to do by law but had never previously done.

As noted earlier, steps were also taken to concentrate Pertamina's activities on oil production and marketing and to streamline
its internal organisation, so providing the opportunity to incorporate internal controls within the company. The new President-
Director, Piet Haryono, managed to establish a delicate balance
between the economic requirements of the technocrats and the
political obligations of the military-dominated uppermost stratum
of the ruling establishment. The replacement of Haryono by Judo
Sumbono in April 1981 was regarded, however, as a tilting of this
balance towards the latter group, and in particular, President
Soeharto. Soeharto took the opportunity provided by his appointment of Sumbono to strengthen his control over Pertamina, dis-
missing its entire management board and replacing them with new
directors who would pay greater regard to the political requirements of financial support and allegiance to himself.[11] Four of the
six new directors were close associates of Sutowo, who after the
Pertamina débâcle had demonstrated their personal loyalty to
President Soeharto by cooperating with his policies, and who therefore owed their rehabilitation to the President. Their appointment
also suggested that the view advanced within government circles,
that the Pertamina financial crisis derived solely from mismanagement and not from personal corruption or the misdeeds of any individual, had been endorsed by the Presidential establishment.

Haryono himself had come to disagree increasingly with government policies, especially where these were justified by political or other non-economic criteria. For example, the hydrocracker expansion planned for the Dumai refinery was questioned on the grounds of its overall feasibility, the involvement of President Soeharto's business associates in the scheme's financing, and the technical competence of the foreign firms selected as contractors by a specially constituted government commission outside Pertamina. Pertamina found its position on the Dumai project undermined when it was removed from the decision-making process, even though Haryono's dissent was not made publicly explicit. The dispute may have persuaded Soeharto of the need to ensure that Pertamina would be more susceptible to his political control by appointing subordinates who would implement his directives loyally.

Sumbono's replacement in turn by General Abdulrachman Ramli in June 1984 represented a further development in this process of politicisation. While Sumbono was blamed for Pertamina's lacklustre performance in a weak oil market, and it was further pointed out that the company still fails to produce audited accounts,[12] it was also believed that Sumbono had himself become less than compliant towards Presidential directives and in consequence had succeeded in upsetting the country's political élite. The changes resulting from this emphasis on political considerations in oil-sector policy formulation spread outside Pertamina with the subsequent dismissal of the Director-General for Oil and Gas, Wijarso.

A more general consideration evoked by the Pertamina crisis is the issue of financing development with foreign and domestic loans. While there can be no question of Pertamina returning to the headlong growth of the Sutowo years financed largely by borrowed money from every available source, there is the danger of over-reacting by adopting an antithetical position. It may be argued that the issue should not be that of incurring debts, but rather what the capital so raised is used for. Obviously any project to be implemented should be carefully evaluated. This investigation should not only comprise a feasibility study based on narrow financial considerations but also relate the nature of the project to broader social costs and benefits. It is particularly necessary to consider the project within the overall strategy of development.

Following the Pertamina crisis, with its aftermath of heavy debt burdens, the government was resolved to avoid incurring further debts as far as possible. It therefore favoured a policy of structuring all commercially feasible petroleum-related projects as joint ventures with 'off-balance-sheet' financing which would not affect the official debt service ratio. This particular method required a contribution of equity from the foreign contractor backed by foreign government export credits, but with further guarantees coming from the joint-venture company to be set up rather than from the Indonesian government. It was aimed at keeping the Indonesian government out of direct state financing by refusing to provide official support, and to keep the debt incurred out of the government's debt portfolios by placing the responsibility on the joint-venture company.

This strategy, introduced in 1978, had in the event to be abandoned by 1980 when foreign banks proved reluctant to risk funding projects without host-government financial guarantees. In returning to more conventional forms of government financing through funds from its own reserves, inter-governmental loans and commercial loans raised on the international market, the Indonesian government was helped by the 1979 oil price increases which had substantially boosted foreign exchange reserves. Indeed, the potential inflationary pressures inherent in these additional governmental funds led the government to utilise them for capital purchases as a way of injecting the money into the economy without producing direct inflationary results.

The obverse aspect of the issue of raising loans to finance development is its effect on the country's debt situation. Until 1975, the Indonesian government, in planning its investment programme and consequent debt-servicing obligations, had assumed that Pertamina would service its own debt created by its own investment projects. The Pertamina financial crisis, however, obliged the government to commit a substantial proportion of its future non-Pertamina development resources to complete Pertamina projects and repay or service outstanding debts. In taking over responsibility for petroleum sector investment, the government had been aided earlier by the 1979 oil price rises. But by 1983 the government found that falling oil prices and demand (together with a drop in export earnings from non-oil products)[13] required it to take measures to limit its rising foreign debt burden. Its decision in May 1983 to rephase or postpone the implementation of development schemes which required a high level of foreign currency financing included four major petroleum and energy-related projects.[14]

The Pertamina crisis made clear as well that while negotiations with foreign companies should be carried out with the best available expertise and management, this ability should also be applied to projects under consideration. Although Pertamina may have been able to bring together such skilled personnel as were available in the country's petroleum industry, when it moved into areas outside its main concern their specialisations may not have proved so relevant and hence so useful in the grasping of technical details and in the negotiating of contract terms. Furthermore, Pertamina as an agency whose primary concern is limited to the Indonesian petroleum sector would presumably not have the necessary overview of the whole economy to compare the rate of return on its capital investment in any of its projects with the opportunity cost of that capital within the economy as a whole. For it is not sufficient to ensure that the capital yields a rate of return greater than the rate of interest on the loan used to raise the funds (provided it is not a tied loan). It may be argued that such broader considerations would be more prevalent in an institution with a wider purview such as the National Planning Board, Bappenas, which therefore should and did assume responsibility for such overall decisions.

Finally, it may be observed that the measures taken to rein in Pertamina after the financial crisis it engendered, while succeeding in introducing a measure of accountability into the central-government–state-company relationship, did not resolve the underlying political situation which enabled Pertamina's prodigality to occur in the first place. For so long as Indonesia is governed by a military régime in which the army has come to rely on the perquisites of office, and whose style of government emphasises patronage and close personal ties at the expense of public accountability, political considerations will limit the government's ability to establish a viable and efficiently run petroleum sector within the country's economy. And a fundamental weakness of the governmental organisation in dealings with foreign oil companies will persist, as political and personal demands have to be met and extra-economic considerations taken into account. The problem of ensuring proper accountability within the government will continue to weaken the governmental structure in foreign company negotiations, even if not so blatantly as in the past.

APPROACHES TO NEGOTIATION

A country's negotiating configuration may be shaped, as indicated above, by forces outside the strict foreign-company–host-government relationship, and which derive from the dynamics of internal politics or the need to stimulate economic growth. Its attitude towards the negotiating process may well depend also on extraneous factors, perhaps crucially on its legal code and cultural traditions.

From the analysis of provisions in Indonesian oil contracts, it is evident that some contractual terms have been loosely worded and the rights and obligations of both parties to the contract have been in part vaguely phrased. These ambiguities may of course be attributed to an insufficiency of negotiating skills on the part of the government, or to a lack of information critical for it to effectively assess the economic and business context within which negotiations proceed.

Yet there is also a cultural consideration to bear in mind. Where a cultural heritage, as in the Indonesian case, stresses the avoidance of open conflict, this value may come to colour the agreements reached, with a desire to eschew confrontation finding expression in a blurring of legal terms. It has been argued on the Indonesian side that the seeming emphasis on 'mufakat' in their society, that is, the reaching of a consensus based on goodwill and compromise, is alien to the western concept of adversary bargaining. This Indonesian attitude 'has led to a lesser concern with protective clauses spelled out for specific contingencies than is the case in the American tradition'.[15]

Such a consideration may well be significant in any examination of the foreign-company–host-government relationship. For if Indonesians do have a quite different understanding of the nature of contract negotiation from that of the foreign companies with whom they deal, then the relationship between host government and foreign company would for them be jeopardised. This relationship is not exclusive, there being other determinant factors and influencing parties; nor is it static, as over time it takes the character of a bargaining process. Nevertheless the relationship assumes basically a legal contractual form, with a division of benefits between two parties. Each side is expected in theory to promote its own interests and to defend its gains against the legitimate attacks of the other side. If, though, one party relies implicitly on some traditional belief in good faith, preferring to avert acrimonious argument by means of a careful choice of oblique phraseology, then the theoretical premise of adversary bargaining underlying the whole process is invalidated. And the relationship itself is thrown out of kilter as both sides interpret their actions from wholly different standpoints.

This anomaly has a counterpart within the Indonesian legal system where the traditional attitude of glossing over and thereby avoiding unseemly disagreements results partly in vague and deficient laws. Indeed foreign firms complain that 'no comprehensive modified edition of the law exists, and when the actual text can be found the meaning can be difficult to clarify'.[16] Furthermore, though government guidelines on investment may appear rigorous, foreign companies cannot take them at face value as the policies set out are vague and conflicting.

With the legal framework consisting of general principles, the foreign company will try to pin down its conditions of operation, seeking to elaborate the relevant legal codes through detailed provisions within its agreement which safeguard its interests. Assuming that it manages to do so, the situation which results gives specific protection for the company's position with only a vague endorsement of the government's rights, thus sowing the seeds for future dispute. This legal imbalance is aggravated by a further incongruence. The foreign company typically concerns itself with its own interests and assumes that the government does likewise. But this assumption may not be valid if Indonesian negotiators are predisposed to play down the adversary aspect of their relationship with the foreign company, leading them to seek out common rather than singular interests. With both sides proceeding according to different modes based on contrary beliefs as to the nature of their mutual dealings, a stable agreement is less likely to be achieved.

While attitudes towards negotiation may reflect cultural predispositions, their influence should not be overstated. Examination of successive generations of Indonesian oil contracts does show that the increasing experience gained in this long-established industry has given government negotiators a more sentient ability to identify those issues of particular danger to government interests, and to cover them with increasing, if as yet not totally effective, precision. Nonetheless the need for still greater care in the drafting of provisions cannot be gainsaid. Such efforts to be specific will help limit the grounds for later disagreement by forcing both sides to be more open as to their intentions. Moreover if the agreement is couched in clear and precise terms, both sides are likely to be more inhibited in breaching its provisions than when ambiguous terms give scope for some excuse to be contrived.

It is as well therefore for both sides to appreciate such different cultural approaches before coming to the negotiating table. Yet differences in legal traditions may be so deep-rooted that it may be easier to preach than to practise mutual cultural empathy. As a European lawyer noted, 'There is indeed a certain tendency among American lawyers coming to Europe in order to negotiate an international contract – and this is true even of those who have had a fairly wide experience abroad – to try to impose their style and techniques as if they were not only the best, but also the only possible ones in the world.'[17] The problem here is similar to that of the Indonesian experience. Anglo-American lawyers, with their common-law tradition, feel the need to be extremely thorough in the drafting of a legal instrument, it being indispensable to envisage all possibilities, including the most unlikely ones. But European continental law, based on civil law, traditionally emphasises the notion of 'bona fides' or good faith in negotiations, leading to the use of a more general legal idiom, a rejection of 'legal perfectionism', and a greater trust in the discretion of the judge or arbitrator.

It should be apparent that both sides need to carry out as much preliminary investigation as is possible. For the government, negotiating priorities can only be established after having analysed all data relating to the industry and the position within it of the foreign company in question. The situation of Pertamina, as inheritor of the country's historical involvement in oil production, is here advantageous. For Pertamina's accumulated experience has helped provide it with a basic fund of knowledge of oil industry characteristics, thus enabling it to determine those issues of greatest concern to itself and to lay out a strategy which stresses its principal priorities. As for the company, it is important to have not just some general idea of the political, social and economic climate of its intended host country, but to know specifically what limitations are placed on foreign companies, what protection is afforded to them and what position is taken by the state with respect to the field of the intended investment. The provisions of the 1967 Foreign Investment Law, together with details of land law and land use policy, labour policies, corporate and personal income taxes, the international agreements reached with the Indonesian government providing investment guarantees against nationalisation and expropriation, and the priority economic sectors for foreign investment, would in this respect be of special interest.

This preliminary preparation being completed, the government will have a considerable influence in shaping the bargaining process which follows, and the manner in which it conducts these negotiations is likely to crucially affect the final result. In the Indonesian petroleum industry, it is Pertamina, and not the foreign company, which provides the draft contract to serve as the basis for negotiations. The Indonesian side is thus able to put forward its own point of view first, and in this way to take the initiative; for the draft contract would naturally reflect the position of the party which prepared it. Allowing the foreign investor to submit its initial proposals for discussion would on the other hand place any government in the difficult position of having to negotiate from a framework set out by the company, and very likely to feel impelled to oppose many specific provisions that reflect the company's point of view.

Going into the negotiations with a prepared draft presupposes that the government side has a clear policy on what it intends to achieve. Here another advantage of having a single negotiating body with sole responsibility for concluding agreements with foreign companies becomes apparent. For by having Pertamina virtually independent of the governmental bureaucracy, conflicts of interest between various government departments with different priorities may be avoided, and specific objectives together with a reasoned policy to justify them may be worked out.

Pertamina further uses a bidding procedure together with its first draft approach, opening the contract for general bidding and then commencing negotiations by selecting the company with the best offer. The method generally used is to take a specific area or 'block' within which no oil operations are proceeding, and to open it for bids from foreign companies. Which blocks are chosen to be put up for tender and how these areas are outlined is decided by Pertamina's Exploration and Production Directorate on the basis of available geological data. Companies on Pertamina's list who have expressed interest in oil exploration within Indonesia are then invited to tender bids. This offer is accompanied by a draft of the proposed agreement prepared by Pertamina and based generally on a model production-sharing contract, together with an exposition of the supposed worth of the contract area as seen by Pertamina. Prospective contractors are then interviewed and bids received. A specified fee has usually to be paid for each application, and companies are also required to provide a full record of their financial standing and operational experience. While there is no set criterion for judging the bids, Pertamina would naturally take greater heed of those items on which it does not propose a figure, such as the signature bonus and the various production bonuses which the applicant is prepared to offer, the capital investment it intends to make annually (especially in the initial years of the con-tract operation), and the share of the operation which it is prepared to turn over to local participation. These figures would reflect how attractive the applicant perceived the block on offer to be, and the degree of commitment it would hence be prepared to make.

While competitive bidding on an initial draft allows Pertamina to begin negotiations from a set of favourable terms, such an approach may not be a feasible proposition in many instances. This method is only suitable where at least a few companies are attracted by the contract areas put out for tender, and where they may be expected not to collude with each other, coming together for instance into a single consortium or cooperating to submit single bids for different blocks on offer. When the first production-sharing contracts were negotiated in 1966, Sutowo chose not to employ a scheme of competitive bidding because he feared that the hitherto tightly oligopolistic structure of the oil industry would enable the major companies to oppose his proposed new contrac-tual scheme as a group. He decided instead to negotiate on an ad hoc basis with selected 'independent' companies, even though this probably meant receiving less revenue than would have been the case with competitive bidding.

Having received tenders from all interested parties, the manner in which the government side responds can help ensure reasonable and cooperative behaviour from the chosen applicant. If for instance the range of prospective contractors is reduced to just one company after evaluating the different bids, the chosen company is well placed to drive a hard bargain in the subsequent negotiations. On the other hand, if the government side chooses to negotiate with several companies together on the basis of their tenders, it might find it possible to pit potential applicants against each other, matching their intentions and the offers which they make. In the Indonesian petroleum industry, Pertamina takes a position intermediate between but closer to the first of these two possibilities. After reviewing the different tenders submitted, it makes a single proposal for award, inviting just one party for the first round of negotiations. However if agreement cannot be reached with the chosen company, Pertamina then has recourse to a reserve list in which it continues to keep other applicants. While this procedure does put pressure on Pertamina to secure an agreement as soon as possible, it also helps Pertamina conserve the resources of its negotiating team which will not have to divide its time and attention between different sets of negotiations with various applicants.

One other approach encountered in the Indonesian petroleum industry is for the foreign company to request a specific area from Pertamina. In this case the company conducts its own preliminary research before going to Pertamina, though this does not generally include exploration work on the ground in the intended contract area. A standard production-sharing contract is then usually concluded providing for the exploration of and, if possible, production from the given contract area. In such cases, it might be thought that the host government would do better to seek out other potential investors and then offer the contract block to the highest bidder. Or else the host government could refrain from negotiating terms for the extractive operation until after the foreign company has conducted an extensive survey of the contract area. By increasing the amount of information available and hence reducing the initial uncertainty, it may then be possible for the government side to obtain a more favourable agreement if commercially viable production is proved possible. It would have to be conceded though that especially in the petroleum industry, the foreign company is likely to be reluctant to invest the technical skills and financial resources necessary to explore for oil in rough and not easily accessible terrain unless it was reasonably sure of benefiting from any consequent production. In any case, by granting the surveying company first option to conclude an agreement with the government, the latter's freedom of action during negotiations is at least partially circumscribed.

In the negotiations which take place between foreign company and host government, the way in which both sides conduct themselves may be crucial if an effective and enduring agreement is to be reached. Given that a prime objective of such a negotiation should be to achieve full understanding by both sides of the implications of the agreement being constructed, a negative aspect of company attitudes which derives from a short-sighted view of the negotiating process, has been the adoption of what might be termed a caveat emptor approach. If the company is not sufficiently responsible to brief the host government of the true nature and scope of the agreement, any resulting misunderstanding or perceived misrepresentation may redound back at some later date to the company's disadvantage. This attitude was, for instance, evident in the contracts reached for the Krakatau steel project, where one of the contracting firms was later to justify the high cost of the plant it supplied by claiming that the Pertamina negotiators had demanded the highest standards of safety and the most modern equipment available. But by taking the view that the Indonesian side could have whatever it wanted no matter how expensive or inappropriate the equipment, if not indeed encouraging the Indonesians to adopt such a profligate attitude, the company only found itself kept waiting for substantial arrears of payment as a result of the Pertamina financial crisis. And it was forced eventually, after much adverse publicity, to renegotiate its contracts with the government. It is therefore important for the negotiating company to lay down a firm groundwork of understanding at the outset so that the government side is less likely to attempt later to nullify the agreement or to use its governmental powers to retaliate against the company.

Company representatives should not on the other hand underestimate the experience and abilities of their opposite numbers on the government side. To do so might not only result in a patronising attitude being taken towards the government team, which would at the least irritate the latter for no useful purpose, but possibly also prejudice the outcome of negotiations from the company's viewpoint through the over-confidence of its negotiators.

An important contributory factor to the sense of uncertainty which company negotiators often feel is the level of corruption encountered within the government bureaucracy. Potential investors may be unsure how to respond if asked for a bribe; or given that the request may be delicately phrased or made in an oblique manner, they may even be uncertain if a bribe has been sought from them. A delay in negotiations may be caused by a myriad of reasons not often readily apparent to company negotiators, who may be left uneasily wondering if some private payment was required to oil the wheels of the negotiating process.

Within the Indonesian oil industry, Pertamina is generally regarded by foreign companies as having freed them from the nagging concern of having to cope with continual petty corruption. By shielding its contractors from a notoriously corrupt government bureaucracy, Pertamina has significantly eased their day-to-day operating conditions through reducing the necessity for contact between contractor companies and government departments. Oil-company executives on the whole agree that Pertamina has never sought from them the sort of pay-offs that are commonplace for most business transactions in Indonesia. This does not, however, mean that Pertamina has been free of corruption. Persistent charges by domestic critics were denied by Ibnu Sutowo, though the line between his own public and private activities seemed extremely ill-defined. Further light was shed on corruption within Pertamina's management by the case of Achmad Thahir, Sutowo's general assistant and personal aide at Pertamina, who died in July 1976 leaving a private fortune of over 52 million Deutschmarks plus US$1 million in a Singapore bank account.[18] This sum was contested between various surviving relatives and Pertamina. One of the former submitted an affidavit detailing a web of corruption ranging through the middle to upper levels of Pertamina, with Sutowo and the Indonesian government being aware of and conniving in the amassing of private fortunes by various Pertamina officials. And Pertamina itself admitted that the disputed money had been acquired corruptly, largely from bribes on contracts for the Krakatau steel project.[19] Pertamina's reputation suffered a further blow in October 1980 with the discovery of substantial systematic thefts by employees from its oil stocks.[20] While these incidents clearly showed that Pertamina had no claim to financial probity, it has, though, to be pointed out that they were not part of those of its activities connected with its supervision of foreign-company extractive operations.

During negotiations with a prospective investor, the host government may interweave a number of considerations which are just as complex as those which company negotiators have to make. Government negotiators may have to balance the different interests of various ministries and, where the government team is itself drawn from different ministries, ensure that the other side does not attempt to divide it by siding with one subgroup against another. Pertamina's unified negotiating structure again obviates this danger. In any case, the government's chosen goals are likely to be partly inconsistent. A strategy of maximising its overall gains may result in contract provisions that are difficult to administer. And if some subtly refined and intricate arrangement desired by the government cannot be effectively administered, it may be less beneficial than at first apparent. Given that its supervisory resources are finite, the government has to phrase contract provisions so as to match its abilities to enforce them.

Examples may be readily given which illustrate this need to ensure terms within an arrangement which can be enforced. Production-sharing contracts lay down a time limit on the right of both sides to audit the operation's books and accounts. Such an audit would have to be made within a period of one year from the financial year that is the object of the audit, and cannot take more than a year to complete. While it would appear fair to set some limit to the retrospective powers of auditors, such narrow constraints could strain the auditing resources of Pertamina (acting for the host government) which, if it fell behind schedule in its carrying out of audits, would lose an important check on company activities.

Indonesian income-tax policies for foreign residents provide an example of a compromise between the partly incompatible demands of the practicable and the reasonable. The Indonesian government taxes foreign residents on all their world-wide income from whatever source while granting them credit for taxes paid abroad, a policy which is capable of being enforced as it basically involves the application of the domestic tax system. To meet possible objections from foreign employees should they find themselves paying higher taxes in Indonesia than they would pay in their home country, the nominal tax rates for personal income are limited to a maximum of 50 per cent, on which special tax deductions are allowed.[21] Such an arrangement may not be optimal but is at least feasible to administer. The alternative of guaranteeing that the foreigner would not have to pay higher taxes locally than he would in his country of origin is quite unrealistic, requiring the Indonesian authorities to evaluate the regulations existing in other countries' tax jurisdictions and to assess how these would work out in practice.

The Indonesian approach to foreign participation in its petroleum industry uses methods which may be considered to help ease the administration of contracts. To begin with, production-sharing contracts take a basic form, thus helping to standardise provisions from different agreements and hence simplifying administration. Within contracts, some requirements are phrased in a manner which warns in advance of possible difficulties. For example, the contract provisions which call for sales of oil to be valued at third-party prices and also provide a straightforward definition of what constitutes a third party, at least warn contract supervisors to look out for transfer-pricing practices (even if they lack the power to prevent the company from attempting such measures beforehand). Pertamina itself has a clearly established process for obtaining regular work reports from companies, and would not therefore have to request such reports on an ad hoc basis. And the Indonesian government through Migas has also helped to ease the supervision of oil contracts by issuing administrative regulations covering such matters as safety practices and export and import requirements. Where contracts could be improved with regard to their administration would be to incorporate clear sanctions in the event of the company's non-compliance with any of its contractual obligations. For this might encourage the company to act on its responsibilities, while otherwise it would have little incentive to conform unless pressed by the supervisory authorities.

Negotiations between host government and foreign company establish a range of possible outcomes whose limits are set by the economic and political considerations discussed in earlier chapters. As this chapter shows, the point within this range where the final bargain is struck may depend crucially on the negotiating skills and organisational configurations of the two sides involved. But the negotiating process is not exclusive and need not be a zero-sum game. Other groups can be brought in and will then have to be considered, and the final result may in consequence be altered. The host government, for instance, may have to consider the interests of other governments, or may indeed derive support from them. It is to such broader considerations, beyond the strict foreign-company–host-government relationship, that the discussion finally turns.

7. SOME REGIONAL CONSIDERATIONS FOR SOUTH-EAST-ASIAN OIL-PRODUCER GOVERNMENTS

THE SEARCH FOR APPROPRIATE MODELS

The relationship between host state and foreign corporation has been the central concern of this analysis. This contractual relationship is only part of a triangular framework of which the foreign company's home country forms the third apex, and this factor has at times worked to shape the considerations of the other two actors. However, the scope of their concerns goes beyond this basic structure to encompass other such triangular frameworks formed by contractual relationships which are perceived to be relevant. The vast majority of the community of states act as hosts for transnational corporations, establishing contractual relationships whose terms may become the points of reference for later contract agreements between companies and governments, whether as a result of the investor attempting to secure contract terms equivalent to those agreed before for fear of establishing a precedent, or of the host government seeking new ways to increase its bargaining power. A more complex construct is required to reflect all the relevant extraneous facts for any particular contractual negotiation. It would prove too unwieldy for productive analysis. Nevertheless, in considering the problems faced by both foreign investor and host government in negotiating any one contract, the wider considerations posed by those features of other investment agreements which the negotiating parties regard as relevant, do have to be taken into account.

Contract negotiations take place within a system which is essentially bilateral in nature, with no overall framework such as exists theoretically in a free market in which the behaviour of other market participants provides relevant information and induces competition among buyers and sellers. Hence the process of contractual negotiation may well not take account of the behaviour of other firms or host governments within the relevant mineral industry, and the contractual bargain which is struck could be far from what might otherwise be expected from a consideration of earlier agreements reached in that field. Yet both participants do not act in vacuo. Even if the system is not fully multilateral, the host government is increasingly gaining access to a significantly greater volume of information.

This information is unlikely to come from the home government of the foreign enterprise, given the correspondence of interests that generally exists with home countries as consumers of the resource produced. The home government might, however, consider such a move to be in its long-term interests should the result serve to ensure a stable supply of the mineral. Other producing countries, and also other countries in which the same foreign company is operating, may provide assistance to a particular producer government so long as they do not consider themselves to be in competition with it to attract foreign investment. Regional groupings too may share a sufficient community of interests to encourage them to pool the sort of information needed to negotiate with foreign investors. These groupings need not necessarily be formally organised, but may act on an ad hoc basis through informal mechanisms, or perhaps merely through one country's achievements exerting a demonstration effect on others. Each individual country within such a regional grouping may not be in a position, however, to emulate a more successful neighbour, and it will have to be realistic in assessing to what extent it can assimilate the experiences of other countries and to effectively employ such acquired knowledge in dealing with its own foreign investors.

South-east Asia emerged as a coherent region for oil companies in the late 1960s when offshore drilling technology had developed sufficiently for them to prospect extensively in continental-shelf waters. Their interest was sharpened by a number of factors which laid the foundation for the subsequent exploration boom: the oil-price rises of the early 1970s, the perceived political instability of the Middle East, the desire of local governments to become oil exporters rather than importers, the low sulphur content and hence non-polluting quality of South-east-Asian crude oil, the proximity of the region to the Japanese market, the favourable physical environment for offshore oil development (with shallower waters and, occasional typhoons apart, generally more clement weather than, say, in the North Sea), and the large increase in oil consumption expected for South-east Asia itself. The embryonic South-east-Asian offshore oil industry also offered extremely low acquisition costs to companies considering alternative investments in different oil-producing regions.[1]

While interest in the oil reserves of South-east Asia dates back to the last century, the exploration boom that began in the late 1960s was different from the level of activity that had preceded it, both quantitatively in the number of companies involved and the level of investment funds committed, and qualitatively in the exploration technology employed and the companies' own high expectations of the region's resource potential. This euphoria was subsequently dampened in the mid 1970s when, despite concentrated exploration, very few large fields were discovered (though in compensation, a large number of smaller fields were found), and furthermore what the companies regarded as adverse legislation was introduced in Indonesia and Malaysia. The amelioration of these government-imposed terms helped induce a consequent revival of oil-company activity; though it would appear that the companies have always taken a favourable view of the region's long-term potential as a major oil-producing province within the scope of their global operations.

The mere physical presence of oil deposits does not ensure that production will take place. The economic appraisal made by the company which will determine its operational decisions is a function of two broad groups of variables, technical and legislative. The former encompasses such considerations as the level of technology which is available, the regional infrastructure and environmental conditions, and the company's perception of the resource potential of the area based on geological and geophysical studies. The latter involves the company's calculations of expected future profits, based on cost and price estimates, which would accrue to it given the legislative framework imposed by the host government, and the risk of change within this legislative framework which might entail a new set of profitability criteria.

With a given set of technical constraints, it is the host government's contractual and institutional framework which therefore decides how the company will conduct itself through defining its terms of operation, and hence determining the parameters of the company's financial calculations and its estimation of the viability of the project under consideration. In order to appreciate the behaviour of foreign oil companies in South-east Asia, it is necessary to review the contractual frameworks and conditions of operation imposed by individual host governments.

Host governments have not readily appreciated how volatile companies can be in reacting to changes in legislation and policies, and how sensitive to such changes is their willingness to commit risk capital for exploration ventures. As the Indonesian experience has shown, a revision of fiscal arrangements can quickly cause a substantial drop in company activity. With offshore oil operations, exploration can rapidly switch its commitment through moving of exploration rigs from one location to another. This sensitivity is heightened by foreign oil companies treating the East Asian region as a single whole in planning future investment, for while this regional purview contributed to the high level of oil-company activity in the late 1960s and early 1970s, it also makes company investment decisions highly susceptible to the attractions of alternative areas for investment.

This volatility is, however, least apparent in the small British-protected state of Brunei, which achieved independence in December 1983. The country has a symbiotic relationship with its dominant foreign oil company, Brunei Shell Petroleum, the locally incorporated subsidiary of Royal Dutch Shell. Shell remains the sole oil exporter and has secured the bulk of the country's onshore and offshore contract areas, while it in turn enables Brunei to exist as an independent state. The government is dependent on oil and natural gas exports for almost its entire income.

Brunei retains the traditional concession system, the companies enjoying exclusive rights over their operational areas and over resources discovered. The Petroleum Mining Enactment of 1963 (amended in 1969 and 1972) sets out long-term agreements lasting 38 years for onshore and 40 years for offshore concessions, with further 30-year renewals. The government imposes a 50 per cent tax on net profits which are calculated from a jointly determined posted price,[2] and it also charges a royalty which ranges from 8 to 12.5 per cent of the value of output, though this royalty is credited against the 50 per cent tax. A system of area relinquishments and various minimum expenditure obligations (which are deductible from costs in the calculation of net profits for tax purposes) provides apparent safeguards for the government's interests. The minimum expenditure requirements can, however, be set off against royalty payments as well, which therefore negates the value of the royalty as an assurance of a minimum payment regardless of company costs.

The terms of operation are patently favourable to Shell, and given the ineffectiveness of the government in supervising the operation of contracts, the latter's ability even to ensure that it obtains its full half-share of profits has been doubted.[3] In an effort to improve its supervision, the government has been steadily increasing its equity ownership of Brunei Shell Petroleum from 25 per cent in 1973 to 50 per cent in 1975, and of Brunei Liquefied Natural Gas (an equity joint venture between Shell, Mitsubishi and the Brunei government, which is the sole LNG exporter) from 10 per cent in 1972 to one-third in 1977. In addition, the government acquired 50 per cent of Brunei Shell Marketing which undertakes the domestic distribution of petroleum products. While the Brunei government has ample financial resources to make these purchases and, by this means, be represented at director level within these companies, it has not managed to translate this representation into effective control because of its shortage of technical and managerial expertise. The formation of a Petroleum Unit within the Chief Minister's Office in 1982 may be the beginning of an attempt to acquire such expertise, though this would be very much a long-term process.

Although Brunei profits handsomely from its oil industry, given its minuscule size and population, which enables its autocratic government to provide generous welfare and economic benefits, the obvious differences in operational terms for oil companies between Brunei and its neighbouring states of Indonesia and Malaysia could provide a focus for any latent political dissent in the future. Given the finite nature of Brunei's oil resources and its own increasing energy needs, differences could also arise between the government and the foreign company over the rate of exploitation or the use to which oil production is put.

The difficulty which host governments have encountered in retaining the interest of foreign oil companies may be illustrated by the examples of Burma and Vietnam. Both host governments have been fundamentally averse to accepting the presence of western companies within their domestic economies, but yet have made a conscious decision to exempt development of petroleum resources from this general policy by inviting the participation of foreign oil companies.

In the case of Burma, the oil industry was nationalised in 1963 and therefore came under direct government control. The Burmese government did, however, follow developments in Indonesia with great interest in the late 1960s and early 1970s, sending several official missions there in order to gather information on the new production-sharing contracts then being introduced. In 1973, the state oil company, Myanma, opened a number of offshore contract areas to foreign companies under the terms of service contracts which resembled the Indonesian production-sharing model. The companies which came in then withdrew in 1976, dissatisfied with their allocated areas of operation and put out by the difficulties of coping with Burmese attempts to supervise and manage their activities and also with the idiosyncratic functioning of the Burmese governmental system. Another attempt in 1978 to attract foreign participation in offshore oil exploration under terms similar to those of 1973 failed to reach any agreement with foreign companies. In 1979 however, Myanma concluded a joint venture agreement with the Japan National Oil Corporation, JNOC, for joint offshore exploration in the Gulf of Martaban. Natural gas deposits were discovered in 1982, though further capital will be needed for their commercial development.

The Burmese service contract ceded management control to Myanma, in planning, formulating work programmes and budgets, and in procuring equipment and supplies. It expressly stipulated that all operations would be supervised jointly, leaving the company with little room for manoeuvre if this condition was interpreted literally. The company's remuneration came from a share of the proceeds realised from the sale of any oil or gas produced. This procedure required all sales proceeds to be remitted to Burma, from where the company's cost-recovery allowance and payment for services rendered would be received by the company and transmitted abroad. When difficulties were encountered with implementing this method, the government agreed to allow crude oil production rather than income to be divided, thus bringing the terms of operation closer to the Indonesian model. The company was allowed to recover costs from 40 per cent of production, and was then paid for its services from the 'profit' component of production by a 70:30 division in favour of Myanma, this ratio rising to 72.5:27.5 above a production threshold of 100,000 barrels per day. Three years were allowed for exploration (renewable for a further three years) and twenty years for exploitation. The company was required to allocate up to ten per cent of its share of crude oil for domestic use, to pay various production bonuses and data purchase fees, and to meet area-relinquishment and minimum-expenditure obligations. While this contractual scheme followed the Indonesian production-sharing contract to a large extent, it proved unacceptable to the companies in the Burmese case, perhaps through an over-exact interpretation by the host government of its powers of control.

As for Vietnam, it is wider political factors which have constrained the government's freedom to engage foreign companies within its petroleum industry. The North Vietnamese government reached agreement in April 1973 with Ente Nazionale Idrocarburi (ENI)[4] for joint offshore prospecting. In July 1973 and again in May 1974 the South Vietnamese government signed contracts with several foreign oil companies for offshore concession areas on a royalty-tax basis. While the South Vietnamese contracts were repudiated following the victory of the North in 1975, the new Vietnamese government was avowedly amenable to foreign investment within its domestic economy. In early 1978 it entered into agreements with three exploration groups, Deminex (West German), Agip (Italian) and Bow Valley (Canadian) on a service contract basis for offshore areas within that of the former South Vietnamese concessions.

Under these contracts, all exploration risks were borne by the foreign company, which would not be recompensed if unsuccessful. Should commercially viable reserves be discovered, exploration costs were to be recoverable from any subsequent oil production. Further development costs were to be treated as an interest-bearing loan from company to government, and would be repaid in cash at market rates within ten years of the commencement of production. As an incentive, the government undertook to pay a risk premium, allowing the company to purchase up to 50 per cent of production at a preferential price ranging from 5 to 11 per cent below the prevailing international price.

The Vietnamese also considered entering production-sharing arrangements with several companies, but eventually rejected this idea in favour of service contracts. They attempted to introduce a different form of service contract in mid 1978, which came closer to being a contract for the supply of services at a fixed price, with the company being given no share of profits, nor on the other hand having to bear the risk of exploration. The Vietnamese side was to assume both operational responsibility and risk, the foreign company investing capital and providing equipment and services. Any subsequent oil production was to be used to cover the company's costs at international market prices and interest rates. If the venture was unsuccessful, repayment was to be made in cash. Negotiations on the Vietnamese proposal, however, fell through, which was not altogether surprising given the difficulty for countries, other than established producers, of securing a contract agreement without offering any premium as incentive.

The progress of the various service contractors proved disappointing, bureaucratic obstruction being encountered and no commercially exploitable oil reserves being found. They eventually withdrew at the end of 1981, after failing to obtain a more favourable renegotiation of their contracts. The ability of the Vietnamese government to attract foreign oil companies was, moreover, severely impeded by a US-government prohibition on economic links with Vietnam which prevented American firms from entering into negotiations. The Japanese company JNOC, which had also been seeking exploration rights, suspended negotiations after Vietnam invaded and occupied Kampuchea in December 1978. These negotiations were terminated by the Vietnamese in May 1980.

The Soviet Union had meanwhile been pressing Vietnam for access to its oil and gas resources, which it formally obtained in July 1980 with the signing of an agreement for Comecon 'cooperation in geological prospecting and extraction of oil and gas'.[5] A joint Vietnamese–Soviet enterprise was set up to conduct surveys and explore for oil and gas on the continental shelf off Southern Vietnam and further north in the Red River delta. Though the Soviet Union had been intermittently involved in Vietnamese oil exploration onshore since the early 1970s, considerable scepticism has been expressed over the Russian ability to carry out offshore exploration given its inadequate technological capability in this field.[6] Indeed its limited abilities could pose a dilemma for the Vietnamese government. For while Vietnamese dependence on the

Soviet Union has enabled the latter to apply pressure for closer political and economic ties, with access to Vietnamese port and airbase facilities and a stake in its mineral resources, should it prove unable to effectively develop these resources, then Vietnam will be unable to acquire a stronger capacity to reduce this dependence. In this regard, recourse to western help to achieve this end through the employment of foreign companies would be difficult under prevailing political circumstances.

Both Thailand and the Philippines may be cited as examples of countries which have managed to sustain exploration activities by foreign oil companies only through offering generous terms of operation. They illustrate the weak bargaining position of governments with unproven reserves on the periphery of the world petroleum system. In each case, though, the government has tended to adopt a position in accordance with the generally market-oriented philosophy of its ruling establishment.

The case of Thailand is a straightforward one. Being a negligible oil producer without a lengthy history of foreign involvement in oil exploration, it has not come into conflict with foreign companies on this particular issue. Thailand retains the concession form for its oil exploration contracts. The concessionaire acquires ownership rights over his concession area, and is subject to a net profit tax of between 50 to 60 per cent as well as to royalty payments which are, however, deductible expenses for tax purposes.[7] These royalties are charged both in cash, at either 8.75 per cent (where the water depth of the offshore block is over 200 metres) or 12.5 per cent of the gross realised value of output, and in physical volume at either 7/73 (9.6 per cent) or 1/7 (14.3 per cent) of output. Contracts cover an exploration period of up to 8 years (extendable to give no more than 9 years in all) and a further production period of 30 years (extendable for another 10 years), and incorporate relinquishment, work obligation and minimum expenditure requirements.

Difficulties have, however, been encountered with the oil companies, especially since Thailand became a significant producer of natural gas. The 1973 oil crisis, in which the established companies were unable to ensure adequate oil supplies for the domestic market, spurred the government to assume formal responsibility for oil imports. When oil-supply difficulties were again experienced in 1979, the government further tried to reduce its dependence on the major oil companies by securing alternative sources of supply on government-to-government contracts. Its attempts to do so showed only how weak its influence on oil-producer governments was. While some help was obtained with direct oil supplies from the Middle East, Malaysia and Indonesia provided little assistance, and China agreed to institute regular supplies of a particularly heavy crude oil for which Thailand had only limited refining capacity. The government also attempted to increase its control over domestic refining. It already owned the country's three refineries, which were leased out to operating companies. In 1981, the government took a 51 per cent interest in one refinery, previously run as a private joint venture by Shell, with the intention of substantially increasing the refinery's capacity. It also terminated the lease on another refinery run by the Thai military by re-routing the refinery's crude-oil supply contract from Saudi Arabia direct to the Thai government instead of to the operating company.

The country's total dependence on foreign sources of supply for petroleum gave added urgency to its offshore search for oil and gas. Exploration has been more successful for the latter, with commercially viable reserves being discovered by Union Oil in the Gulf of Thailand in 1972. Differences between government and company arose, however, over the pricing of the expected gas production, with the government attempting to impose an administered price. The gas eventually came on-stream in September 1981, but a further dispute followed when the company reduced its reserve estimates after encountering problems with the field's geologic structure. The government was compelled to accept a redetermination of effective reserves in December 1983, but the company thereupon sharply increased production the following year. This has raised difficulties with the government on agreed gas supplies for domestic use.

Another commercially viable gas discovery was subsequently made by Texas Pacific, though it encountered difficulty in obtaining government permission to export the gas production, which has delayed the field's development. The main disagreement again centred on an appropriate pricing formula. The problem with pricing natural gas is that there is no open trading market in gas with arm's length prices to provide a yardstick for comparison. And despite the substitutability of oil with gas as a source of energy, there is no clearly defined link between gas and oil prices. Unless the government manages to establish a clearly defined pricing procedure, differences with operating companies are likely to recur as new gas fields are discovered and brought on-stream.

As for the Philippines, oil exploration has received added urgency from the country's drive to reduce its dependence on costly oil imports. The first commercially viable discovery was made in 1976, but the Philippines remains an insignificant oil producer. Under its Oil Exploration and Development Act of 1972, the Philippines adopted a service-contract system, this replacing an earlier concession system laid down by the 1949 Petroleum Act.

The government claimed to have based its new service contracts on the Indonesian production-sharing model, but significant differences may be discerned between the two contractual forms. The crucial difference in the Filipino contract is that it cedes management of the extractive operation to the company, with the government merely overseeing the company's activities. Also significant is that the government party to the contract is not the state oil company PNOC,[8] but the Ministry of Energy, which is therefore responsible for supervising the implementation of contracts.

The financial provisions of the Filipino service contract provide handsome incentives to the companies, reflecting the government's weaker bargaining position as compared to the Indonesian case, rather than any desire to be generous to the companies. While the companies assume all exploration risks, they are allowed to recover costs out of 70 per cent of any subsequent production (reduced in some later contracts to 55 per cent). The remaining 'profit' component of production is divided in the ratio 60:40 in the government's favour (raised in some later contracts to a 65:35 split), the government's share including all the company's tax obligations. The company may also claim an allowance for Filipino participation in the extractive venture, thus skewing the 'profit' division in its favour.[9] Other incentives include exempting the company from tariff duties on all imported equipment, and allowing it to freely remit abroad all foreign exchange earnings and to repatriate its capital investment. Later contracts have, however, introduced signature, discovery and production bonuses. And the company is required to allot a part of its share of production to supply the domestic market; though, unlike Indonesian contracts, it receives the full international market price for such production.

As for the service contract's regulatory provisions, these appear especially weak. The company may be authorised to market the government's share of production both domestically and internationally. In doing so, it can virtually decide the posted price at which petroleum would be sold, being bound only to consult the Energy Ministry on this matter. Service contracts do incorporate area reduction and minimum expenditure and work obligations, but these are on the whole quite liberally phrased. A seven-year exploration period is allowed, which may be extended for up to a further five years, and an additional 25 years is granted for production, extendable for another 15 years. Area limits of 7,500 square kilometres for onshore and 10,000 square kilometres for offshore contract areas are set, and the contracting company is required to progressively relinquish half its contract area after seven years, and to retain only the producing area (plus an additional small percentage for further exploration) should commercial production be achieved. Work expenditure obligations, which are set in proportion to the size of contract area held, do, however, specify a drilling commitment as well.

The government's relations with foreign oil companies have not generally involved any argument over management or distribution of benefits. When the government introduced signature and production bonuses and drilling requirements in 1976, the companies protested, but disagreements have always been contained and have never degenerated into open conflict. Indeed the government has been careful to exclude the petroleum industry from its more nationalistic directives. And while PNOC has tried to develop an ability to engage in oil extraction, the government still requires foreign companies to undertake the risk-bearing function and to provide the required technology.

The case of Malaysia, to which we finally turn, provides by contrast a history of conflict between host government and foreign oil companies over a variety of issues. The government itself remains favourably disposed towards foreign investment, pursuing a basic development strategy of investment-oriented economic growth supported by the continued presence and indeed encouragement of foreign multinational enterprises, which have enjoyed a secure position within the country's primary product and mineral export-based economy since colonial times.

These attitudes have, however, been complicated by the political necessity within the country's multi-racial society of redistributing its economic resources in favour of the politically dominant Malay community. Malaysia's New Economic Policy sets a target for ownership of the corporate sector along communal lines, stipulating that, by 1990, 30 per cent of equity ownership should be held by Malays, 40 per cent by the other communities and 30 per cent by foreign concerns. In 1970, when the policy was formulated, the share of equity ownership held by the different groups was 4.1 per cent, 33.8 per cent, and 62.1 per cent respectively.[10] The policy therefore implies an extensive running-down of the apparent concentration of power of foreign multinational concerns. While the government intends this transfer of ownership to be effected not by expropriation, but by the purchase of existing firms and the creation of new ones in the context of general economic growth, its basic desire to gain greater control of the economy for the Malay community has undoubtedly coloured the government's attitude towards its relations with foreign business interests. More specifically within its oil industry, the government has been concerned to reduce the control of foreign oil companies over domestic oil supply and downstream activities, and has encouraged the state oil company, Petronas, to play an active part in regulating the petroleum sector.

Petronas, set up in 1974, was explicitly modelled on Indonesia's Pertamina, and is regarded by the government as a key instrument for implementing its New Economic Policy. It was hoped that Petronas revenues would finance other Malay development projects and that the experience and expertise gained by Malays through participation in the country's expanding oil industry would galvanise Malay entrepreneurship throughout the country. Furthermore, the first chairman of Petronas, Tunku Razaleigh, also had wider personal political ambitions, and in implementing government policy he seized the opportunity presented by his Petronas appointment to establish his nationalist credentials and advance his position within the United Malay National Organisation (UMNO), the dominant political party within the ruling National Front coalition.

Although Malaysia is only a marginal oil producer in global terms, its petroleum industry holds an important position within the country's economy, crude oil being the largest export product since 1980. In East Malaysia, the industry dates back to the beginning of the century when oil was discovered at Miri in Sarawak, from where Shell has since maintained a modest production. But the present importance of oil production in Malaysia as a whole derives from the offshore search for oil and gas from the late 1960s onwards, when a total of seven companies were licensed to prospect in offshore waters. The first discovery was made by Shell off the Sabah coast in September 1971 (and proved commercially viable in December 1972), followed by more discoveries offshore from Sabah and Sarawak in 1972 and 1973 by Shell and Exxon. Off the east coast of West Malaysia, the first discovery was made by a consortium led by Continental Oil (Conoco) in May 1973, and a second by Exxon in February 1974.

The principal area of contention between government and foreign oil companies has been over their terms and conditions of operation. Previously, within Malaysia's federal system of government (formerly Malaya and the two Bornean states of Sabah and Sarawak), mineral extraction had been the responsibility of the individual state governments, each of whom was free to negotiate its own contracts with the oil companies for petroleum exploration and development. The system was subsequently unified in the 1966 Petroleum Mining Act and 1967 Petroleum Income Tax Act which laid out a typical concession arrangement under which the company retained control over the extractive operation. It paid royalties of between 8 and 11 per cent of the value of its output into both state and federal treasuries, and was subject in addition to a tax of 55 to 60 per cent of its profits.

The passing of the Petroleum Development Act by Parliament in July 1974 endowed the newly established Petronas with ownership of all Malaysia's petroleum resources. It provided the basis for Petronas to negotiate with the state governments to surrender their exploration and production licences granted to foreign oil companies, thus transferring company–government relations from the state to the federal level, and the basis for Petronas to negotiate with the companies as well to convert their concession contracts into production-sharing agreements. The Act allowed six months for this renegotiation of company contracts; but in the event a lengthy argument between the major oil companies and Petronas ensued over the terms proposed by the latter.

The chief point disputed was a provision incorporated in an amendment to the Petroleum Development Act passed in May 1975, which required all oil companies with downstream operations in Malaysia (in effect Shell, Exxon and Mobil) to transfer to Petronas a block of what was termed 'management' shares, equivalent to one per cent of their total equity, but with 500 votes per management share (as compared to one vote for each ordinary share) in all decisions relating to the appointment or dismissal of company directors or other staff. The companies interpreted this move as constituting the first step towards nationalisation. And since Petronas could have secured an automatic voting majority by giving management shares 100 votes each, its demand instead for a 5:1 voting majority aggravated already strained relations by giving not just the impression that Petronas intended to control the companies on this issue, but that it wished to provoke them for no apparent reason.

The negotiating atmosphere was further complicated by the inexperience of the Petronas negotiators and what appeared to be ineffective lines of communication between the two sides, which led to a prolonged situation of considerable uncertainty in which the companies found themselves unable to obtain any clear proposals from Petronas. In July 1975, Exxon, which had been on the point of making major new investments off the east coast of West Malaysia, suspended all further exploration, cancelled contracts for the delivery of equipment, and withdrew the bulk of its personnel from the country. The company claimed that its moves were intended only to secure clarification from the government side of terms under which it could continue to operate. Two other companies, Mobil and Oceanic Exploration, gave up exploration efforts and relinquished their contract areas in August and September 1975 respectively. While most companies were cutting back their exploration and development programmes, Shell on the other hand had already made substantial investments and gone into large-scale production. It therefore proceeded more cautiously, only seeking clarification from the government of proposed terms, while continuing to operate much as before.

With negotiations still unresolved, the then Prime Minister, Hussein Onn, intervened, meeting company representatives in July 1976, and appointing a special mediator to secure a consensus, while the 'management' shares provision was retracted. Final agreement was eventually reached, with Shell signing production-sharing contracts for its operational areas in November 1976, followed by Exxon in December.

The contracts which were reached gave Petronas formal management control over the extractive venture, with the companies acting as contractors to Petronas. The companies were required to submit annual work programmes and budgets for approval, and Petronas had the power to decide on the subcontracting of work and the purchase of goods and services for the companies' operations. The duration of contracts was set at 20 years (2 years for exploration, 3 for development and 15 for production), with possible extensions of 4 years for oil and 14 years for gas.

Companies could recover exploration, development and production costs out of 20 per cent of total production in the case of oil and 25 per cent in the case of gas. A royalty payment was required, set at 10 per cent of gross production per annum for crude oil and 10 per cent of gross sales for natural gas. It was to be paid in equal shares to the federal government and to the appropriate state government. After deducting royalty and cost recovery payments, the 'profit' oil component of production was split according to the ratio 70:30 in favour of Petronas, and both parties to the contract were liable to pay income tax on their respective shares to the federal government. An amendment to the 1967 Petroleum Income Tax Act passed in 1976 reduced oil company taxes to 45 per cent charged on their share of 'profit' oil. The tax payment therefore modified the 'profit' split in effect to 83.5:16.5. The companies were further obliged to pay Petronas 0.5 per cent of their proceeds from the sale of their 'cost' and 'profit' oil for use in a research fund.

A system of bonus payments was also laid out: a signature bonus to be determined prior to the offer of new areas, an information bonus set in line with the value of the data already collected, a discovery bonus of Malaysian $2.5 million (about US$1 million) for each commercially viable field discovered, and a production bonus of Malaysian $5 million (about US$2 million) when output reached 725,000 kilolitres per quarter (about 50,000 barrels per day). Furthermore, a price increase arrangement to catch 'windfall' profits arising from oil-price escalations, provided that, should prices exceed US$80 per kilolitre (about US$12.72 per barrel), 70 per cent of the whole of the increase in sales proceeds would go to Petronas (though this base price was allowed to rise at a rate of 5 per cent per year). All royalty and bonus payments, together with the companies' research contributions were, however, deductible from tax payments.[11]

The drawing up of contracts with Shell and Exxon did not, however, bring to an end Malaysian government disputes with foreign oil companies over their extractive ventures. Conoco, the third company operating in Malaysia with potentially profitable oil production in its contract area, judged its estimated reserves as too marginal to justify accepting the terms granted to Shell and Exxon. It held out for a larger share of production to be determined according to a sliding scale based on the number of dry or 'marginal' wells drilled. This procedure proved unacceptable to Petronas, which had in any case tied its negotiating hands by stipulating in Exxon's contract that any better terms obtaining in other contracts automatically applied to Exxon. After some two years of negotiation, Conoco eventually withdrew in June 1978, this act only strengthening the already dominant position of Shell and Exxon.

Just prior to pulling out, Conoco apparently reversed its position, claiming the presence of substantially greater oil reserves in its contract area, in an effort to improve the terms under which it was to withdraw. A Petronas subsidiary, Carigali, took over the contract area, intending to operate the field with the help of foreign drilling contractors. It confined itself initially to carrying out further assessment drilling, which by 1981 confirmed that the field held significant oil deposits. Development of the field has, however, proceeded at a leisurely pace, partly because the government has not wished to depend unduly on petroleum revenue, and production is not expected to begin till 1987.

More difficulties arose in 1980, when the government imposed a 25 per cent export duty on the companies' portion of 'profit' oil, in order to gain a larger share of the increased profits arising from the 1979 oil price rises and despite the price increase arrangement already incorporated in the companies' contracts. The companies argued that the government move constituted a breach of their contracts, which included a clause prohibiting any charge which affected their earnings, but they were nevertheless overruled.

A range of other problems was also encountered by the government in implementing policy for its petroleum industry. Petronas's negotiations with the individual state governments to relinquish their petroleum rights proceeded with little difficulty for 12 of the 13 state governments, who were both subject to political pressure from the central government and to offers of financial inducements from Petronas. But negotiations with the Sabah state government, led by a highly independent Chief Minister, proved extremely protracted, agreement only being secured in mid 1976 after his contrived fall from power.

The stated intention of Petronas to assume control of all domestic processing, refining and distribution of petroleum, despite the withdrawal of its 'management' shares demand, also engendered persistent difficulties with the companies. Petronas eventually agreed to buy a controlling interest in the companies' local refining and marketing operations through the purchase of ordinary shares. Following oil-supply shortages in 1979 (because, like Indonesia, Malaysia imports heavy Middle-Eastern crude oil for domestic consumption, exporting its own more valuable light crudes to Japan and the United States), Petronas moved to begin planning to build two refineries of its own for processing local production. The oil companies opposed this move for fear that Petronas might then squeeze their existing refineries by undercutting prices, but were unable to make Petronas withdraw its plans.

The government introduced a national oil depletion policy at the end of 1979 to reduce the country's oil production by about 10 to 15 per cent, and so conserve the life of its oil reserves. This policy was not welcomed by the oil companies, who would have preferred a higher extraction rate so as to maximise production, though Petronas pressed on regardless of their objections. Petronas also specified production rates for certain oil-fields in order to reduce the wastage of related gas through flaring. Because of the country's relatively prosperous economy, with a diversified range of commodity exports, the government could afford to introduce such restrictive measures as it was then not overly dependent on oil revenues. In any case the 1979 rise in oil prices more than offset the financial reduction resulting from its depletion policy. From 1981, however, this policy had to be relaxed when prices in international commodity markets slackened. With income from oil-related activities rising to almost 25 per cent of all revenue by 1984,[12] the government had indeed to push extraction rates upwards in order to counter falling oil prices. This rise was, however, checked in December 1984 when, under pressure from Indonesia and other Moslem oil-producing countries, Malaysia agreed to trim down its projected production for 1985.

Malaysia has also come to assume growing importance as a natural-gas producer. The consequent setting up of a large processing plant at Bintulu, Sarawak, to liquefy natural gas for export to Japan, also provided a cause of further disputes with foreign companies. The project was of major importance to Malaysia, being the largest industrial venture so far undertaken by the government in terms of its required financing. Agreement on a joint venture was reached by Petronas with Shell and Mitsubishi in March 1978, only after long and difficult negotiations over a period of some four years. Of crucial concern to both sides was the technical consultancy contract, eventually awarded to a Shell subsidiary, Shell Internationale Petroleum Maatschappij (SIPM). While Shell wished to maintain control over the technical coordination of the project, Petronas feared that, with SIPM in charge of all technical matters, Shell would have an effective hold over the whole operation, even though Petronas held a 65 per cent equity interest (as against Shell's 17.5 per cent) in the Bintulu project. Although negotiations were delayed by this dispute, the company responsible for transporting the LNG, the Malaysian International Shipping Corporation (MISC),[13] had gone ahead and prematurely ordered five LNG tankers from French shipyards. The tankers began to be delivered from late 1978 and, with production from Bintulu not scheduled to commence till 1984, they had to be laid up for the interim period. This situation led to further negotiating difficulties, when Petronas tried but failed to make Shell and Mitsubishi responsible for the additional expenses incurred, by agreeing to pay an inflated freight charge.

With the Malaysian government striving so strenuously to assert its authority over foreign oil companies, it has to be asked how effective the exercise of this control has proved to be. The answer is not an encouraging one for the government.

As early as 1973, the Minister of Primary Industries, Abdul Taib, who was then responsible for the oil sector, stated that under existing arrangements, the government was not well-informed about oil company operations. When questioned about offshore oil developments in Sabah and Sarawak, the Minister admitted that he had no information, adding, 'This is what I mean. Members of parliament ask me about these things and what am I to tell them?'[14] The establishment of Petronas was intended to remedy this situation, but with a shortage of qualified local staff with the necessary technical and managerial expertise, supervision of oil-company activities has turned out to be less effective than originally hoped for. During the

1975 contract renegotiations, Petronas officials were reportedly reduced to approaching Shell in order to ask the company what 'profit' split it needed to continue operating, before formulating their own negotiating proposals.[15] And when Petronas invited bids from foreign companies in 1976 to draw up a detailed 'Master Plan' which would draft short- and long-term investment programmes for the development of the country's oil, natural gas and petrochemical industries, it found itself unable to interpret the highly technical proposals submitted.

In 1980, the Malaysian parliamentary opposition leader, Lim Kit Siang, charged Exxon with taking more than its entitled share of oil production, and alleged that Petronas lacked the competence to monitor and effectively police oil company operations. Lim's allegations, made in detail, asserted that Exxon was drawing an additional 23,000 barrels per day from its oil-field off the east coast of West Malaysia, the extra production going undetected by Petronas because the latter depended on Exxon for operational information. A metering system for Petronas to monitor production was maintained by Exxon, and was in any case deficient. Lim also cited various examples of inadequate control by Petronas and the Malaysian government, including the use of substandard work practices by Exxon which had been barred in the Middle East, large cost overruns on inferior equipment, company deviations from Petronas-approved work plans, and the use of expatriate personnel for jobs different from those specified in their work permits. Examples were also given of governmental negligence in failing to collect oil-company taxes and royalties which were due to it. Exxon's failure to effectively refute these charges led the government to acknowledge that Petronas had an inadequate supervisory capability. Petronas subsequently revised and substantially expanded its control procedures,[16] though the effectiveness of these new measures must continue to remain in doubt.

This survey of host-government–foreign-oil-company relations in South-east Asia has shown a diverse range of experiences in which difficulties between governments and companies have, however, proceeded along established lines, with disputes largely centring on management of company operations and on the division of the economic rents deriving from oil and gas development. The Malaysian case in particular illustrates the tortuous difficulties encountered by governments of less-developed countries in attempting to assert their sovereignty and to restrict the financial advantages enjoyed by foreign companies in an industry of which the government has little knowledge. Its incapability to achieve effective control also provides a warning (as does the Indonesian example) to other host governments wishing to set out on the same path of economic nationalism, of how difficult it is to translate formal control into successful practice, even if that formal control has been wrung from the companies after great effort.

It has to be expected that more difficulties will emerge, leading to further disputes between host governments and foreign companies. Not all host governments have attempted to achieve even a formal control over foreign company operations. They may well initiate a process of bargaining in order to do so; and other governments, who have progressed further, are likely to try to invest their exercise of sovereignty with some significant content. To the extent that host government objectives are determinedly pressed, future conflict will be likely. In addition, of course, the bargaining positions of the two sides in each individual extractive operation are continually changing, and the degree of control and division of profits at any one point will always be subject to query at the margin, tending to draw both parties into a continuing process of negotiation.

As host governments contrive new arrangements to take account of these shifting positions, they will have to bear in mind various considerations. In drawing up new contractual forms, they must recognise that the assertion of their sovereignty may well be at the cost of economic efficiency. Indeed it may not even be achieved, if they lack the necessary expertise to bring to bear against the companies' own understandable desire to maintain effective control over ventures in which they have committed substantial investments. Furthermore, a decision to accept the presence of foreign companies involves an evaluation of a wide range of costs and benefits, a process of judgment which must to some degree be subjective. Consequently it will be difficult for host governments to agree on where the balance should be struck; and even within individual governments, unanimity of opinion may be hard to achieve.

The production-sharing contract which has been adopted in several countries has proved to be a flexible instrument in bridging the gap between economic nationalism and foreign company participation. It does however, contain substantial weaknesses, and those provisions which have been devised and incorporated within it to overcome these deficiencies have not proved adequate to safeguard the specific interests of the governmental party to the contract. It would not, on the other hand, appear that strategies of coercion are particularly effective. Indeed host governments may well have to recognise that if they wish to carry out effective and efficient development of their oil resources, the skills and technology of foreign companies will continue to be needed, especially so as extractive operations move towards oil production from marginal reserves located in areas which are difficult to exploit.

Finally, as host governments move to integrate their petroleum sectors more closely into general plans for economic development by expanding into downstream operations, new areas of disagreement between governments and companies will arise, as governments attempt to gain control over processing, supply and marketing functions. These arguments over downstream activities may for the moment be regarded as quite separate from disputes over the upstream extractive ventures. But as the Malaysian experience shows, the two areas of disagreement may begin to encroach on each other as the demarcation between them becomes less distinct.

THE POTENTIAL FOR AGREEMENT: COOPERATIVE MEASURES BY GOVERNMENTS

If the goals of host governments are broadly similar to each other, one possible strategy which they might employ in improving their regulation of multinational enterprise activity would be to cooperate with each other, extending assistance where possible and presenting a unified front in their dealings with foreign companies. Such cooperation may develop in two ways: either through intergovernmental organisations incorporating most if not all producer governments of one particular commodity (and sometimes the governments of the major consumer countries as well), or through regional groupings of host governments with similar economic aims.

In looking at the South-east-Asian oil industry, it would appear that the relevance of intergovernmental commodity organisations is negligible. Only Indonesia is a member of OPEC (though Malaysia has observer status), and it has been content to play an inactive role on pricing issues within that organisation. And while some other OPEC countries have on occasion offered technical and negotiating assistance to various South-east-Asian governments, such help has not improved the latter's bargaining or supervisory capabilities to any perceptible extent.

The process of regional cooperation may on the other hand hold more promise for ultimately improving the economic prospects of individual governments. Cooperation at the regional level may be more easily achieved if there is some sense of regional coherence, or if the countries of the region are at a similar stage of development and hence are more likely to share common interests. One possible objective might be to mobilise a collective countervailing power to pit against the multinational companies, which, however, is less relevant for the South-east-Asian petroleum industry where, in the context of individual foreign-company–host-government bargaining, the problem is not basically one of coordinating joint government action through harmonising trade and investment policies. Working towards more limited aims, such as an exchange of information or the establishment of regional marketing outlets, may, though, eventually make a greater contribution to host governments' bargaining power.

In South-east Asia, a regional impetus to the development of off-shore oil reserves which began in the late 1960s was provided by the United Nations Economic Commission for Asia and the Far East (ECAFE)[17] which set up the Committee for Coordination of Joint Prospecting for Mineral Resources in Asian Offshore Areas (CCOP) in 1966. Membership of CCOP comprised nine South-east and East Asian countries with substantial marine shelf areas adjoining their coasts; and the Committee was responsible for organising and coordinating regional offshore mineral surveys with financial and technical assistance from a number of extra-regional industrial countries. Offshore geophysical surveying began in 1968 and a programme aimed specifically at assisting oil exploration began in 1972. The data obtained were made available through CCOP's technical secretariat to foreign companies interested in the mineral potential of the region.

While this information has proved useful in stimulating foreign company interest in offshore oil development, through being made generally available it has also helped regional host governments, by giving them some idea of the extent and value of their resources. For if a host government has little information on the quantity and quality of its oil reserves, the initial agreement which it reaches with the foreign company is likely to give the latter more favourable terms, reflecting the high risk and considerable uncertainties which the venture is presumed to face. And even after the operation has proved profitable and the uncertainty dissipated, there will usually be a time-lag before the government becomes aware of the imbalance in the relationship and begins to take steps to rectify it. The exploratory work undertaken by CCOP has allowed more knowledgeable assessments of resources to be made by both parties before negotiations begin.

Within South-east Asia, indigenous efforts at regional cooperation in oil-related affairs found expression in the setting up by the Association of South-east Asian Nations (ASEAN) of the ASEAN Council on Petroleum (ASCOPE) in October 1975. ASCOPE is made up of the heads of the state oil companies or government oil agencies of the five ASEAN member states: Indonesia, Malaysia, the Philippines, Singapore and Thailand. Its establishment was reinforced by ASEAN's heads of government in February 1976 when they issued their Declaration of ASEAN Concord which specifically called for increasing regional cooperation in energy production. The principal aim of ASCOPE is to promote mutual assistance and collaboration between its members in the development of their oil resources, primarily through facilitating the exchange of information and the exchange of government personnel in training programmes.

In order to implement this objective, ASCOPE established technical, economic and legal committees charged with identifying and assessing areas for cooperation. As yet ASCOPE primarily fulfils a documentary and information-supply function. A regular mechanism for the exchange of information was set up following a meeting of ASEAN energy ministers in September 1980. Comparative studies of member-government petroleum policies and the training of state company and other government administrative personnel have also been undertaken. Pertamina had earlier helped advise both the Philippine and Malaysian governments in setting up their state oil companies, and it has technical cooperation agreements with both PNOC and Petronas, under which officials of the latter two companies are able to study Pertamina's drafting and implementation of its production-sharing contracts. These measures may appear modest when set against such possible objectives as initiating joint investment projects or establishing united negotiating fronts and production quotas, but they should nevertheless not be disparaged.

Mutual assistance and the exchange of information can help provide knowledge critically needed by host governments in dealing with foreign companies. Indeed as the survey of South-east-Asian oil-company–host-government relations made clear, a lack of information and experience may seriously handicap the negotiating and supervisory abilities of governments. Terms of agreements reached in other countries can give some idea of what the host government might seek to achieve for itself, an important consideration when sometimes it does not even possess the most basic information on the subject. Being able to draw upon the experience in administering agreements of other governments can alert the host government to potential pitfalls in the phrasing of contract terms. And assistance in training can help the host government's bureaucracy to assimilate and make effective use of the information received. Recognising the importance of providing such information is an important step in establishing effective host-government cooperation, especially so as governments in the past have not always been inclined to assist each other if they viewed other producer governments as potential competitors. Although the benefits to be derived from such mutual assistance may not be immediately obvious, as they form part of a gradual learning process, they can still prove to be significant in the long term.

One other area of possible cooperation to which ASCOPE has addressed itself is that of ensuring stable oil supplies for each of its member states. This task might not be thought difficult to achieve, given that of the five ASEAN members Indonesia and Malaysia are both net oil exporters, while Singapore has extensive processing and refining facilities. However, both Indonesia and Malaysia import the bulk of their own crude-oil requirements from the Middle East and choose deliberately to export their higher quality low-sulphur crude-oil production to Japan and the United States, thus saving the price differential between delivered Middle-Eastern oil and their own production. Hence all five countries crucially depend on oil imports to meet domestic consumption. Their oil-refining capacity is largely geared towards processing heavier Middle-Eastern crude oils, and therefore unsuitable to refine local production. Indeed given that the bulk of their oil supplies comes through the international oil companies, both Indonesia and Malaysia have ironically found themselves vulnerable to production cutbacks in the Middle East, despite being designated as 'friendly' nations because of their Moslem character by the Arab oil-producing states.

Following the 1973 oil crisis which brought in its train higher prices and temporarily limited deliveries, the Philippines called for the establishment of an ASEAN energy market. Indonesia at first responded that it could not help without cutting its own consumption, as the bulk of its production was committed under long-term agreements to the American and Japanese markets. Then, after continued pressure from the other ASEAN states, it agreed in January 1974 to allocate a mere 5,000 barrels per day to help ease the short-term supply difficulties of other ASEAN countries.[18] Subsequently, agreements were signed with the Philippines and Thailand, in 1975 and 1976 respectively, to supply them with limited quantities of Indonesian oil. The sales were made at c.i.f. prices no higher than those of Middle East oil imports, which Indonesia regarded as a concessionary act to its fellow ASEAN states.

The 1979 oil shortages induced a greater realisation in both Indonesia and Malaysia of the economic costs of depending on the Middle East for their domestic oil requirements. Both countries initiated plans to build new refineries and to convert a part of existing refining capacity to handle local crude-oil production. In June 1980, ASCOPE agreed that Malaysia and Indonesia would, in an emergency, divert a proportion of their oil production to Thailand, the Philippines and Singapore whenever oil supplies to the latter group fell 10 per cent below their normal requirements because of extra-regional production cutbacks. The modus operandi of this cooperation was not made public.[19] How effective these measures aimed at sharing regional production will prove still remains to be tested. It is, however, important for the region's economic stability that South-east Asian oil producers take further steps to extend their cooperation so as to reduce dependence on imported oil from outside the region.

THE POTENTIAL FOR CONFLICT: DISPUTES OVER
TERRITORIAL RIGHTS

One other contingency needs to be entertained, namely that host governments, instead of cooperating, may find themselves in rivalry or even in conflict with each other. The process of petroleum production may give rise to intergovernmental disputes at various stages of the extractive operation. The principal source of conflict is, however, disagreement over sovereign rights to land territory or ocean areas, deriving basically from any incompatibility in the perceptions by different states of the validity of jurisdictional boundaries, sharpened by the knowledge or expectation of the presence of petroleum reserves.

Within South-east Asia, a number of territorial disputes have arisen, largely because of the desire to gain access to potential oil-producing areas. Although no major conflict has yet arisen, given that there are so many overlapping claims within the partially enclosed South China Sea, the complex political question of sea boundaries could prove a major constraint to the development of offshore petroleum resources. As the littoral states have advanced claims to extensive tracts of water, and given the poor state of relations between some of them, the issue of sea boundaries has become tied up with strategic considerations related to broader political disputes. The main areas of contention are over the Spratly Islands, the Paracel Islands, the Indonesian–Vietnamese continental shelf boundary, and within the Gulf of Thailand.

The Spratlys, which comprise more than 100 islands scattered over an area of some 450,000 square miles, are claimed in their entirety by China, Taiwan and Vietnam, and parts of the island group are also claimed by the Philippines and Malaysia. Their claims are based on a variety of historical and legal grounds and, however specious they may appear, are at least in part of somewhat dubious validity. Each of these countries, with the exception of China, maintains a physical presence in the area, with the Philippines garrisoning seven of the islands, Vietnam five and Malaysia and Taiwan one each.

In 1975 and 1976, the Philippines granted several oil contracts in the Reed Bank area at the eastern end of the Spratly Island group. When a Swedish–Philippine consortium began exploratory drilling (with little success), both Vietnam and China protested. The Philippines declared its willingness to defend these contract areas militarily if necessary. The US government, however, warned American companies that, for its part, it was not in a position to protect them and was not prepared to become involved in any territorial dispute. One company, Amoco, subsequently withdrew from its section of the disputed area. The Philippines also tried to argue that any interference by other claimants would activate the US–Philippines defence treaty, an interpretation which the Americans rejected, though the presence of American military bases in the Philippines could make it difficult for the United States to keep out of any military conflict.

Further north, the Paracel Islands are claimed principally by China and Vietnam, with Taiwan making a parallel claim to that of China. The archipelago is, however, under firm Chinese control, the Chinese having maintained a continuous presence on some of the islands since 1950, and having dislodged a small South Vietnamese garrison from the area in a military attack in January 1974.

When in March 1979 China concluded contracts with foreign oil companies to prospect in offshore areas stretching down to the Gulf of Tonkin, Vietnam warned that any company so doing would have to bear the consequences. In their award of concessions, the Chinese placed two American companies, Amoco and Atlantic Richfield (Arco) around the Hainan Island area, thus forming an American buffer on the southern flank of their offshore oil-exploration efforts, presumably to discourage any future Vietnamese or Russian intervention. The tension in the area was, however, so high that Amoco, which was positioned on the Gulf of Tonkin side of Hainan Island, suspended its operations till December 1979. Although the companies involved are only engaged in seismic survey work with a limited physical presence in the area, if commercial production begins, they will have to commit more substantial assets and may well find themselves as hostages in any future conflict between China and Vietnam.

Problems over the Indonesian–Vietnamese boundary centre on overlapping claims to an area of the sea north of Indonesia's Natuna Islands (part of which also lies within China's claim to the South China Sea). In June 1971, South Vietnam claimed this area of the continental shelf between the two countries on the basis that it lay on the Vietnamese side of the median line between them (drawing this median line between the Kalimantan and Vietnamese coasts, and hence excluding the Natuna Islands themselves). Indonesia engaged in talks to resolve the matter with the newly reunified Vietnam, which then wished to apply the Thalweg Principle to a trench off the continental shelf in determining the disputed boundary (drawing the boundary line along the deepest part of the waters between the two countries, a method traditionally used only for the delimitation of river boundaries, and which further extended the Vietnamese claim). These talks began in June 1978, and have continued without agreement. Vietnam has since withdrawn the Thalweg Principle, reverting to the median line position. But the sticking point still remains the basis of the Indonesian claim, the archipelago principle, which enables the Indonesians to draw the baseline for their claim along the outermost points of their outermost islands. This Vietnam finds inequitable because the Natunas are so far from the Kalimantan coast.

In November 1979, Vietnam protested after Indonesia's Pertamina signed production-sharing contracts with five American companies to explore offshore around the Natuna Islands, three of whom had contracts covering the sea area under dispute. Indonesia remained adamant, and proceeded to sign a further two contracts in and near the disputed area, while carrying out a series of military exercises around the Natuna Islands and building a new military airfield on one of the islands. From late 1980 onwards, oil and gas deposits were located in the area, though none has as yet been developed. The Vietnamese for their part countered the Indonesian moves by concluding an agreement with the Soviet Union for oil exploration in the disputed area, though this remained a formal agreement and was not given any practical effect.

In the Gulf of Thailand, all three littoral states, Thailand, Cambodia and Vietnam have overlapping claims to their respective exclusive economic zones and their share of the continental shelf. While in the past difficulties arose between Cambodia and South Vietnam over offshore oil-exploration activities by the former, conflicting claims by the two countries are no longer actively pursued. And with the installation of a pro-Vietnamese Kampuchean government by unified Vietnam in January 1979, this quiescent state of affairs is likely to continue, even if the rival claims within the gulf have yet to be fully resolved. Indeed, in July 1983 Vietnam and Kampuchea reached agreement on the principles under which they will begin to undertake the limitation of their land and sea boundaries.[20]

Other territorial disputes in the region include differences between Malaysia and Singapore over the island of Batu Puteh, between Malaysia and the Philippines over two areas of the South China Sea, and the dormant Philippine claim to the Malaysian state of Sabah. In the last case, while the Philippines has indicated that it will no longer pursue its claim, it has not, on the other hand, formally withdrawn it; and the development of Sabah as an offshore oil-producing state in the 1970s has undoubtedly enhanced its economic attraction should the claim be revived in the future.

All the territorial disputes discussed above have been greatly exacerbated by the general trend of littoral states to claim expanded offshore boundaries. The United Nations Law of the Sea convention of 1982, if ratified, will legitimise a country's right to claim territorial waters extending to 12 nautical miles, a 200-mile exclusive economic zone, and a 350-mile continental shelf, and also the right for an archipelagic state to claim as its internal waters all the sea enclosed by a boundary connecting the outermost points of the outermost islands of its grouping. Such claims would transform the South China Sea into a mosaic of various national controls, fencing off large blocks of what was once considered to be open sea. South-east-Asian states have already anticipated these legal rights, most having staked their claims to 12-mile territorial seas, 200-mile economic zones and continental shelf rights extending well beyond 200 miles. And the two archipelagic states of Indonesia and the Philippines have achieved increasing recognition of their sovereignty over waters between their islands.

But it should not be thought that all territorial claims in the region have been pressed to the full. Indeed Indonesia, recognising the importance of clearly defined and internationally accepted boundaries for offshore oil development, took an early initiative to demarcate its offshore boundaries, reaching agreements with Malaysia and Thailand in 1968, with Australia (over West Timor) in 1972, with Papua New Guinea in 1973 and with India (over the Andaman Sea) in 1974. Since Indonesia's military invasion of East Timor in 1975, however, the problem remains of settling with Australia the sea boundaries south of East Timor. Meanwhile both countries are considering a jointly administered zone in the disputed area to allow oil and gas exploration to proceed.

The process of oil production, moreover, requires inter-governmental cooperation not only in resolving boundary disagreements, but also over a wide range of activities, failing which international controversy could well arise. Even if political and economic boundaries have been agreed upon, the natural accumulation of oil deposits occurs without respect to such man-made limits.

In the exploratory phase of operations, it is important for the host government to determine the nature of any geological research taking place within its offshore waters. It has to distinguish between purely scientific research into the physical or biological characteristics of the seabed, for which its consent should not normally be withheld, and actual exploration of the continental shelf for mineral deposits, for which it claims to have exclusive rights.

Should commercial production be reached, difficulties may then arise if the oil reserves being recovered are spread out over two or more national jurisdictions. This may easily come about if the oil discovery is near the limits of the host country's economic zone, for there is no reason why the underlying deposit should fall within or be conterminous with the country's economic boundary line. In such cases, one government may, for instance, fear that the operating company on its neighbour's contiguous territory is draining oil from its own side. Or even if there is an agreement on joint extraction, the two governments may still disagree on such matters as the optimum rate of extraction. Such a joint agreement was concluded between Malaysia and Thailand, when they signed a 'Memorandum of Understanding' in 1979. The Memorandum, intended to run for 50 years, provides for joint development of a 2,100 square mile disputed area east of their common land border. However, while exploration for oil and gas has commenced, no commercial production has ensued, as agreement has still to be reached on the tax régime to be applied and on an appropriate division of both expenses and earnings between the two governments.[21]

Furthermore, there is always the possibility of marine pollution arising, perhaps from oil spills in drilling operations or from tanker accidents, and spreading across maritime boundaries. Such transfrontier pollution is an especially serious problem in South-east Asia, with its extensive fishing industry easily harmed by oil pollution, and the dependence of a large part of the indigenous population on fish and marine products for a major source of protein. South-east-Asian governments have on the whole been aware of the danger of marine pollution and have imposed various anti-pollution measures and safeguards on their operating companies.

In February 1977, as part of an agreement to safeguard the safety of navigation in the Straits of Malacca and Singapore, the bordering countries of Indonesia, Malaysia and Singapore agreed to formulate a joint policy to deal with marine pollution.

Finally, we have to consider the possibility that extra-regional governments may play a part in regional disputes over oil operations. The home governments of foreign oil companies might for instance be brought into regional intergovernmental conflicts. As yet, this has not come about because home governments have been careful to keep their distance from any nascent regional dispute. With, for example, American companies operating in the East China Sea and the Soviet Union in the Gulf of Tonkin, both sides have exercised considerable caution. Given, however, that an increasing number of state-owned companies are becoming involved in South-east Asian oil operations, it may be more difficult for home governments to avoid such entanglements in the future. Such state companies may act in part like private companies, but place greater emphasis on securing sources of oil supply rather than on engaging in commercially profitable production. Others play more active roles. Algeria's Sonatrach, Britain's BNOC (British National Oil Corporation), Norway's Statoil and Mexico's Perminex have advised South-east-Asian governments, while state oil companies from Kuwait, Saudi Arabia and Iran have become involved in refinery investments and oil-supply agreements. With closer government-to-government relationships, the consequences of any regional dispute which their activities may stimulate and in which they may become involved are likely to be more widespread and serious.

Whether or not regional intergovernmental disputes become intensified in the future may well depend on the assessment by governments of the likely gains from pursuing their claims. The United Nations Law of the Sea convention, even if ratified, does not necessarily resolve these issues, given that various countries have entered reservations on its provisions, and may therefore not feel bound by it; while these provisions have themselves to be interpreted and negotiated for each particular set of circumstances. There is, however, no reason why disagreements should not be resolved, if an amicable solution entails lower costs and provides at least a measure of benefit for both parties. On the other hand, disputes over ownership of oil reserves may well be pursued more prominently if South-east-Asian countries face internal political instability or have to adjust to the regional implications of changing relationships between the major global powers.

8. THE VIABILITY OF TRANSNATIONAL MINERAL AGREEMENTS

The experience of Indonesia in the development of its petroleum industry underscores the differences in outlook and objectives which must be appreciated in any analysis of the interaction between transnational companies and local host governments. Both oil companies and the Indonesian government have been pre-occupied with achieving an accommodation of interests which could provide a viable basis for cooperation over the extractive process. Yet what the Indonesian example also shows is that, while there may appear to have been a basic shift in favour of the host government in the content of agreements for oil extraction, when one begins to examine the precise terms and operational conditions of these agreements, it has at the least to be questioned if this presumed shift in favour of the host government has in fact occurred.

There may indeed be a trend towards an apparent new accommodation between foreign company and host government, but this does not mean that the latter has necessarily secured a markedly greater share of the benefits from the extractive operation. Pre-occupation with obtaining formal ownership and control over the extractive operation has not meant that real control has in fact been exercised. Formal ownership may of course be desired as an end in itself, and is a legitimate objective if it serves to confirm the host government's authority. But there remain significant problems for the host government if it wishes to achieve effective control over the use of its oil resources. The gains from better negotiation of contracts could in some respects be considerable, though they are more likely to be incremental. For the effective limits imposed on government action are set ultimately by the finite extent of its technical and supervisory capabilities.[1] Whatever strategy the government chooses to pursue, there can be no alternative to the necessity of developing a national competency in the field of mineral, specifically petroleum, development.

In looking at the experiences of other South-east-Asian producer governments, it may again be seen that it is their limited capabilities which set the conditions under which oil extraction proceeds. Of these governments, Indonesia and Malaysia have been most prominent in seeking a more active policy to strengthen their bargaining power towards the oil companies. Indonesia in particular sought explicitly to create a contractual framework for oil-company operations which could stimulate the learning process under which the government side could build up its supervisory abilities and negotiating skills. Yet its inability to develop an effective indigenous capacity in the overall management of its petroleum industry has in the end constrained its de facto regulation of oil-company operations.

But if the trend towards a shift of power from foreign company to host government should not be overstated, at least so far as the South-east-Asian experience seems to indicate, it nevertheless still remains that governments such as that of Indonesia have not been deterred from increasingly attempting to assert more autonomous policies within their mineral sectors. And given the dynamic nature of the 'concessions process' between company and government, it may be expected that any increase in governmental abilities to exercise real control will eventually find opportunities opening up for it to assert itself and achieve practical effect. Indeed, in examining the evolving relationship between a foreign company and a host government, shifts in bargaining power either allow both sides to act to increase their relative gains from the extractive process or require them to defend their existing positions. Such shifts therefore open up new sources of instability as existing arrangements are threatened. But threats to the existing order need not be to the benefit of either side unless on the other hand it were possible to work out an amicable agreement ensuring stable prices and markets, to their joint advantage.

Arrangements for mineral extraction in general have in the past reflected and reinforced the vertically oligopolistic position held by foreign multinational companies which allowed them, to a large degree, to control the activities in which they were involved from the extractive operation through to the marketing stage. Where bargaining power has shifted has been in the opportunities which have arisen for host governments to breach this oligopoly, and thus erode the privileges of the foreign firms. The success of these host-government attacks may in some crucial respects be more apparent than real, given the necessity of governments to establish their legitimacy within the domestic politics of their particular states by means of asserting their nationalist credentials. Nevertheless opportunities may arise for host governments to establish real gains, through obtaining access to capital funds or formerly closely guarded technology or through establishing points of entry into overseas markets to compete directly with private-company sales. Perhaps the principal obstacle to such host governmental efforts to establish themselves within mineral industries has been their limited technical, managerial and entrepreneurial capabilities. These limitations are not readily overcome, as it is difficult to acquire a capacity for organisation or a nucleus of technical expertise. Nor do they allow for effective supervision and control of foreign companies, even though the host government may have formally arrogated such functions to itself.

Indeed even if the host government succeeds in eroding the bargaining power of the foreign company, this achievement may be self-defeating if it also results in destroying the carefully regulated market for the mineral production built up through the companies' oligopoly. Furthermore the development of new technology, such as that required for offshore oil production, may serve as a means for the company to restore its bargaining position. The host government may then find that, despite its improved abilities, the control it desires always remains just one step beyond its grasp. It may therefore serve host governments better to recognise the limits of their abilities and, if possible, to seek contract arrangements in which they can cooperate with foreign companies to secure mutually agreed shares of a larger, possibly expanding cake than to attempt to increase their share of a much reduced one.

Quite apart from the intransigence of many foreign companies, who may not be prepared to accept a secure if reduced position within the mineral-production structures of their host states, the difficulty which the host government faces in adopting such cooperative policies lies in reconciling them with the political tensions generated by the activities of the foreign company within its host society. The dictates of domestic politics typically require the host government to assert its national autonomy against what is perceived as a foreign element operating within its midst. Hence governments have become more assertive in challenging these companies. Foreign companies, however, tend to be in stronger bargaining positions in less-developed countries than in developed ones and, so long as they possess some unique asset or strength which the host government would find difficult to obtain, they may effectively resist the controls which the government attempts to apply.

This situation promises little stability, and is further disturbed by the continuing insecurity of a host government which feels threatened by its need to rely on foreign multinationals. If, however, the host government can improve its administrative capacity to some extent, it is just possible that the tension between it and the foreign company may be held in check. In this regard, those contracts of operation which formally grant the host government nominal management and other ambiguous controls over the extractive process, may fulfil a useful function if they provide the host government both with a public display and with a sense of increased control over the foreign company, together with a semblance of authority with which to ward off domestic criticism. Even if the real role of the foreign company does not alter in its critical aspects, the atmosphere and form of participation on the part of the host government could change sufficiently to help to ease tension. This could allow each side to pursue arrangements which build on common interests, in place of strategies of obtaining more for itself to the exclusion of other objectives.

The interaction between foreign company and host government may be analysed from many different standpoints; and generalisations about the behaviour of foreign multinational companies are difficult to make, given the vast and varied nature of the evidence.

Positive evidence is difficult to collate. For example, how many different factors need to be considered in quantifying the various costs and benefits to the host government from the operations of the foreign company? The financial figures submitted by the company are unlikely to reflect its 'true' profits, given the internal pricing policies of the multinational network of which the local foreign company is but one subsidiary. And in calculating the social cost–benefit ratio, any figure which purports for instance to stand for such elements as the social value of local labour or the use of local inputs, must to some extent be arbitrary.

The only conclusion which may safely be drawn is that no simple causal explanation motivating the process of foreign-company–host-government relations is possible. Both parties to the relationship are powerful in their own right. But, in a very important sense, they do not compete with each other. They operate in different spheres and according to different principles. The foreign company cannot take on the sovereign powers and functions of an autonomous national government; nor can the government be expected to operate according to the strict profitability criteria of a business enterprise.

Some further inferences drawn from the process of contract relations between foreign company and local host government may be made. To begin with, the course of negotiations between foreign company and host government is determined in large part by the balance of bargaining power between them. Yet analysis of this balance at any one point in time gives an essentially static picture of the relationship, which is a dynamic process. Nor does it encourage stability by leading both sides to seek collaborative solutions aimed at joint maximisation to increase the absolute returns from the operation as a whole. An appreciation of bargaining power is more likely to encourage confrontation, with each side seeking to increase its own individual proceeds, possibly even at the expense of overall returns. Yet the competition of both parties will only achieve a fragile temporary equilibrium, and it may be preferable for them to collude to maximise joint returns at the possible expense of third parties such as the consumer or the company's home government.

To comprehend the development of the foreign-company–host-government relationship, it is necessary to introduce an element of change into the terms governing the extractive operation, allowing for the evolution over time of the balance of power between the two sides. The foreign investor may try to uphold the sanctity of his original contract, but this would only be to argue that the agreement should be frozen on terms favourable to himself. The host government can be expected to attempt to revise such a contract when it feels it has built up sufficient countervailing power. Difficulties arise when this process of change is not accepted by the company, for resistance can generate considerable tension and perceptions of injustice.

This pattern of company–government relations has been characterised as an obsolescing bargain,[2] because while the foreign company may be enticed by advantageous terms to make an original investment under conditions of considerable uncertainty, once the project is a going concern, its terms appear overgenerous and the company finds itself forced to accept the less generous conditions of a revised bargain. It follows from this model that the foreign investor's initial uncertainty that the extractive operation might be hampered by host-government attempts to establish new terms at a later stage, should be replaced by an expectation of certain revision once the project establishes itself as commercially viable.

The company may seek to protect itself by various strategies through which its local profile is lowered and its capital and risk commitments reduced, but these will not remove its basic vulnerability. The method of 'unbundling' corporate services separates the provision of capital from the provision of technical and managerial services and it shares capital commitments with customers and their intermediaries. This strategy does help to spread risk, but cannot avoid it so long as the company retains formal ownership of operational assets, mineral production or resources in the ground. Furthermore it is aimed at building transnational alliances in marketing and finance in order to cut off host governments from potential markets or sources of international finance, which will only cause further tension and instability in the foreign-company–host-government relationship.

A basic paradox underlies the extractive process. For one thing, no company would be prepared to make an initial large investment commitment at considerable risk and uncertainty without using whatever bargaining strength it has to secure the best possible terms for itself. And few host governments would give up the opportunity to redress the balance once the uncertainty and risk are dissipated. Yet host governments are generally unwilling and usually in no position to pay the international market price for scarce business and technical skills under the high-risk conditions prevailing at the start of the mineral operation. The idea of companies contracting out their services through management and technical assistance contracts without assuming the initial risk, if strictly applied, therefore appears impracticable. Multinational companies would never make an investment commitment at the start if they were restricted to the extent host governments may desire. On the other hand, the companies cannot expect to restrain the later exercise of their sovereign powers by host governments who, unless highly unstable, cannot credibly constrain themselves in the way foreign companies may wish.

Indeed within the foreign-company–host-government process, the primacy of governmental decision-making should be stressed. This of course is an ineluctable tenet of international life, deriving from the sovereignty of nation-states. Companies on the other hand cannot be expected to acquire the viewpoint of governments, for corporate social responsibility is inherently limited. The primary concern of the companies remains the yield on their investments, their efficient functioning, and their competitive positions with respect to each other. They will only pursue an unprofitable activity, unless forced to, so long as it is regarded as essential for securing their other operations, or if it is expected to become profitable in the long term. Companies can hardly be required for instance to take on such governmental concerns as the provision of full employment or the establishment of distributive justice. These are properly the responsibilities of government which must direct the companies to achieve these ends. It is therefore up to the host government to establish a clear national policy governing foreign transnational companies, gearing their activities to its goals of development. In this regard, even ordinary regulation requires a degree of administrative competence and objectivity if government agencies are not to turn into instruments of bureaucratic obstruction.

The company's economic power cannot of course be compared to the government's sovereign power. Ultimately the government can regulate the foreign companies operating within its territorial boundaries, or else nationalise them. Nevertheless an important constraint on the effectiveness of governmental policies towards foreign companies is the relatively weak bargaining position of governments in most less-developed countries. Many host governments lack precise knowledge of the topics and issues which they are bargaining about. They are frequently unsure of their own capabilities and uncertain of the strength of the company with which they are negotiating. And they are often unaware of the alternatives open to them.

What specific policy prescriptions may be deduced for the oil industry in particular? As the oil industry operates in different countries under a wide variety of circumstances and company–government régimes, it is not possible to lay down a set of rules governing host-government policy in every situation. Nevertheless it is clear that for any significant oil-producer government its petroleum industry will form such a vital component of the national economy that it will have a large part of its attention constantly focused on the industry's functioning. Host-government anxieties are further intensified by the multinational character and apparent strength of the companies with whom it deals. As the host government attempts to assert its right to query the activities of these companies and to intervene in the industry's affairs, its relations with the companies are hence never easy.

In approaching this problem, the host government has first to establish a clear legal framework, which reflects the policies it has determined for the oil industry's functioning and defines its intended relations with foreign companies. In so doing, its freedom of action may be constricted by domestic political pressures and by the actions of other producer and consumer governments. The government must decide its position on such issues as how dependent it should allow the country's economy to become on oil production, and which governmental administrative organs should be responsible for regulating the oil industry. It must judge to what extent the national interest, however defined, is served by relying on foreign companies, and what position these companies should occupy within the domestic economy. In this regard the government has to determine if it wishes to establish a state enterprise whose primary concern is control of its oil industry. If the country largely depends on foreign companies, setting up such a national concern may well help to build an indigenous capability in an important industry, provide a sense of local participation, and give some means of assessing the performance of the foreign companies. But close scrutiny of the state corporation itself is essential, and the nature of the autonomy granted to it must be carefully assessed. Such issues as these form the basis for governmental policies, setting the terms of reference under which it will intervene in its oil industry.

The government has then to determine what objectives it wishes to achieve and, in working out its negotiating strategy, what relative importance it should attach to each of these goals. The exploitation of its oil reserves cannot simply be left to the commercial self-interest of the companies but must be measured against the overall national interest. The pace of resource development, the issue of local processing, and the decision whether to export crude-oil production or utilise it for domestic consumption, are all topics which closely affect this broader interest.

In ensuring that it maintains ultimate control over oil production, the government will have to monitor issues of pricing and supply with especial care. Its concern with prices covers a wide spectrum of problems: company transfer-pricing practices, government tax rates and their implications for company behaviour, and the price of the country's oil production in international markets. The question of supply requires the government to decide on the number and type of companies engaged in oil exploration and production, to set a desired rate of production from the country's estimated reserves, and to determine the manner of and extent to which local participation in oil production should be achieved.

For many host governments, it may be expected that oil production will remain largely in the hands of foreign companies. The problem for host governments is therefore to create a climate in which the companies are induced to operate effectively, while at the same time ensuring that their own interests are taken into account.

As for the companies, their paramount consideration is obtaining what they regard as a reasonable rate of return from the operation in question. Agreement between governments and companies as to what constitutes such a rate will never be easy to reach so long as each side doubts the motives of the other. The problem is that no one outside the companies possesses reliable and precise information of their operations and the proceeds which they acquire. The companies themselves are parsimonious with the data which they choose to release, tending for instance to understate oil reserve estimates, as they have no interest in provoking the sort of hopeful expectations which might undermine their own arguments for a better financial deal from the host government. Yet they are commonly the sole source of government information on such matters as estimated reserves, oil-field characteristics and production. These are facts which might readily be used by the host government against the companies' own interests, but which the government perforce relies on them to supply.

Oil companies generally argue in favour of reducing the overall level of taxation through taxing net profits rather than physical production, for providing incentives to encourage the development of smaller higher cost oil-fields, for more flexibility in the amortisation and depreciation procedures which they are allowed, for issuing new contract areas on a regular basis for exploration, and for greater consistency in and simplicity of governmental tax and regulatory policies. While room for improvement cannot be denied, this would not necessarily be in the direction indicated by the companies. The pitfalls for the government in some of their recommendations have been dealt with already. Taxing profits alone would, for example, give the companies much greater scope for creative accounting procedures to minimise tax payments. And if the terms of a given division of financial proceeds appear complicated, they only reflect the fine balance resulting from the trade-offs struck by company and government during the negotiating process; and which in any case may enable the host government to pursue a number of governmental objectives unconnected with narrow profit considerations.

What is required are host-government policies which manage to coax a steady rate of exploration and development activity from the companies at a level desired by the government. In this regard, the companies' claim that maintaining production levels requires a continual effort to explore for and develop new oil-fields does need to be seriously taken into consideration by host governments in structuring oil taxation policies. Remaining oil reserves, those as yet undiscovered, tend to be located in remote areas, at great depths, both onshore and offshore, and within difficult geological formations and harsh physical environments. The long lead times before commercial production is attained, the technological difficulties and mounting development costs associated with such smaller marginal fields, requires the provision of sufficient financial incentives tailored to encourage their development.

The companies' willingness to engage in oil exploration is not just dependent on government taxation policies. What matters is their estimated costs and expected future profits. The level of oil prices is therefore a very important consideration as well, though this is a factor not generally within the ability of any one producer government to influence. The higher the oil price, the more readily can the larger financial outlays required for exploration and development of marginal deposits be justified, as their economic viability is enhanced. On the other hand, the host government's interests are not always served by a higher production rate, given the difficulties of absorbing the financial proceeds into its domestic economy and the structural changes which may result.

For their part, the companies are not usually unwilling to threaten to pull out of the oil-producing country concerned for other alternative production areas. While they have done so in the past, it still remains that no company can afford to rely on one possibly insecure region for its oil production. In the interest of stability, companies would feel compelled to extend their operations across different oil-producing regions as far as is feasible, for the implication to them of the greater risk involved in developing marginal deposits is that they must spread this risk by being involved in several areas simultaneously. So host governments may be assured that the oil companies will not easily pass over the opportunity to explore for and produce oil so long as they view the investment and political climate of the country under consideration as reasonably stable.

Finally we turn to a consideration of the future development of foreign-company–host-government relations in general through the implications of certain trends which may already be discerned. Of central concern to the future of this relationship is the increasing involvement of host governments, superseding the companies themselves in the decision-making process for the operation being undertaken. This shift has resulted in operational decisions being informed by considerations of an essentially political nature. Foreign companies may still attempt, as they always have done in the past, to maximise economic and corporate efficiency, and governments remain responsible for carrying out a wide variety of social objectives. But political considerations now require in addition the achievement of broader national goals of political status, independence and social autonomy, which, even more so than the government's social objectives, are inimical to the efficiency criteria by which multinational companies operate. Within this socio-political framework, the foreign company has to demonstrate its effectiveness to the host government as an instrument for the accomplishment of governmental policies.

Such host-government determination of the activities of foreign multinational companies may perhaps be most readily apparent in the case of the oil industry, and there remains a wide spectrum of corporate susceptibility to government interference; but it is generally true that the trend is towards greater governmental regulation and tighter control, however effective, over foreign investment. And as a consequence of this trend, the multinational company is increasingly having to modify its privately determined economic interests to suit the public purposes laid down by host-government decree.

Two qualifications need to be made in evaluating this perceived trend. First, the more enthusiastic proponents of a steadily expanding intervention by governments in foreign-company operations have discerned a need for international codes of conduct which comprehensively cover all aspects of the activities of multinational companies.[3] Their argument holds that national regulation by host governments needs to be supplemented by international measures and directives so as to match the global perspective of the multinational companies themselves. Moves have therefore been set in train to lay down new rules governing foreign private investment at the international level. It is, however, unlikely that such agreements will be closely observed, given that they cannot be made binding on their signatories. It remains to be seen to what extent relations of such variety and intricacy as those between host governments and multinational companies will lend themselves to the kind of blanket legal regulation which is envisaged. Changes in relative bargaining power and different perceptions of self-interest, which derive from the considerable diversity in political and economic interests of host governments and differences in their relative dependence on multinational companies, will act to hinder and ultimately obstruct the overall applicability of such intended codes. It may be possible to achieve some modification of the companies' modes of behaviour and to reinforce the bargaining position of host governments, but the basic character of multinational companies as profit-oriented business entities will remain unaltered. They will still have to be provided with appropriate stimuli in the form of incentives to induce the desired responses.

Second, the institutional framework governing foreign-company–host-government relations has come to receive increased attention with a variety of new contractual models being proposed and implemented as host governments devise new legislation to regulate multinational enterprises. These arrangements include joint ventures, 'fade out' policies aimed at ensuring a transition to full national ownership, 'unbundling' of investment packages so as to acquire only the goods and services needed, negotiating and paying for each item separately, and 'repackaging' of investment contracts to bring in international agencies and third-party and home governments with an interest in the venture. Host-government contracts with foreign companies basically provide a framework for cooperation between a state and a transnational entity, which interweaves both public and private interests by pursuing a dual policy of national development on the one hand and the implementation of a transnational business strategy on the other. The new contractual structures are attempts at modifying this framework, to take into account the current tendency for the former purpose to attain a formal predominance over the latter.

Multinational companies initially resisted but eventually proved willing to enter into such agreements. But whether or not these new approaches will provide significant pointers to the future will depend on the ability of host governments to invest these structures with a real as opposed to a merely formal content. Limiting foreign ownership in individual companies or key industries to minority positions will not effect a fundamental transformation of the foreign-company–host-government relationship so long as the company can effectively override governmental initiatives, continuing to take key policy decisions and possessing resources and abilities which the government cannot hope to obtain. If, however, host governments can assume the entrepreneurial risks of such projects, this transfer-of-risk assumption will shift the basic function of the multinational company from an entrepreneurial role to the sale of corporate capabilities and services, thus changing the nature of its functioning and altering its structure of profit incentives. Such an achievement may prove a decisive first step in providing the host government with long-term control of foreign operations; but it can only be consolidated if the government itself has the organisational capability to coordinate its powers and manage the operation as an efficient whole, and if its administration at the level of the operation's functioning has the knowledge to effectively assess the company's performance. Such abilities are indeed scarce in most less-developed countries.

A related consideration is the legal basis which will underlly future contractual forms. Despite attempts in the past to apply international law to state contracts with foreign entities, it would appear that foreign-company–host-government relations will in future be governed by municipal or national law. The most likely prospect is for continued bilateral relationships between foreign companies and the governments in whose jurisdiction they function. Indeed as host governments have attempted to tighten their supervision of foreign companies, this has acted to 'nationalise' rather than 'internationalise' contractual relations between states and transnationals.[4]

In transnational economic relations of the kind we have considered, what is required is a more objective recognition by both sides of each other's nature and interests. Satisfying the claims of the one need not be at the expense of the other. Host-government negotiators may believe that the essential point is to know where to draw the line or to strike the balance, so as to engage the cooperation of the multinational enterprise on the best possible terms. And foreign companies may attempt to draft detailed provisions on the conditions of their involvement and to secure host-government agreement over these terms. But such views present only part of the whole picture. While contracts regulate current relations and circumstances, they also have a potential for renegotiation and contain within themselves elements capable of sparking off future conflict. The temporal nature of such relationships, therefore, points to the need for a continuing dialogue, possibly even an argumentative one, between foreign companies and host governments. Only in this way can a more satisfactory and enduring relationship be built up between the two sides.

NOTES

1. The impact of the foreign company on government policies in less-developed countries

1 Radetzki argues that the perception of 'political risk' by mining firms crucially determines investment decisions in less-developed host countries. M. Radetzki, 'LDC Policies towards Foreign Mineral Investors', in *Mining for Development in the Third World: Multinational Corporations, State Enterprises and the International Economy*, eds. S. Sideri and S. Johns (New York: Pergamon Press, 1980), p. 290.

2 See J. Martin Rochester, 'The Paradigm Debate in International Relations: Data in Search of Theory', in *Transnationalism in World Politics and Business*, ed. Forest L. Grieves (New York: Pergamon Press, 1979), pp. 3–19.

3 Lall and Streeten go further in asserting that host-government policies implemented on behalf of foreign investment may correspond to the interests of particular sections of the dominant classes. Sanjaya Lall and Paul Streeten, *Foreign Investment, Transnationals and Developing Countries* (London: Macmillan, 1977), p. 221.

4 See, for instance, Raymond F. Mikesell, ed., *Foreign Investment in the Petroleum and Mineral Industries: Case Studies of Investor–Host Country Relations* (Baltimore: Johns Hopkins Press, 1971), p. 424.

2. The Indonesian petroleum industry: form and content of agreements

1 Schelling points out that if mutual dependence is part of the logical structure, some kind of collaboration or accommodation might be necessary so as to avoid mutual loss. Thomas Schelling, *The Strategy of Conflict* (London: Oxford University Press, 1963), p. 83. In the case of oil extraction, this would apply insofar as the absolute level of profits, in which both sides share a common interest, depends to some degree on mutual action.

2 Article 33, sections 2 and 3 of the 1945 constitution in *The Indonesian Revolution: Basic Documents and the Idea of Guided Democracy* (Jakarta: 1960), pp. 59–83.

234

3   Law No. 44 in *Business Prospects in Indonesia Today* (Hong Kong: Indonesian Consulate General, 1975), pp. 129–33.

4   See Indonesia, Department of Information, *Investment: The New Procedures of Foreign Capital Investment* (Jakarta: 1968). A former Pertamina official candidly admitted, while interviewed, that the law resulted in 'a very strange situation' as it studiously ignored any reference to production sharing. Indeed production sharing could only be justified on the grounds that, with the system only just being established, to acquiesce in other forms of contract would only 'open the door to mayhem'.

5   As the post of Managing Director is termed by Pertamina.

6   Article 12 of Law No. 8, 1971 (Pertamina Law) in *Pertamina: Indonesian State Oil Enterprise: Reference Book: Second Edition* (Jakarta: Pertamina, 1974), pp. 13–29. The preamble to the law makes it clear that it is intended to supplement rather than supplant Law No. 44 of 1960. The anomaly of not having production-sharing contracts approved by Parliament remained unaffected. An accompanying elucidation of article 12 merely states that Parliament would be notified after the President had approved each contract.

7   The situation is actually somewhat more complicated in practice. Hossain points out that individual agreements could incorporate a clause binding the company to accept all future legislative changes, thus obviating the need for complex and elaborate renegotiation clauses. See Kamal Hossain, *Law and Policy in Petroleum Development: Changing Relations between Transnationals and Governments* (London: Frances Pinter, 1979), pp. 103–4.
    The government may therefore seem to hold the advantage in either case. On the other hand, Brown argues that a contractual clause which sets out to nullify any future legislative changes insofar as they affect that particular contract is legally dubious. See Roland Brown, 'Choice of Law Provisions in Concessions and Related Contracts', *Modern Law Review* 39 (1976): 625–42.

8   1899 Law in Robert Fabrikant, ed., *Oil Discovery and Technical Change in Southeast Asia: The Indonesian Petroleum Industry: Miscellaneous Source Material* (Singapore: Institute of Southeast Asian Studies, 1973), pp. 1–108.

9   'Contract of Work between P. N. Pertambangan Minjak Indonesia (Pertamin) and Pan American Petroleum Corporation, June 15th, 1962' (Singapore: Institute of Southeast Asian Studies). Pan American is a subsidiary of Standard Oil of Indiana.

10 While Sutowo is generally credited with this innovation, many persons from both company and government sides were in fact responsible for devising the form of early agreements. They were therefore collectively responsible for the substance of production sharing as it emerged.

11 Quoted by Louis Kraar, 'Oil and Nationalism Mix Beautifully in Indonesia', *Fortune*, July 1973, p. 99.

12 Ibnu Sutowo, *Prospect of Oil for our National Prosperity* (Jakarta: Pertamina, 1972), p. 12.

13 'Production Sharing Contract between P. N. Pertambangan Minjak dan Gas Bumi Nasional and Independent Indonesian American Petroleum Company, September 6th, 1968' (Singapore: Institute of Southeast Asian Studies).

14 Ibid., sec. VI, par. 1.5.

15 For descriptive purposes, production is here divided into a 'cost' oil element, representing that part of production from which the company can recover its operating costs, and a 'profit' oil element, which is the balance from which the division of production takes place.

16 Ibid., sec. VII, pars. 1.2 and 1.3. An adjusted weighted average of net prices realised on such sales was to be taken for the three months preceding the sale in question, with third parties limited to companies with no direct, indirect or joint interest with IIAPCO.

17 Ibid., sec. VII, par. 1.4.

18 It should be noted that the terms of LNG contracts were also modified in 1976, for the same reason as petroleum contracts, to enable the computation of company costs and profits to be accepted by the US Internal Revenue Service. The issue is discussed in the context of petroleum operations in chapter 3, section 6. The other incentives introduced by the government in 1976/1977 did not, however, apply to LNG production in general, though they were applicable to natural gas condensates.

19 'Technical Assistance Contract between P. N. Pertambangan Minjak dan Gas Bumi Nasional and Rehabilitation, Engineering and Development Company (REDCO), October 15th, 1968' (Singapore: Institute of Southeast Asian Studies).

3. Financial provisions and consequent areas of dispute

1 The discounted cash flow is the future income on the investment discounted by the relevant rate of interest (or annual costs of capital to the company) to obtain its current value. This enables the company to estimate the present value of future earnings from the later stages of the extractive operation when commercial production is generating income, to set against development costs in the earlier stages when no oil is produced.

2 Hong Lan Oei, *Petroleum Resources and Economic Development: A Comparative Study of Mexico and Indonesia* (Ph.D. dissertation, University of Texas, 1964; Ann Arbor, Mich.: University Microfilms, n.d.), pp. 91–3.

3 Murray Clapham, 'Some Difficulties of Foreign Investors in Indonesia', *Bulletin of Indonesian Economic Studies* 6 (March 1970): 73.

4 Indonesia, The Java Bank, *Report for the Year 1951–1952* (Jakarta: 1952).

5 Art. 26 par. a(6) of 'Contract of Work between P. N. Pertambangan Minjak Nasional (Permina) and P. T. Stanvac Indonesia, September 25th, 1963' (Singapore: Institute of Southeast Asian Studies). This was taken as a percentage of 'New Area' production, and could only be expensed if such production was available.

Depletion is here taken to mean the cost to the firm of acquiring and bringing the petroleum deposit into production, treated as a company expense, and hence deductible against income once commercial production begins. More usual in resource-extractive operations is for the depletion cost to be calculated as a fixed sum and then set as a ratio against estimated total reserves of the mineral. That proportion of the originally estimated reserves which is produced in any one year would then also be the proportion of the depletion cost which is deductible for that year. See Charles T. Horngren, *Introduction to Management Accounting* (Englewood Cliffs, N.J.: Prentice-Hall, 1981), p. 518.

6 See, for instance, art. III par. 2 of Exhibit 'C' in 'Production Sharing Contract between P. N. Pertambangan Minjak dan Gas Bumi Nasional (Pertamina) and Texaco Overseas Petroleum Company and California Asiatic Oil Company, August 9th, 1971' (Singapore: Institute of Southeast Asian Studies).

7 The reason for this continued reliance on the companies lies in Pertamina's lack of accounting expertise, a disability admitted by it. Indeed when Pertamina attempted at one stage to take over record-keeping for company operations, the companies resisted on the grounds that these records would not be of a standard to satisfy their shareholders and home governments. A former government minister also claimed in the course of interviews that Pertamina was never able to produce a balance sheet for him without reservations, as its own bookkeeping was not in order.

8 Exhibit 'B' art. I par. 2 of the 'Contract between Pertamina and IIAPCO, September 6th, 1968'.

9 Exhibit 'C' art. III par. 1 of the 'Contract between Pertamina and Texaco/Calasiatic, August 9th, 1971'.

10 Ibid., Exhibit 'C' art. II par. 2 subsec. 2.2.

11 International Bank for Reconstruction and Development, *Indonesia: Economic Report* (Washington D.C.: 30 November 1973), cited by Sritua Arief, *The Indonesian Petroleum Industry: A Study of Resource Management in a Developing Economy* (Jakarta: Sritua Arief Associates, 1976), pp. 220–1.

12 Sec. VII par. 1.4 of the 'Contract between Pertamina and Texaco/Calasiatic, August 9th, 1971'.

13 This is recommended by David N. Smith and Louis T. Wells Jr., *Negotiating Third-World Mineral Agreements: Promises as Prologue* (Cambridge, Mass.: Ballinger, 1975), p. 78.

14 Exhibit 'B' art. II par. 8 of the 'Contract between Pertamina and IIAPCO, September 6th, 1968'. Later contracts extended the prohibition to money borrowed for 'petroleum operations' in general, and some qualified it by applying it to loans incurred after the date the contract became effective.

15 The term 'independent' is used merely for convenience to denote companies other than the accepted seven 'major' non-state international oil companies (Exxon, Mobil, Gulf, Texaco, Socal, B.P. and Shell).

16 Examples of both types of procedures may be given. The IIAPCO contract area of 6 September 1968 has been farmed out to four other

companies, each bringing in its train connections with various associate companies and affiliates; and Petromer Trend, operating in Irian Jaya on a contract signed on 15 October 1970, only has 25 per cent of its assets owned by the original parent company, the remainder being held by various American and Japanese companies and groups.

17 Some Pertamina officials have expressed the view that the more complicated a contract is, the more favourable it becomes for the companies, because of limited supervisory resources on the Indonesian side. One described how details in a contract could not be grasped by staff responsible for its execution. It would therefore seem that Pertamina is itself unsure how far the joint participation contracts are in its interests, in terms of ensuring the companies' compliance with their provisions.

18 See *Petroleum News Southeast Asia* 4 (December 1973): 18–19.

19 The change in the base price was calculated, directly proportional to the change in both the U.N. Price Index and the weighted average value of crude oil using the first quarter of 1974 as the starting point for calculation, and the lower of the two figures was then taken. The base price was in fact raised twice, first to US$5.42 and then in June 1975 to US$5.83, reaching its highest point before contract terms were revised again in mid 1976. The system remained operational for companies operating under contracts of work, and the base price for them reached US$9.48 by November 1982.

20 Sec. VI par. 1.7 subsecs. (a) and (c) of 'Production Sharing Contract between P. N. Pertambangan Minjak dan Gas Bumi Nasional (Pertamina) and Trend Exploration Limited, October 15th, 1970' (Singapore: Institute of Southeast Asian Studies).

21 Sec. VI pars. 1.7 and 1.8 of 'Production Sharing Contract between P. N. Pertambangan Minjak Nasional (Permina) and Continental Overseas Oil Company, May 12th, 1967' (Singapore: Institute of Southeast Asian Studies).

22 The legal arguments behind the assignment of ultimate responsibility for tax payments are discussed by Robert Fabrikant, *Oil Discovery and Technical Change in Southeast Asia: Legal Aspects of Production Sharing Contracts in the Indonesian Petroleum Industry* (Singapore: Institute of Southeast Asian Studies, 1973), pp. 39–57.

23 Law no. 8, 1971, arts. 14 and 15 in Indonesia, Pertamina, *Undang-Undang Pertamina: Pertamina Law* (Jakarta: 1975).

24 Indonesia, Department of Information, *Presidential Decree No. 33 Year 1971: On State Revenue from P. N. Pertamina* (Jakarta: 1971), arts. 1 and 2.

25 Dividend tax of 20% on remaining income after corporate tax of 45% is equivalent to a tax rate of (20×0.55) or 11% on pre-tax income. Total tax is therefore $(45 + 11)\%$ or 56%.

   The company's post-tax percentage share of the 'profit' oil is therefore $(34.09 \times 0.44)\%$ or 15%.

   Pertamina's share is $(65.91 \times 0.44)\%$ or 29%; giving a total Indonesian 'take' of $(56 + 29)\%$ or 85%.

26 Indonesia, Ministry of Mines, *Minerals and Mining in Indonesia* (Jakarta: 1969), p. 27.

27 The method is outlined by Bierman and Drebin as follows: 'The declining balance procedure involves the application of a constant depreciation rate to the decreasing book value of the asset. With the straight-line procedure a constant rate was applied to a constant depreciation base. With the declining balance method, the use of book value instead of the constant base results in diminishing charges over the lifespan of the asset . . . With the declining balance procedure any depreciation rate could conceivably be used, but the rate is generally expressed as a function of the straight-line rate. A rate equal to twice the straight-line rate . . . is frequently called the double declining balance method of depreciation.' Harold Bierman Jr. and Allan R. Drebin, *Financial Accounting: An Introduction* (Philadelphia: W. B. Saunders, 1978), p. 225.

28 Art. 26 par. a(4) of the 'Contract of Work between Permina and Stanvac, September 25th, 1963'.

29 It would appear that this provision covered the bulk of companies' capital investment, as much of the equipment used in offshore extractive operations, such as drilling rigs, would be regarded as 'movable'.

30 Fabrikant, *Legal Aspects*, p. 64.

31 *Far Eastern Economic Review*, 6 August 1976 and 27 August 1976; *Straits Times*, 15 March 1977. The differences between old and new contract terms are illustrated graphically in fig. 2.

32 A parent company and its wholly- or majority-owned subsidiaries and affiliates are here treated as one enterprise. This rule will be followed whenever figures for numbers of companies are given.

33 See *Straits Times*, 22 July 1976 and 3 August 1976; and *Petroleum News Southeast Asia* 7 (January 1977): 19–20. Only 7 of these 20 companies had actually commenced production, but the 13 non-producers were subject to Group I depreciation procedures under the 1977 incentives programme for new production, which in effect placed them in Group I.

34 This works out at 28.6% on the book value of assets.

35 The term used by Pertamina; see Indonesia, Pertamina, *The Production Sharing Contract: Current Status* (Jakarta: Pertamina Public Relations for the Foreign Contractors Coordinating Body, BKKA, 1980), p. 10.

36 Interviews.

37 The aim of both payments, supplementary to standard depreciation, is to recover all investment made by the firm. Thus the mining operation is viewed as an ongoing concern, and provision is therefore made for the maintenance of capital in some fashion.

38 It would seem though that preproduction development costs as a necessary expenditure can still be charged to operating costs. This would cover expenditure on geological and other exploratory surveys, test drilling and infrastructure costs. Elimination of the distinction between depletion and amortisation does not therefore remove the

basis for charging for the former, but rather subsumes it under the latter.

39 See United Nations, Department of Economic and Social Affairs, *United States Income Taxation of Private Investments in Developing Countries* (New York: 1970), pp. 120–5.

This privilege was eroded from 1975, when American oil companies were required to use an 'overall' method in determining the limitation imposed on the foreign tax credit granted to them by the US government. Each oil company had to combine its total foreign gains and losses, and then deduct only net foreign losses from its domestic US income. Previously, companies had been allowed to use a 'per-country' method in determining this limitation. Under this method, exploration, development and drilling costs in any one foreign country could be subtracted from the domestic income of the American parent company, regardless of profits earned in third countries. American oil companies finally lost this privilege when legislation was passed in 1982 allowing them to deduct all losses abroad only against income earned in the countries where the losses were incurred.

It has been noted that mineral investments show huge initial losses, largely because exploration and development costs are deductible immediately, company accounting practices treating amortisation as a current expense. These costs should fairly be amortised over the life of the oil-field being developed, and should therefore be dealt with together with capital depreciation. C. Fred Bergsten, Thomas Horst and Theodore H. Moran, *American Multinationals and American Interests* (Washington D.C.: Brookings Institution, 1978), pp. 463–5.

40 Ch. II art. 3 par. 1 of Act No. 1 Year 1967 re Foreign Capital Investment, in Indonesia, Department of Trade, Directorate-General of Marketing and Commercial Development, *Basic Documents on Economics and Finance* (Jakarta: 1967), pp. 31–48.

41 See U.S., Internal Revenue Service, *Indonesia: Oil and Gas Production Sharing Contracts: Corporation Tax and Dividend Tax* (Washington D.C.: IRS Rev. Rul. 78–222, 1978–1 C.B. 232).

42 According to the then Minister of Mines and Energy, M. Sadli. *Petroleum and Mining Report* (Jakarta), 18 May 1976.

43 *Asian Wall Street Journal*, 7 February 1977; *Bulletin of Indonesian Economic Studies* 13 (July 1977): 16–17.

44 Indeed the system of bonus payments works to ultimately reduce, not increase, the level of oil-company competition. For the higher the bidding price expected, the smaller is the number of companies capable of paying it. Thus only the larger firms are able to acquire the choicest areas for exploration, as the barriers to entry which prospective companies face are increased. See Charles F. Doran, *Myth, Oil, and Politics: Introduction to the Political Economy of Petroleum* (New York: Free Press, 1977), p. 80.

4. Provisions for development and national control

1 Art. 15 of the 'Contract of Work between Permina and Stanvac, September 25th, 1963'.

2 Companies usually follow a policy of purchasing locally insofar as this is practical. Food supply especially tends to be a problem in the remote and sparsely populated areas where they operate, and petroleum companies with onshore contract areas generally themselves initiate farming projects within the vicinity.

3 Sec. IV par. 1.2 subsec. (q) of 'Production Sharing Contract between P. N. Pertambangan Minjak dan Gas Bumi Nasional (Pertamina) and P. T. Caltex Pacific Indonesia, August 9th, 1971' (Singapore: Institute of Southeast Asian Studies).

4 The act of setting up a company (usually with limited liability) under local law.

5 'Dutch subjects' would refer to citizens of the Netherlands and Netherlands Indies, and later of Indonesia.

6 This statement needs to be qualified by noting that training of Indonesians was initiated by the Japanese during their Second-World-War occupation, and began to be more widely practised in the post-war years by companies operating under the concession system. This, however, was not a binding requirement formalised in their contracts.

7 Sec. XII par. 1.1 of the 'Contract between Pertamina and IIAPCO, September 6th, 1968'.

8 The number of expatriates employed by registered foreign oil companies rose from 826 in 1969 to a peak of 9,781 in 1975, before dropping to 6,199 in 1977.

9 Thus according to the Directorate General of Oil and Gas, the number of foreign oil companies (including companies engaged in supporting services for oil operations) rose from 40 in 1969 to 235 in 1975, before falling to 190 in 1977.

10 Arief, *Indonesian Petroleum Industry*, p. 283.

11 Ibid., p. 284.

12 For the additional investment figures, see Piet Haryono, *Challenges for the Indonesian Petroleum Industry* (Jakarta: Pertamina, 1979), p. 7.

13 Indonesia, National Development Information Office, *Indonesia: Fact File* (Jakarta: 1980), p. 14:3.

14 Ibid., p. 14:3.

15 Under production-sharing arrangements, Pertamina undertakes to discharge all import duties for equipment imported by the companies; and investment credits formed part of the incentive package introduced by Pertamina in 1977.

16 Art. 15 of the 'Contract of Work between Permina and Stanvac, September 25th, 1963'.

17 Constructed by the foreign contractor as a complete viable operation, and then handed over to Indonesian management.

18 Pertamina had found it necessary to supplement its own production of

refined products by entering into a processing deal with the Singapore Petroleum Company in 1973. Under this arrangement, Indonesian crude oil was refined in Singapore for re-export to Indonesia, to meet the demand for certain products with high domestic consumption rates. From 1984, however, Indonesia discontinued long-term arrangements for refining crude oil in Singapore, though short-term contracts continue to be made.

19 A simplified numerical example, not intended as an accurate reflection of the actual Indonesian industry structure, may help to clarify this requirement:

Assume the total national production of crude oil in Indonesia in any given year = 500 million barrels,

the total domestic consumption requirement for crude oil (including the total refinery intake) = 100 million barrels,

and the company's production of crude oil from its contract area = 50 million barrels.

Therefore the company's share of overall national production = 50/500 million barrels = 10%.

The company is therefore required to supply 10% of its crude oil production for domestic use, or 5 million barrels.

This quantity to be supplied is not to exceed two limits:

First, the limit imposed by the same percentage share of the total domestic consumption requirement = 10% of 100 million barrels = 10 million barrels.

Second, the limit imposed by 25% of the company's crude oil production from its contract area = 25% of 50 million barrels = 12.5 million barrels.

The company therefore supplies for domestic use the original quantity worked out, i.e. 5 million barrels, as this is below the two limits.

20 Sec. V par. 1.2 subsec. (p) of 'Production Sharing Contract between P. N. Pertambangan Minjak Nasional (Permina) and Kyushu Oil Co. Ltd., November 22nd, 1966' (Singapore: Institute of Southeast Asian Studies).

21 Sec. V par. 1.2 subsec. (p) of 'Production Sharing Contract between P. N. Pertambangan Minjak dan Gas Bumi Nasional (Pertamina) and Continental Oil Company of Indonesia, October 28th, 1971' (Singapore: Institute of Southeast Asian Studies).

The phrases within brackets were added to clarify the procedure, the working of which may also be illustrated by a simplified numerical example:

Assume the total national crude-oil production in Indonesia in any given year = 500 million barrels,

the overall domestic crude-oil consumption requirement = 100 million barrels,

and the total production of crude oil from the contract area = 50 million barrels.

Then under stage (i), $(100 \times 50)/500$ million barrels $= 10$ million barrels.

And under stage (ii), 25% of 50 million barrels $= 12.5$ million barrels.

(The lowest quantity is therefore 10 million barrels from (i).)

In stage (iii), assuming that, of the total contract production of 50 million barrels, the company takes 20 million barrels to recover its costs, and the remaining production is subject to a 'profit' oil split of 85:15 in Pertamina's favour,

then the required quantity $= 10$ million barrels $\times [0.15 \times 30$ million]$/[1 \times 30$ million] $= 1.5$ million barrels.

(It should be noted that the domestic supply requirement computed under (iii) is not dependent on either the deduction of 'cost' oil from production or the amount of 'profit' oil remaining, but only on the ratio of the 'profit' oil division.)

22 Interviews.
23 Indonesia, Antara, President Soeharto, *Government Statement on the draft state budget for 1979–1980 to the House of the People's Representatives* (Jakarta: 1979), p. 39.
24 Anderson G. Bartlett III *et al.*, *Pertamina: Indonesian National Oil* (Jakarta: Amerasian, 1972), p. 291.
25 Ibnu Sutowo, *Oil for National Development* (Jakarta: Pertamina, 1973).
26 Badan Koordinasi Kontraktor Asing.
27 Interviews.
28 It should be noted, though, that there has been one instance in which a company decision not to proceed with production from its extractive operation was overruled by Pertamina; and another case where a company wishing to go ahead with commercial production was ordered not to do so by Pertamina.
29 Some production-sharing contracts define allowable costs more narrowly as the amount spent in conducting 'exploration' operations.
30 Smith and Wells, *Mineral Agreements*, p. 113.
31 Sec. V par. 1.2 subsec. (d) of the 'Contract between Pertamina and Continental Oil, October 28th, 1971'.

5. Problems of negotiation and contractual change

1 It should be noted that international law takes a far more flexible attitude towards this issue than is commonly supposed. See Henry J. Steiner and Detlev F. Vagts, *Transnational Legal Problems: Materials and Text* (Mineola, N.Y.: Foundation Press, 1976), p. 499; and J. G. Starke, *An Introduction to International Law* (London: Butterworths, 1977), pp. 324–6.
2 Art. 84 of the 1930 Law in Fabrikant, ed., *Miscellaneous Source Material*, pp. 62–3.
3 Art. 25 of the 'Contract of Work between Permina and Stanvac, September 25th, 1963'.

4 Sec. XI par. 1.2 of the 'Contract between Pertamina and IIAPCO, September 6th, 1968'.

5 Weigel and Weston note, however, that the principle of partial compensation has been accepted by the foreign investment community and has in effect been sanctioned in international law. See Dale R. Weigel and Burns H. Weston, 'Valuation upon the Deprivation of Foreign Enterprise: A Policy-Oriented Approach to the Problem of Compensation Under International Law', in Richard B. Lillich, ed., *The Valuation of Nationalized Property in International Law: Volume I*, 3 vols. (Charlottesville: University Press of Virginia, 1972), p. 9.

6 *Far Eastern Economic Review*, 17 July 1981.

7 The term 'let alone' referred to the companies' foreign exchange earnings, they being still required to pay taxes and royalties.

8 The Indonesia Project, Center for International Studies, Massachusetts Institute of Technology, *Stanvac in Indonesia* (New York: National Planning Association, 1957), p. 42. Stanvac is a joint subsidiary of Exxon and Mobil Oil.

9 These concessions included valuing crude oil on realised rather than posted prices, having all Indonesian taxes incorporated within the government's 60 per cent share of operating profits, and, most importantly, allowing the companies to pay the government partly in rupiahs and not exclusively in hard foreign currency, as the Indonesian side had originally insisted upon. Alex Hunter, 'The Oil Industry: The 1963 Agreements and After', *Bulletin of Indonesian Economic Studies*, 2 (September 1965), 28.

10 Indonesian officials have attempted retrospectively to claim a greater legitimacy for their action against the companies. The then Minister of Mines and Energy Mohammad Sadli ascribed the main reason for the Indonesian action to a desire to capture the economic rent from oil price rises. *Petroleum and Mining Report* (Jakarta), 27 May 1977, p. 3. And President Soeharto asserted that there was no direct connection between the Pertamina crisis and the question of foreign oil company investment. *Asian Wall Street Journal*, 21 February 1979.

11 Indonesia, Department of Information, President Soeharto, *Government Statement on the draft state budget for 1976/1977 to the House of the People's Representatives* (Jakarta: 1976).

12 Kuhn Loeb Lehman Brothers, Lazard Frères, and S. G. Warburg, *The Republic of Indonesia* (London: n.p., 1979), p. 26.

13 *Petroleum News Southeast Asia* 7 (January 1977): 19.

14 *Petroleum and Mining Report*, 23 April 1976, p. 13; 18 May 1976, p. 20.

15 For companies, given the short estimated life of Indonesian oil fields, the differential between their average 'take' and their average cost may tend to be higher during the early productive years but lower in later years due to production decline. Removing the 40% provision would both lower the rate of cost recovery in general and substantially reduce 'front end' cost recovery (the recovery of preproduction costs from the initial production). A lowered cost recovery would force companies to recover costs out of expected profits on investment, reducing reinvest-

ment in further development. This negative impact is sharpened by the reduced 'front end' cost recovery, by further squeezing the smaller profits in the later years of the field's development.

The companies, however, stated publicly that the new profit split was 'tolerable'. *New Straits Times*, 15 August 1976.

16   Interview in *Business Times*, 13 October 1976; speeches in *Petroleum and Mining Report*, 18 January 1977, p. 3, and in Indonesian Petroleum Association, '6th Annual Convention, Jakarta 23–24 May 1977 (Programme and papers)' (Singapore: Institute of Southeast Asian Studies).

17   Such a comparison as the alleged report made, pointing to a significant differential in company profit margins in different regions, would to some extent be inappropriate. Profit margins would have to be weighted to account for differences of quality between various crude oils. And Indonesian operations have higher overall costs, and hence require higher capital outlays. Also while Indonesian oil contracts require the foreign company to bear all costs and assume all the risk, new arrangements in other OPEC countries have allowed for a sharing of both risk and cost.

18   Negotiations were formally between the companies and Pertamina, yet Indonesian proposals could equally be presented by other government bodies concerned with the petroleum sector.

19   *Bulletin of Indonesian Economic Studies* 12 (November 1976): 30–1.

20   Caltex operated under a long-standing contract of work in Central Sumatra where, principally from its Minas field, it produced some 40% of total Indonesian crude-oil production. It also operates offshore under production-sharing arrangements.

21   The major producing field, Minas, is ageing, and an eventual decline in production may only be delayed in the short-term through a comprehensive secondary water-flood recovery operation, which would maintain production at around 350,000 barrels per day for the next few years. In the long term, Caltex intends initiating a major programme of steam-flood injections for its Duri field, aimed at pushing production from 40,000 barrels to a projected 300,000 barrels per day.

22   Eugene B. Mihaly, 'Is Adverse Oil Policy Shift near in Indonesia?', *Oil and Gas Journal*, 14 December 1981, pp. 146–8.

23   Bartlett *et al.*, *Pertamina*, p. 301.

24   *Petroleum and Mining Report*, 5 October 1976, p. 1.

6. Organisational structure and the negotiating process

1   Dewan Komisaris Pemerintah Pertamina.

2   Direktorat Jendral Minjak dan Gas Bumi.

3   The 1968 Law setting up Pertamina as a state enterprise made its President-Director directly responsible to the relevant Minister. The 1971 Law did not remove this responsibility, but made Pertamina responsible in addition to the DKPP. Compare art. 19 pars. (2) and (3) of Pertamina, *Pertamina Law* with art. 7 par. (3) of Government Regu-

lation no. 27 Year 1968 in Fabrikant, ed., *Miscellaneous Source Material*, pp. 263–74.

4 See, for instance, Sevinc Carlson, *Indonesia's Oil* (Boulder, Colorado: Westview Press, 1977), pp. 53–63.

5 Ibnu Sutowo, *Prospect of Oil for our National Prosperity* (Jakarta: Pertamina, 1972), p. 17.

6 *Bulletin of Indonesian Economic Studies* 13 (March 1977): 5.

7 The reasons for Pertamina wishing to avoid seeking formal government approval have their origin in the complex informal network of personal relationships characterising the Indonesian power structure. Sutowo often acted at the personal request of government ministers, and the formal authorisation for his undertaking various projects was at times unclear. He was also aware of the opposition of the so-called technocrats (mainly US educated Indonesian economists) within Bappenas (the National Planning Board) and the Finance Ministry, who disagreed with the capital-intensive projects implemented by Pertamina. Furthermore, while the major part of funds for economic development comes from the petroleum sector, Bappenas was responsible for the implementation of national development plans, so competition inevitably arose for control of these resources. Sutowo was alleged to have stated that he did not agree with Bappenas and was therefore not prepared to surrender oil revenues to it.

8 The Republic National Bank of Dallas.

9 *New Nation* (Singapore), 11 March 1976.

10 *Asiaweek* (Hong Kong), 18 August 1978, p. 39.

11 These requirements have proved difficult to meet, even given the willingness of Pertamina officials to assist the Soeharto family's business dealings. A long-term LNG contract to South Korea was, for example, held up when one of Soeharto's sons agreed to ensure that a South Korean shipyard build one of two LNG tankers required, while another son and a son-in-law had a stake in a rival plan under which both tankers would be leased from third countries. Pertamina officials did not dare to cross any of Soeharto's sons, nor did they know which one to support. *Wall Street Journal*, 22 August 1983.

12 *Petroleum Economist* 51 (August 1984): 305–6.

13 This process began in the early 1980s, the 1979 price rises inducing the industrialised countries to reduce oil consumption and to develop alternative energy sources to the OPEC countries; while Saudi Arabia, the largest OPEC producer, was quite prepared to allow the oil price to fall. However, the lower oil price brought considerable financial difficulties to other OPEC producers, forcing them to limit development plans and to restrict governmental spending.

14 These comprised two petrochemical complexes, an oil refinery and an alumina plant. *Far Eastern Economic Review*, 26 May 1983 and 23 June 1983.

15 Soedjatmoko, 'Foreign Private Investment in a Developing Nation: An Indonesian Perspective', in *Symposium: Private Investors Abroad: Problems and Solutions in International Business in 1969*, ed. Virginia Shook Cameron,

for International and Comparative Law Center, The Southwestern Legal Foundation, Dallas, Texas (New York: Matthew Bender, 1969), p. 322.

16 *Indonesia: Business Opportunities* (London: Metra Consulting, 1977), p. 201.

17 Jean-Flavien Lalive, 'Negotiations with American Lawyers – A Foreign Lawyer's View', in *Symposium: Private Investors Abroad: Negotiating and Drafting International Commercial Contracts*, ed. Virginia Shook Cameron, for International and Comparative Law Center, The Southwestern Legal Foundation, Dallas, Texas (New York: Matthew Bender, 1966), p. 6.

18 It was believed that Thahir had similar substantial deposits in other bank accounts which had already been withdrawn by his second wife after her husband's death. *Straits Times*, 7 February 1980.

19 *Asian Wall Street Journal*, 5 February 1980.

20 *Business Times* (Singapore), 31 October 1980. The method used was to transfer oil at sea from Pertamina tankers carrying fuel oil from Singapore to Indonesian ports for domestic distribution.

21 Indonesia, Investment Coordinating Board (BKPM), *Indonesia: A Guide for Investors* (Jakarta: 1980), p. 82.

7. Some regional considerations for South-east-Asian oil-producer governments

1 While oil leases on 850 square miles of continental shelf off the United States coast cost US$845.8 million in initial payments when bid for in November 1970, companies acquired 800,000 square miles of Indonesian offshore concessions in the late 1960s and early 1970s for a total initial payment of under US$80 million. Leon Howell and Michael Morrow, *Asia, Oil Politics and the Energy Crisis: The Haves and the Have-nots* (New York: International Documentation, 1974), p. 60. The financial outlay required for new oil exploration ventures within South-east Asia may since have risen, but their relative value in comparing interregional costs has not altered significantly.

2 Prior to 1969, taxes were levied on profits calculated from realised prices declared by the company. The change therefore made transfer pricing practices less easy.

3 B. A. Hamzah, 'Oil and Independence in Brunei: A Perspective', in Institute of Southeast Asian Studies, *Southeast Asian Affairs 1981* (Singapore: Heinemann, 1981), p. 97.

4 The Italian state-owned petroleum company.

5 Cited by *Petroleum Economist* 47 (August 1980): 348.

6 Far Eastern Economic Review, *Asia 1981 Yearbook* (Hong Kong: 1981), p. 267.

7 As royalties are expensed instead of being credited against tax, as in the Bruneian case, the income allocation is more favourable to the government in the Thai case.

8 Philippines National Oil Corporation.

9 This allowance was suspended in 1979, though the government indicated that it may be re-introduced in the future.
10 Malaysia, *Second Malaysia Plan 1971–1975* (Kuala Lumpur: Government Press, 1971), p. 40. The Malay share is inclusive of nominee companies and federal and state government holdings.
11 The royalty payment was therefore both tax deductible (as an expense) and deductible prior to dividing the 'profit' oil.
12 *Far Eastern Economic Review*, 10 January 1985.
13 This is not a state company, though the Malaysian government has a substantial equity interest in it.
14 Howell and Morrow, *Asia, Oil Politics*, p. 87.
15 *Straits Times*, 26 August 1975.
16 Planned facilities for the new Dulang oil-field include a data-acquisition platform that will link by computer all production platforms with Petronas headquarters, in order to monitor production. *Far Eastern Economic Review*, 31 May 1984.
17 Now ESCAP, the Economic and Social Commission for Asia and the Pacific.
18 *Asia Research Bulletin* 3 (31 January 1974): 2387–8.
19 *Business Times*, 30 September 1980.
20 *Summary of World Broadcasts*, 23 July 1983 (FE/7393/A3/1).
21 Such an agreement, modelled along Malaysian production-sharing lines, dividing revenues equally between Malaysia and Thailand, was announced in February 1985, yet joint development of the area continues to be postponed. See *Petroleum News Southeast Asia* 15 (February 1985): 18; 16 (June 1985): 8.

8. The viability of transnational mineral agreements

1 From a study of three commodities (bauxite, iron ore and copper), Radetzki concludes that the market structure for the mineral product is much less important in determining host-government bargaining strength than commonly presumed. See M. Radetzki, 'Market Structure and Bargaining Power', in *Mining for Development*, eds. Sideri and Johns, p. 141.
2 Raymond Vernon, *Sovereignty at Bay: The Multinational Spread of US Enterprises* (Harmondsworth, Middx.: Penguin, 1973), pp. 53–60.
3 United Nations, Economic and Social Council, Commission on Transnational Corporations, *Transnational Corporations in World Development: A Re-examination* (New York: E/C.10/38, 1978), pp. 28–33, 146–8.
4 Juha Kuusi, *The Host State and the Transnational Corporation: An Analysis of Legal Relationships* (Farnborough: Saxon House, 1979), p. 165.

SELECT BIBLIOGRAPHY

Journals

Asia Research Bulletin
Asian Wall Street Journal
Bulletin of Indonesian Economic Studies
Business Times (Singapore)
Far Eastern Economic Review
New Straits Times (Kuala Lumpur)
Petroleum Economist (formerly *Petroleum Press Service*)
Petroleum Intelligence Weekly
Petroleum and Mining Report (Jakarta)
Petroleum News Southeast Asia (Hong Kong)
Straits Times (Singapore)

Books

Arief, Sritua. *The Indonesian Petroleum Industry: A Study of Resource Management in a Developing Economy.* Jakarta: Sritua Arief Associates, 1976.

Bartlett, Anderson G., III; Barton, Robert John; Bartlett, Joe Calvin; Fowler, George Anderson, Jr.; and Hays, Charles Francis. *Pertamina: Indonesian National Oil.* Jakarta: Amerasian, 1972.

Bergsten, C. Fred; Horst, Thomas; and Moran, Theodore H. *American Multinationals and American Interests.* Washington, D.C.: Brookings Institution, 1978.

Booth, Anne, and McCawley, Peter, eds. *The Indonesian Economy during the Soeharto Era.* Kuala Lumpur: Oxford University Press, 1981.

Bosson, Rex, and Varon, Bension. *The Mining Industry and the Developing Countries.* New York: Oxford University Press for the World Bank, 1977.

Carlson, Sevinc. *Indonesia's Oil.* Boulder, Colorado: Westview Press, 1977.

Cooper, Bryan, ed. *Far East Oil and Energy Survey.* London: Petroleum Economist/Petroconsultants, 1981.

Cowhey, Peter F., and Aronson, Jonathan David, eds. *Profit and the Pursuit of Energy: Markets and Regulation.* Boulder, Colorado: Westview Press, 1983.

Fabrikant, Robert. *Oil Discovery and Technical Change in Southeast Asia: Legal*

Aspects of Production Sharing Contracts in the Indonesian Petroleum Industry. Singapore: Institute of Southeast Asian Studies, 1973.

Fabrikant, Robert, ed. *Oil Discovery and Technical Change in Southeast Asia: The Indonesian Petroleum Industry: Miscellaneous Source Material.* Singapore: Institute of Southeast Asian Studies, 1973.

Garnaut, Ross, and Ross, Anthony Clunies. *Taxation of Mineral Rents.* Oxford: Clarendon Press, 1983.

Hossain, Kamal. *Law and Policy in Petroleum Development: Changing Relations between Transnationals and Governments.* London: Frances Pinter, 1979.

Lall, Sanjaya, and Streeten, Paul. *Foreign Investment, Transnationals and Developing Countries.* London: Macmillan, 1977.

May, Brian. *The Indonesian Tragedy.* London: Routledge and Kegan Paul, 1978.

Mikdashi, Zuhayr. *The International Politics of Natural Resources.* Ithaca, N.Y.: Cornell University Press, 1976.

Mikesell, Raymond F., ed. *Foreign Investment in the Petroleum and Mineral Industries: Case Studies of Investor–Host Country Relations.* Baltimore: Johns Hopkins Press, 1971.

Noreng, Øystein. *Oil Politics in the 1980s: Patterns of International Cooperation.* New York: McGraw-Hill, 1978.

Ooi Jin Bee. *The Petroleum Resources of Indonesia.* Kuala Lumpur: Oxford University Press, 1982.

Palmer, Ingrid. *The Indonesian Economy since 1965: A Case Study of Political Economy.* London: Frank Cass, 1978.

Pearce, David W.; Siebert, Horst; and Walter, Ingo, eds. *Risk and the Political Economy of Resource Development.* London: Macmillan, 1984.

Sauvant, Karl P., and Lavipour, Farid G., eds. *Controlling Multinational Enterprises: Problems, Strategies, Counterstrategies.* London: Wilton House, 1976.

Siddayao, Corazon Morales. *The Off-shore Petroleum Resources of South-east Asia: Potential Conflict Situations and Related Economic Considerations.* Kuala Lumpur: Oxford University Press, 1978.

Siddayao, Corazon Morales. *The Supply of Petroleum Reserves in South-east Asia: Economic Implications of Evolving Property Rights Arrangements.* Kuala Lumpur: Oxford University Press, 1980.

Sideri, S., and Johns, S., eds. *Mining for Development in the Third World: Multinational Corporations, State Enterprises and the International Economy.* New York: Pergamon Press, 1980.

Smith, David N., and Wells, Louis T., Jr. *Negotiating Third-World Mineral Agreements: Promises as Prologue.* Cambridge, Mass.: Ballinger, 1975.

Steiner, Henry J., and Vagts, Detlev F. *Transnational Legal Problems: Materials and Text.* Mineola, N.Y.: Foundation Press, 1976.

INDEX

252   *Index*